Farewell Perestroika

Farewell Perestroika

A Soviet Chronicle

◆

BORIS KAGARLITSKY

Translated by Rick Simon

VERSO

London · New York

First published by Verso 1990
© Verso 1990
Translation © Verso 1990
All rights reserved

Verso
UK: 6 Meard Street, London W1V 3HR
USA: 29 West 35th Street, New York, NY 10001–2291

Verso is the imprint of New Left Books

British Library Cataloguing in Publication Data
Kagarlitsky, Boris, *1958–*
   Farewell perestroika: a soviet chronicle.
   1. Soviet Union
   I. Title
   947.0854

   ISBN 0–86091–292–2
   ISBN 0–86091–508–5 pbk

US Library of Congress Cataloging-in-Publication Data
Kagarlitsky, Boris, 1958–
    Farewell Perestroika: a Soviet chronicle / Boris Kagarlitsky;
translated by Rick Simon.
     p.   cm.
    ISBN 0–86091–292–2, — ISBN 0–86091–508–5 (pbk.)
     1. Soviet Union — Politics and government — 1985– 2. Perestroĭka.
  I. Title.
  DK288.K35   1990
  947.085'4 — dc20

Typeset by Bath Press Integraphics, Bath, Avon
Printed in Finland by Werner Söderström Oy

Contents

Contents

Foreword

This book is based on articles that I wrote for samizdat and Western journals in 1988–89. Not one of them has been published in the official Soviet press, a fact which in itself is not a bad indicator of the limits of glasnost. While liberal theoreticians have been filling the pages of journals and newspapers with discussions of Stalinism or the damage done by Marxism – just when it would seem that government decrees on one question or another could be subjected to the severest criticism – any systematic critical analysis of the political process has remained outside the official press, and a stop has unquestionably been put to any attempt to criticize liberal ideology or practice from the left. Of course, this has applied not only to me but to many of my colleagues and co-thinkers who have their own experiences of the limits of glasnost.

I happened to play an active part in several of the events I describe so I do not aspire to the role of objective historian, especially as the time for definitive historical conclusions about this period is not yet upon us. But as a picture began to emerge from this series of articles and notes, there emerged the potential for combining these texts. While they have been reworked, and new sections written for this book, I have not imposed the wisdom of hindsight on the passing judgements they contain.

Boris Kagarlitsky

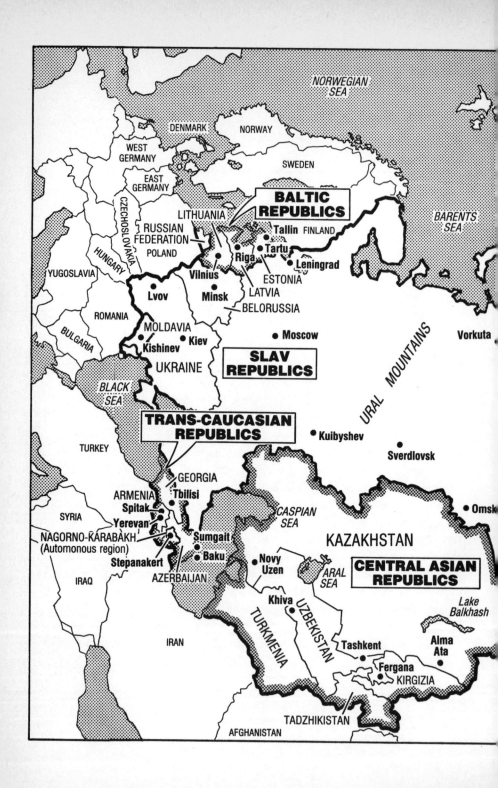

ARCTIC
OCEAN

KARA SEA

LAPTEV
SEA

SIBERIA

RUSSIAN

FEDERATION

SEA OF
OKHOTSK

500 miles

Tomsk

Lake Baikal

Novosibirsk

Mezhdurechensk

Khabarovsk

Prokop'evsk

Irkutsk

CHINA

Vladivostok

MONGOLIA

SEA OF
JAPAN

1

The Hot Summer of 1988

The major event of the year had been announced beforehand. The whole country, the whole world, awaited the Nineteenth Conference of the Communist Party of the Soviet Union (CPSU). All of the happenings of spring were assessed in relation to the approaching Conference and how they might influence its outcome. The many sceptics who tried to suggest that the country's fate would not be settled at a conference were not given credence. The country lived in expectation. Probably never before in the history of Soviet society had the preparations for the next Party forum provoked such universal and lively interest.

The pendulum swung first to the left and then to the right. Liberal hopes had been raised by Gorbachev's speech at the January 1987 Plenum of the CPSU Central Committee and 'informal' left groups had gained the opportunity to organize officially their own conference in the summer of the same year and found a Federation of Socialist Social Clubs (FSOK). But the autumn turned into a 'crisis of glasnost' when Boris Yeltsin, the most popular and radical Party figure, was accused of a multiplicity of political errors and forced to resign his post as First Secretary of the Moscow City Committee (*gorkom*). When, in March 1988, *Sovietskaya Rossiya* published Nina Andreeva's letter – 'I cannot give up my principles' – which contained essentially a call for the restoration of the Stalinist order, many perceived it as a bad omen: was this the beginning of a turning back? No one had any doubts that behind Nina Andreeva stood powerful forces, most probably Yegor Ligachev, who at that time was the Party's chief ideologist.

Mikhail Ulyanov, the President of the Union of Theatre Workers and one of the most visible representatives of the liberal intelligentsia, later acknowledged honestly that 'We were frightened by her letter'.[1] When, about a month later, on 5 April, the pendulum swung in the opposite direction and *Pravda* published a sharp response to Andreeva in an editorial calling her letter 'a manifesto of the opponents of perestroika', there was an outbreak of genuine euphoria in left-liberal intellectual circles.

Meanwhile the conflict between Armenia and Azerbaijan over Nagorny Karabakh had already demonstrated by spring 1988 how unstable the process of liberalization was. Despite the Nagorny Karabakh Soviet's resolutions on unification with Armenia, the mass demonstrations of Armenians in Yerevan, and even reprisals carried out by Azerbaijani extremists against the Armenian population in the town of Sumgait, Moscow remained firm in defence of the old frontiers between the republics. Moderate leaders of the Armenian national movement were called extremists in the pages of the central press, and articles by *Ogonyok* and *Izvestiya* correspondents on the real state of affairs could not get into print (they were finally published by the Socialist Initiative group in their journal *Levyi Povorot*).

The bureaucracy reacted even more vigorously to the fluctuations in the political situation. The publication of Andreeva's letter was accompanied by a wave of persecutions of progressive unofficial groups in the provinces. Here and there the text of Andreeva's letter was reprinted in the local press or distributed to social science teachers as a model of the correct approach to current events. In the wake of *Pravda*'s response, unofficial left-wing groups felt that their position was improving, and it became possible to hold various seminars and meetings, some of which were even publicized in the official press.

In the meantime what was being published in the press was only a pale reflection of the profound struggle going on at the top. The conservative wing, unlike the progressives, did not attach too much significance to the 'Andreeva affair'. Professional apparatchiks know better than anyone that it is deeds and not words that count. Just as the intelligentsia was celebrating the 'defeat of the Stalinists', the conservatives registered two very important successes. First, the theses prepared by the Party leadership for the Party Conference turned out to be an abstract document containing not a single specific proposal. And, second, the procedure for electing delegates in the localities was placed entirely under the control of the Party apparatus. The right to elect delegates was reserved exclusively for plenums of the provincial Party committees (*obkoms*) and, in some instances, for regional committees (*raikoms*). The lower Party organizations had the right to nominate and consider candidates but not to elect them. As a result, the people elected were usually those with the least support 'at the base', or those who had not even made it onto preliminary lists for consideration. In many cases even provincial newspapers began to protest against such anti-democratic procedures. 'What can we say about a delegate who does not know the meaning of the word democracy', wrote *Ust'-Ilimskaya Pravda.*[2] Democracy is the election of all delegates on a competitive basis. In our case there was only one candidate for delegate and the elections had no competitive basis. Analogous situations also arose in Moscow where the most well known commentators of the liberal tendency, even if put forward as candidates, were invariably rejected by the 'electorate' from the Party apparatus.

Dissatisfaction with the electoral process was voiced in a letter signed by a group of eminent Moscow intellectuals (academician Andrei Sakharov, dramatists Mikhail Shatrov and A. Gel'man, historians A. Vatkin, Yuri Afanasyev and others). The authors of the letter demanded the postponement of the Conference until such time as honest and free elections could be held.

The most notable and scandalous event was the 'Afanasyev affair'. The Rector of the Historical Archive Institute, famous throughout the world for his attempts to establish the historical truth and rehabilitate the Old Bolsheviks slandered by Stalin (including Trotsky who was yet to be rehabilitated), Yuri Afanasyev was not even registered as a candidate, although he was supported by many Party members not only in his own Institute but in other institutions in the region. When news reached the students that Afanasyev had been excluded from the elections a veritable revolt broke out. At a stormy gathering of students and lecturers, it was decided to form a committee for Afanasyev's nomination to the Party Conference. Graduates from the Institute began collecting signatures to various petitions in support of Afanasyev in the libraries and institutions

3

where they worked. Almost all the Institute's students signed a similar petition and the younger ones demanded that a demonstration be held. Yaroslav Leontiev, a member of the Socialist Initiative group, with some other students toured various institutes and schools in the region in the hope of gaining the support of the pupils there.

The Institute's professors were taken rather unawares by the students' radicalism. Afanasyev himself cancelled all meetings and interviews and disappeared for a few days. While approving of the students' demands, at least in words, a majority of lecturers sought to achieve the same end by quite different methods; they made every attempt to find 'their own' people in the Central Committee apparatus and induce them urgently to add Afanasyev to the 'central list'.

Worried by the students' actions, the *raikom* agreed to consider the popular historian's candidature, although the 'election' procedure was strange to say the least. Afanasyev was summoned to a plenum of the *raikom* where, *Moskovskie Novosti* has admitted, he was subjected to a humiliating and prolonged interrogation, after which his candidature was unanimously rejected. Some time later, to the great joy of liberal intellectuals, this injustice was put right. Behind-the-scenes manoeuvring in the apparatus had been successful and Afanasyev received his delegate's mandate centrally. The problem was that such a solution had almost no influence on the overall character of the elections across the country.

Preparations for the Party Conference brought about a sudden revival even among unofficial organizations and groups. Right-wing liberals from the 'Democracy and Humanism' seminar were the first to take advantage of the situation. In May they held the First Congress of the Democratic Union (DU) and proclaimed themselves a new opposition party. DU supporters declared their readiness to unite 'all democratic forces' within their organization, although a majority of left groups either were not present at the congress or had sent observers. On the whole the platform the DU adopted at the congress reiterated the traditional slogans of Western liberalism: a multi-party parliamentary democracy, a mixed economy, respect for human rights, and so on. As the DU leader, Valeriya Novodvorskaya, declared: 'a real political force is being created in this country which rejects the illusory character of the advantages of the socialist system and looks to the West on a number of issues, and some of the opposition do so on absolutely all of them'.[3] Of course, the DU did not become a real political force: by summer 1988 its supporters totalled a few hundred people throughout the entire country, significantly less than in the left groups. Nevertheless, information about the DU was quite widely disseminated both by Western radio and by the official mass media.

Official newspapers were naturally critical of the DU but their coverage did serve to provide it with a degree of publicity. Moreover, criticism of the DU in the press was initially rather more muted and careful than criticism of the left groups. Thus for right-wing liberals there had arisen a unified political centre capable of rallying their forces to the maximum. This was a very important lesson for the Left.

The left-wing movement, while more broadly and firmly rooted in many Soviet cities (Sverdlovsk, Saratov, Krasnoyarsk, Omsk, Krasnodar, and so on), suffered, particularly in the provincial capitals, from the traditional disorders of the radical Left across the whole world: fragmentation, sectarianism, splits and internal rivalry. Although, in the provinces, the constant pressure of the local bureaucracy served to strengthen the unity of the left groups, in Moscow and Leningrad all of these problems were only exacerbated over the course of time. The emergence of the DU forced a majority of socialist, ecological and left-democratic groups to look at things in a new light. Slogans in favour of unity were placed on the agenda, especially as there seemed to be a possibility of legally registering the new organizations. In Estonia, a Popular Front (PF) began to form at a republican level, uniting both communists and non-party people in the struggle for perestroika. On many occasions, the Estonian PF acted in complete agreement with the national-patriotic faction of the local apparatus, which naturally provoked a variety of suspicions among Muscovites (there were almost no Russians in the Estonian PF and its programme was directed more at gaining greater independence from Moscow than at resolving the social and political contradictions within the republic itself). Nevertheless, the very fact of its foundation and registration in Estonia was an important precedent for other parts of the country.

Discussion of the CPSU Central Committee theses prior to the Nineteenth Party Conference proved an ideal way for left-wing informal groups to formulate their own political platform. In June, a number of left organizations gained the opportunity to discus these questions.

During the official preparations for the Party Conference, meeting halls were twice granted by the authorities to the 'informals'. This fact was perceived by many activists in left-wing groups as being in itself an indication of a new attitude on the part of the authorities towards the independent social movement. Since Boris Yeltsin's removal from the post of First Secretary of the Moscow *gorkom* (city committee) even the most moderate informal groups had encountered numerous obstacles to any attempt to obtain premises for their work. In those cases where premises were granted, the 'informals' were normally asked to agree beforehand to a set of humiliating conditions. For example, in January, FSOK had been permitted to hold a meeting in the Yunost Hotel but the Komsomol apparatchiks who had sanctioned the meeting in reality took control of it. The renowned independent Marxist historian, Roy Medvedev, who was present at this meeting, noted a few months later that he was presented with 'a gloomy picture when these informals had to account for their activity'.[4] Three months later, in April, the Socialist Initiative group together with other FSOK clubs gained the opportunity to conduct a seminar on the premises of a cultural research institute only after a sharp conflict within the apparatus. The Party *raikom* sent the police to the institute building and they should have prevented the seminar from taking place. However, they were successfully prevented from carrying out this duty through the intervention of the propaganda and agitation section of the Party Central Committee.

On this occasion everything passed off without any excesses. A luxurious hall in the Palace of Youth was then placed at the disposal of the 'informals', and all those taking part in the meeting were able to speak quite freely. Such liberalism on the part of the authorities engendered a peculiar reformist euphoria even among leaders of the clubs. A majority of those who spoke appealed not to society, but to the political leadership in an effort to give them as much advice as possible on how to manage the state. Each speaker proposed their own programme. On the whole, such a spectacle had a negative effect on many of those present. After the first day's discussion, Yevgeny Shvarts, one of the ecological movement's ideologues, remarked that he was ashamed both of the meeting and of his own participation in it.

In practice, though, the meeting in the Palace of Youth proved quite useful. Of course, as always happens in such cases, the real work was conducted not in the conference hall but behind the scenes where the editorial group formed from representatives of the leading clubs endeavoured to combine their proposals into a single document. The text which emerged, entitled 'Public Mandate for the Nineteenth Party Conference', was handed to Yuri Afanasyev, who had by this time successfully obtained his delegate's nomination. The 'Public Mandate' constituted a comprehensive programme of general democratic demands: freedom of the press; freedom of movement; reorganization of the security organs; the abrogation of any rules and norms which might serve as a basis for discrimination on national or religious grounds; and free elections to the soviets at all levels. The possibility of creating a multi-party system was also mentioned in the document although this demand was not pushed to the forefront. The authors of the text devoted rather more attention to the founding of a Popular Front, an organization which, unlike the DU, would not proclaim itself an 'opposition party' but would be capable of putting forward its own candidates at elections, of formulating alternative political and socio-economic proposals and of co-ordinating the activity of independent initiative groups in the localities.

The general feeling among participants in the discussion was that official recognition of the Popular Front and its registration as an all-Russian or even all-Union social organization on the Estonian model was just a matter of time. If they had provided a conference hall so readily, it meant there would be no problems with the Front's registration.

Shortly after adopting the 'Public Mandate', eighteen of the Moscow groups which had signed it formed a Popular Front Organizing Committee and set about working on a platform for the future association. Of course, there were sceptics. The well-known sociologist, G. Ya. Rakitskaya, warned the meeting's participants that rapid official recognition of the PF might turn it into a 'Komsomol for grown-ups' and that numerous official 'voluntary societies', which had been preserved since Stalin's time and were far superior to the Party in their bureaucratization, might join the new organization on orders from above. Typically, just such a scenario was considered quite seriously in the Komsomol leadership, and the Komsomol leader, V. Mironenko, was completely in favour of such a solution.

Nevertheless, the overwhelming majority of the leaders of the informal groups were in an extremely optimistic frame of mind. The situation seemed to favour the most radical undertakings. On 28 May, 1988, even

7

before the start of the discussion on the 'Public Mandate', the Commune (*Obshchina*) and Civil Dignity (*Grazhdanskoe dostoinstvo*) groups organized an unauthorized demonstration which, despite the 'temporary regulations' in force in Moscow to restrict citizens' rights to engage in such actions, was not broken up by the police. As a result, Pushkin Square, the end-point of the 28 May march, became a kind of Muscovite Hyde Park. People became accustomed to going there to meet representatives of the 'informals', to learn the latest political news and to express their opinion. The success of the conference at the Palace of Youth and the uninterrupted functioning of the 'Speakers' Corner' on Pushkin Square were evidence of the high degree of official tolerance and reinforced confidence among the 'informals' in a swift and easy success.

Meanwhile, events in the provinces were unfolding rather more dramatically. The election of delegates to the Party Conference provoked mass discontent in the most diverse regions of the country. The composition of the delegations sent to Moscow by the provincial Party apparatus so blatantly failed to correspond to the masses' expectations that the people began to take to the streets. Only a few weeks before, liberal commentators were bemoaning the passivity of broad layers of Soviet society, especially the workers and provincial intelligentsia; now there was a marked change in the situation. People began to protest. Meetings took place in Yaroslavl, Omsk, Kuibyshev, Astrakhan, Yuzhnosakhalinsk and other cities. In some cases the meeting organizers received official permission and sacrificed the most radical of their demands – as, for example, happened in Omsk. In other cases the situation became very strained and an overt struggle with the city authorities began. In Yuzhnosakhalinsk, events went as far as strike action. In Kuibyshev, meeting organizers put up posters all over the city calling on workers to join a demonstration against the local Party leader E. Muravev, who had held his post since Brezhnev's time. According to Mark Solonin, a member of the meeting's organizing committee, they expected, taking into account the general excitement following the elections to the Party Conference, that they would muster around two thousand people. But on 22 June, the day of the meeting, up to thirty thousand demonstrators, comprising mainly workers from local factories, turned out on the streets. The police kept away and the chief headache for the organizing committee proved to be maintaining order and controlling the unexpectedly large crowd.

Such actions could not pass off without consequences. Odious local bureaucrats were removed from their posts in Astrakhan and Yuzhnosakhalinsk. However, it came as an unpleasant surprise to liberal-bureaucratic circles in Moscow that the activity of the masses turned out to be not the result of official appeals but, on the contrary, clearly engendered by a lack of faith in those appeals. The disparity between the slogans and the real state of affairs locally was the prime stimulus of social discontent; meanwhile, in Moscow, all the bureaucratic factions were preparing the latest political compromise.

This new compromise was manifested both in the abstract theses and in undemocratic elections, against which no one at the top could bring themselves to protest. Not one faction wished to 'rock the boat': the liberals were quite content with the successes that had already been achieved and did not want to risk them; and the conservatives, despite their ideological failures, felt sufficiently confident and had no desire to make new concessions – especially as the gulf between the rival groups had never been as great as one was led to believe. The conservatives continued to accommodate themselves to the new slogans and ideas, and the liberals learnt to respect the politics of the apparatus. Both groupings strove to conduct the Party Conference on the basis of a secure compromise, since neither could face an open trial of strength.

In such circumstances, uncontrolled mobilization of the lower orders and the activization of 'informals' not only irritated the conservatives but also progressives. The situation began rapidly to deteriorate. On 18 June the usual Saturday demonstration on Pushkin Square was unexpectedly dispersed by the police. Several of the demonstrators were detained as it was broken up, although all were allowed home the same evening, and criminal proceedings were instituted against eleven of those taking part. Representatives of the Moscow police, who only a few days before had behaved quite liberally, this time categorically declared that infringing the 'temporary regulations' was not permissible and that, during the Party Conference, order would be maintained in the city by the most resolute methods.

For its part, the PF organizing committee was rent by contradictions. The reformist euphoria of its first few days was sufficient for the 'Public Mandate' to be adopted unanimously, but not for the numerous ideological and political differences between the groups to be overcome. Although a majority of the committee's members viewed the new organization as a broad association of left-wing forces under the slogans of self-management and democratic socialism, a minority dreamt of a 'union of all democrats irrespective of ideological differences'. The principled differences between these two tendencies on the most important questions of the development of the social movement had always existed and it was only in the circumstances of the unbridled optimism that had reigned among 'informal' leaders at the beginning of June that the disagreements had, for a short while, been forgotten. As soon as normal work commenced in the organizing committee, the differences immediately came to the surface. Civil Dignity, Perestroika 88 and a few representatives of other groups insisted on the removal forthwith of the word 'socialism' from all Popular Front documents. Essentially it became a matter of turning the PF into a kind of second edition of the Democratic Union. The founders of DU hoped to gather under their banner all 'informals' on the basis of an acknowledgement of a number of elementary principles of Western liberalism. The attempt was unsuccessful because the right-wing views of Novodvorskaya and her colleagues deliberately excluded any possibility of genuine ideological compromise with the Left. Novodvorskaya was an odious figure to the Left and joining her within the DU held few attractions. Meanwhile, it seemed that the moderate liberals of Civil Dignity and Perestroika 88 could, under certain conditions, come to an agreement with the socialists and achieve what Novodvorskaya had failed to do.

In turn, the 'informal' liberals were in dire need of some form of support from the Left as they were incapable of creating any kind of serious organization or of gaining even minimal support among the lower orders. Unless they subordinated themselves to the Left, the liberals could hope for no real success among the masses.

At first, the left groups made concessions quite easily on the organizing committee. But, quite unexpectedly to everyone, the anarcho-syndicalists of the Commune club joined forces with Civil Dignity and resolutely supported the demand that the words about democratic socialism and self-management be removed from the documents of the PF. Representatives of the largest socialist clubs, Democratic Perestroika and Socialist Initiative, capitulated and signed the document in the form prepared by Commune and Civil Dignity. However, all hell broke loose when the delegates returned to their groups and reported on the results of the voting. Activists refused to ratify such a document and a majority of clubs demanded its immediate revision.

Of course, this was not just a matter of two or three words being inserted into the Popular Front's draft platform. The conflict around the document showed quite simply that the socialist clubs had to pay too high a price for 'democratic solidarity' with the liberals and anarchists. An organization with slogans that were too broad and abstract could scarcely hope to win a genuine mass base: Soviet people, weary after decades of generalities and fine slogans, are primarily interested in a concrete programme which is not just political but social and economic as well. On the other hand, socialist ideas, despite the changes in the political environment, are so firmly rooted in the public consciousness that any organization not advancing socialist slogans is perceived by the broad masses as suspicious, if not downright dangerous. The gulf between the pro-capitalist sentiments of part of the privileged Moscow intelligentsia (from where dissidents used to recruit their supporters) and the spontaneous socialism of the masses was one of the major reasons for the isolation and unpopularity of dissidents during the Brezhnev era. Now, in the event of the victory of 'democratic solidarity', the same fate might also befall the Popular Front.

Alternatively, accepting the conditions laid down by the liberals would have meant that the socialists were not only repudiating their own organization and programme but becoming no more than the radical wing of a liberal organization, working for someone else's programme and ideology. Since the socialist clubs constituted the overwhelming majority both in the organizing committee and in the entire democratic movement, such a result was clearly undesirable. At a gathering of Socialist Initiative, one of the group's ideologists, Mikhail Maliutin, spoke of

a liberal liana which is winding itself around the growing socialist tree in order to stifle it. . . . The more the socialist and communist independent Left is today not yet a forest but a few hundred more or less attractive saplings, the more we must care for their well-being.

In the end the draft was revised and words about 'democratic socialism'

11

appeared as in the original text. Commune and Civil Dignity, who had threatened to leave the organizing committee if it adopted 'sectarian' formulations on the need for a struggle for socialist principles, did not carry out their threat and remained happily in their seats. It seemed as though the conflict had been settled but, in fact, it was no longer a question of this word or that. Profound differences in the groups' political thinking inevitably surfaced at the first serious crisis. This happened rather quicker than expected, only a few days after the question of ideological formulations had been finally resolved.

The meeting of the organizing committee on 24 June, at which the question of holding the next demonstration on Pushkin Square was decided, was the first I happened to attend (previously our group, Socialist Initiative, had been represented by Mikhail Maliutin and Vitaly Ponomarev, but now it was my turn). People crowded into the comparatively small flat of the committee's Secretary, Aleksandr Fedorovsky. The general confusion was heightened by the presence of a number of guests and correspondents. A crew from Soviet Central Television efficiently made a film, although it was doubtful whether it would be televised in the near future. Nevertheless, the discussion proceeded in a fairly businesslike manner: the warnings from the police, who had already broken up the demonstration on Pushkin Square on 18 June, were considered and all conceivable organizational problems were discussed.

The most interesting part of the meeting began, however, somewhat later when Andrei Danilov, a member of Democratic Perestroika, suddenly burst into Fedorovsky's flat and reported that Commune and Civil Dignity had just announced to the city authorities their refusal to demonstrate on Pushkin Square. In Danilov's words, these groups had met with the City Prosecutor and capitulated completely, betraying the other members of the PF. 'This meeting was arranged by these two groups practically in secret. ... In other words, it's a case of their going their own way.' The conclusion of Danilov's speech was drowned by cries of indignation. Ponomarev, who was chairing the meeting, tried unsuccessfully to restore order. Soon the actual leaders of Commune, A. Isaev and A. Shubin, turned up followed by Viktor Zolotarev from Civil Dignity. They declared that it was not a matter of capitulation but of an 'honourable compromise'.

The essence of the agreement reached at the meeting between the two groups and representatives of the Prosecutor's Office was that if they refused to participate in the demonstration on Pushkin Square, they would instead be allowed to hold an alternative demonstration, legally and even with the assistance of the Komsomol City Committee, in another part of the City – by the Palace of Youth.

This wasn't the best place for meetings and demonstrations: there were few passers-by, it was a long way from the city centre, and so on. But this wasn't the main problem. Relinquishing demonstrations on Pushkin Square could only be interpreted by the authorities as a sign of weakness, and the many people who regularly came to the Square on a Saturday to participate in the actions of the Popular Front would feel they had been deceived. However, the authorities' threats had a very strong impact on the supporters of 'democratic solidarity'. Although, on 28 May, it was Commune and Civil Dignity who had insisted more than anyone else on demonstrations, stressing that 'there is nothing that can threaten us', Isaev and Zolotarev now changed their tune. 'They'll use rubber truncheons on Pushkin Square!'; 'There'll be arrests!' People were openly afraid.

The arguments grew fiercer with both sides engaging in mutual re-criminations. It seemed that the organizing committee meeting was turning into a scene from the theatre of the absurd. A minority demanded the immediate cancellation of the previously announced rally; the majority categorically insisted that it go ahead. Any attempts to reach a compromise collapsed as the disputants were simply not listening to one another. This culminated in Zolotarev's unexpected statement that 'three minutes ago, Andrei Danilov, whom I respected until today, committed a quite impermissible gesture ... he grabbed hold of my ear'. An embarrassed Danilov explained that he had simply wanted to draw his interlocutor's attention to what he was saying. Zolotarev energetically demanded an apology and threatened to leave the premises. Someone persuaded the excited wranglers to make it up. Some were laughing, others shouting and trying to score points off each other. Even people in the corridor, who had gone out to get some air, soon started fresh arguments. There was clearly no point in continuing the discussion.

Only later in the evening, after the overwhelming majority of groups had voted for the rally to go ahead and representatives of the minority had walked out in protest, did normal organizational work get under way. The red, yellow and green flag of the Popular Front was approved (there was simply no time for members of the organizing committee, wearied by senseless arguments, to concern themselves with the subtleties of political symbolism: the flag was designed to symbolize 'socialism, ecology and freedom'). Agreement was reached on the order of activities, and tasks were allotted for the following day.

In reaching their decision, the majority's starting point was that a significant number of people had already been informed of the forthcoming demonstration and would go there anyway. Transporting an already assembled crowd to another part of town (as supporters of the compromise suggested) was technically impossible. The threats from the authorities had to be met, not with panic, but with organization and discipline.

In reality such threats were just a sign of confusion. The USSR Minister of Justice, V. Kravtsov, later frankly acknowledged this in an interview with *Izvestiya*. In his words, 'the forces of order at times seem defenceless in the face of a crowd. We have no special equipment or experience of how to behave in such situations.' According to Kravtsov's figures, from 1986–88, in Moscow, Leningrad, Sverdlovsk and other cities more than two hundred and fifty unauthorized, sizeable meetings, processions and demonstrations took place, which the police had no power to prevent.[5] Of course, it was not just a question of the police lacking special equipment. Any attempt to break up the meeting on Pushkin Square would have led to an open and, perhaps, prolonged battle between hundreds of PF supporters and the 'forces of order' – before the eyes of Western correspondents in the crowd, who had come to the capital to cover the Nineteenth Party Conference. Although the prospect did not fill members of the organizing committee with delight, the official circles were even more scared.

On the morning of 25 June, there was still much that remained unclear. The telephones of all active members of the organizing committee were constantly ringing. Some members of Commune and other minority groups could not conceal their surprise at the position taken by their own leaders. It quite soon became known that at the start of the day the police had not received their final instructions. Police officers told our activists that the order to disperse the meeting or demonstration had still not come through. Taking advantage of this, the organizing committee directed its representatives to hold discussions with the police.

14

Organizing committee members also went to the Party Central Committee but no one wished to meet them. Long and inconclusive negotiations were held with the authorities at various levels. One way or another, the official organs were now informed of our position. The organizing committee was prepared to guarantee the maintenance of order only on condition that there was no attempt to wreck the meeting.

Meanwhile it became clear that Commune together with the Komsomol had also not received permission for their meeting. The 'honourable compromise' had turned out to be a straightforward swindle. While this sensational news was being discussed in the organizing committee a report arrived that the Democratic Union intended to enter the Square under their own slogans at the same time as we did and to draw the crowd behind them, thus enjoying the fruits of our two weeks of organizational labour. If supporters of the PF had not previously displayed any special sympathy for the DU, this news provoked a real outburst of anger among the socialists. Meanwhile, the police, who had no particular insight into the contradictions between the DU and the PF, began in the morning to block off Pushkin Square and, to be on the safe side, made ready buses for taking arrested trouble-makers to the cells, irrespective of which organization they belonged to. The telephones of leaders of the organizing committee were permanently engaged. It became known that representatives of Civil Dignity were ringing round people to tell them that the square was closed and there was no need to go because nothing was happening there.

It was decided that, right at the start of the demonstration, organizing committee members would gather by one of the shops on the Square for a final explanation of the situation. When I finally got there at half past three, there was no one at the appointed place; however, an excited crowd was already buzzing on the other side of the Square. Police buses and patrols were not so much pushing passers-by to one side as assembling them. No one understood what was going on but everyone was waiting for something. Members of the organizing committee scattered among the crowd, trying to find one another and to make sense of the situation.

The fact was that the DU had appeared half an hour before us, but had failed to achieve anything. At the first attempt to begin a meeting, twelve of the Union's activists were swiftly seized by the police and led away to buses. Naturally, this had only roused the crowd's interest.

15

No one knew why these people had been taken away. 'Who are they? What are they protesting about? Why are they being arrested?', people asked each other and the police. But no one could provide a sensible answer to satisfy the general curiosity.

Yuri Rapmanov, a representative of the Higher Komsomol School, who found himself an accidental participant in these events, later wrote that 'the Square resembled an agitated beehive'. What stuck in his memory most of all was 'how a KGB official carried out "ideological work" (he later turned up showing his papers). He forced himself into the very heart of the people and screamed "Comrades! They're killing them!" The police rushed towards him, trying to arrest the murderers'.[6]

From time to time an activist of the DU would pull out a new placard calling for the disbanding of the KGB or the establishment of a multi-party system. Just as quickly, these placards would be torn to pieces by the police. They were written in uneven letters on small pieces of blue cardboard and, standing in the thick of the crowd, it was quite impossible to read them. There was no co-ordination of any kind between DU activists; it was quite clear that these people saw themselves as victims of tyranny rather than organizers of mass action.

The Popular Front demonstration began, as planned, at four o'clock sharp at the other end of the square. Placards and the red, green and yellow flags of the PF unexpectedly appeared. The police were in some confusion – who should they seize first? The colonel conducting the operation declared that he would give the PF fifteen minutes to have its say and leave the Square, then he added another fifteen minutes, and then another ten. The co-ordination and decisiveness of the PF activists present in the Square made dispersal virtually impossible. The meeting had started and enveloped the Square so speedily that even members of the organizing committee were taken by surprise: they had to run to secure their place among the ranks of the demonstrators or on the improvised 'platform'.

This level of organization was in marked contrast to the chaos which had reigned the previous evening during the meeting of the leading group. This time the speakers spoke one after another, strictly observed their time limit and quickly gave way to their comrades. Calls rang out for free elections to the soviets and the legalization of the Popular Front. The crowd began to chant slogans. For the first time there was in front of us not simply a gathering of 'informals' but a genuine social movement capable of speaking with one voice.

However, when, after the promised forty minutes were up, the organizing committee decided to give in to the demands of the police and leave the Square, only a few hundred activists followed them. The majority of passers-by, who were there by accident, remained in their places waiting to see what would happen next. Some members of the socialist groups also stayed on, losing sight of the hastily retiring organizing committee. I was myself seized upon by Western journalists – Canadians, British, Italians, Brazilians – who grabbed the remaining representatives of the PF and demanded that we give them an interview. Viktor Girshfeld, who headed the Citizens' Diplomacy group and had also been unable to leave the Square, fell into the press maelstrom. Oleg Rumyantsev from Democratic Perestroika got lost somewhere when crossing the street and couldn't find his group. When, having explained to curious foreigners for the last time the essence of the PF's ideas, I finally tore myself away from the Square, the column of demonstrators, which had again been swelled by casual passers-by, had already gone down along Tverskaya Boulevard, and was out of sight. The police accompanied the demonstration for about a kilometre but were forced to stop at the boundary between two city districts: a police unit must not cross the borders of its own district; the other district was unprepared for the arrival of a demonstration.

No one knew whether Commune had agreed to break the ban and go to their own meeting at the Palace of Youth and so those remaining decided to go there. Alas, disappointment awaited them. When I arrived at the Palace of Youth along with other members of Socialist Initiative who were straggling behind the demonstration, there was no sign of Commune and Civil Dignity. Instead of the proposed meeting there was a military brass band, which for some reason was playing a robbers' song from the 1920s. A group of Commune members meanwhile gathered on Kropotkin Street by the memorial to Engels, for whom they had no special love, but they decided not to begin the meeting under the disapproving gaze of the rapidly arriving police. Supporters of the organizing committee, who were walking past, suggested to the 'splitters' that they join the majority demonstration but were decisively rebuffed. In the end, people from the minority faction just went home for dinner.

17

As one might have expected, in marching from one place to another, the organizing committee had lost a significant number of people. The column proceeded in quite an organized fashion until it was decided to go down to the Metro. After this only some of the demonstrators managed to assemble in a new place. Once again some members of the organizing committee itself got lost, and small groups of activists wandered around the city centre looking for their own people. Nevertheless, around two hundred people remained to hold a fresh meeting at six o'clock in a park by Frunze Embankment.

That evening, many citizens began to phone into the studios of Moscow Television demanding to be told in detail about 'the events on Pushkin Square'. The chief ideologist of the Party's Moscow *gorkom*, Yuri Karabasov, insisted on the strict enforcement of the 'temporary regulations' under which the actions on Pushkin Square were unlawful. These are 'legal regulations adopted constitutionally', maintained Karabasov; however, the sociologist V.G. Britvin declared that, according to surveys, the regulations were supported by only 17 per cent of the population, with 26 per cent firmly opposed and the remainder in favour of their review. Representatives of the city authorities promised the capital's inhabitants 'if not a Hyde Park, then a place for citizens to meet with Party propagandists'. Television viewers did not, however, receive more detailed explanations – ostensibly due to 'lack of time'.

Of course, the events of 25 June in Moscow do not bear comparison with the numerous demonstrations in Kuibyshev, Yuzhnosakhalinsk and Yaroslavl, not to mention Armenia and Estonia. But they were still part of a trend which showed that Moscow had not been left on the sidelines by the general rise of the popular movement. This was precisely how both the authorities and PF activists themselves viewed it. It is not surprising, therefore, that for the Left the 25 June demonstration became a kind of political symbol, the day of the real birth of the Popular Front in the capital. The groups who had refused to participate in the actions very soon not only left the organizing committee but distanced themselves in principle from the Popular Front.

Meanwhile, the Nineteenth Party Conference signified the advent of a new stage in the course of perestroika. Everyone awaited it; everyone hoped to receive an answer to their questions. And now, at last, the Conference was open. The liberal press had tried, in the months preceding the start of the Conference, to obtain live transmission of all its sessions on Central Television, but the final decision had been a negative one. Conservative groups in the apparatus, saying that the working sessions should not be turned into a farce, would not allow direct transmission. All the same, Central Television was allowed to film everything it considered necessary at the Conference. As a result the programme editors were constrained to show only the most interesting moments and to compress them into comparatively short reports. As expected, the outcome proved the direct opposite of what was intended. For millions of television viewers, the Conference turned into a fascinating political spectacle – sometimes dramatic, sometimes terrifying, and sometimes even funny.

The first day of sessions proved highly disappointing. The whole country sat by their television sets but there was nothing sensational either in Gorbachev's speech or in subsequent reports. The major event of the first stage of the Conference turned out to be the speech by Leonid Abalkin, the Director of the Institute of Economics of the Academy of Science. Summing up three years of reformist efforts 'from above', the academician asserted that 'a radical turning point in the economy has not occurred and we are not yet out of a state of stagnation'. According to Abalkin, the measures that had been taken were contradictory, inconsistent and inadequate:

> The national income, which generalizes the indicators of the country's economic and social development (I will take only the official figures of the State Committee for Statistics [Goskomstat]), has grown more slowly over the previous two years than during the stagnation years of the Eleventh Five-Year Plan. The target for such a highly important indicator of efficiency as resource conservation has not been achieved. Over these two years, it fell on average by 0.1 per cent; while in the preceding, often criticized Plan, the annual drop in material capacity constituted 0.5 per cent.[7]

The pessimistic picture drawn by Abalkin of shifts in precisely the opposite direction to that desired, could scarcely have generated much enthusiasm among the delegates. Not surprisingly, Abalkin immediately came under critical fire, both from annoyed conservatives for whom the Soviet economy is the best in the world and from liberals indignant at so low an opinion of their reforming efforts. Abalkin was primarily accused of lacking a 'positive programme' although everyone knew perfectly well that he was continually calling for the experience of Scandinavian social democracy to be utilized, for state regulation of the market and for the priority development of the social sphere. In this regard Abalkin fell between two stools: on the one hand the bureaucracy's conservative centralism and, on the other, the liberals' advocacy of the 'free market'. He could find potential allies only on the left, but supporters of the Popular Front were naturally not represented at the Conference. Nevertheless, many rank-and-file delegates, not to mention millions of television viewers, recalled that Abalkin's speech was one of the most apposite.

Economic questions were, however, very quickly pushed into the background. Some delegates demanded an 'expansion of glasnost' and greater autonomy for the press; others, on the other hand, were exasperated by the fact that glasnost had gone too far. The writer, Yuri V. Bondarev, one of the pillars of official literature during the Brezhnev era, spoke out indignantly about the 'immorality of the press', which was exposing everything to doubt and stunning the reader 'with noise, bad language, re-examinations and the distortion of historical facts'.[8] Vitaly Korotich, editor-in-chief of *Ogonyok*, caused general embarrassment to delegates and gained extra popularity among viewers when he laid on Gorbachev's table a list of four participants in the Conference suspected of bribe-taking.

Everyone awaited Boris Yeltsin's intervention, and he certainly didn't disappoint viewers' expectations. Yeltsin called for a sharp cut in the Party apparatus, for the publication of the Party's expenditure figures and spoke about the limitations of glasnost – even he, a member of the Central Committee, had to address his fellow countrymen through the medium of foreign radio. In conclusion, Yeltsin appealed to delegates for his political rehabilitation and for the dropping of the accusations made against him at the Plenum of the Party's Moscow *gorkom* in October 1987. 'Rehabilitation after fifty years has now become commonplace and this is having a beneficial effect on the health of society. But I am personally requesting political rehabilitation while I'm still alive.'[9]

Soon after Yeltsin, Yegor Ligachev had his say, launching fierce attacks against his long-standing opponent. Ligachev's speech made quite a deep impression on both TV and radio audiences. In a public opinion poll carried out after the Conference, Ligachev undoubtedly proved the most unpopular political figure in the country. Particular anger was aroused by his efforts to deny the privileges of the Party apparatus. The intelligentsia, who had not previously complained about Ligachev, reacted painfully to his sharp remarks towards the press.

Overall, Yeltsin was the moral victor at the Conference. Judging by public opinion polls, his popularity had risen even higher just as Gorbachev's was waning. For example, during a survey conducted in Kazan on the results of the Conference, 65.5 per cent responded positively to Yeltsin's report, 32.8 per cent to Abalkin's, and only 6.9 per cent to Gorbachev's. Typically, Ligachev was firmly in last place on the list, having gained only 3.5 per cent positive and 65.5 per cent negative responses. Gorbachev, while not generating any great enthusiasm among the viewers, did not provoke any particular irritation: only 3.5 per cent of those surveyed responded negatively to his report and interventions.[10]

The Party Conference did not take any sensational decisions – the Kazan survey suggested the overwhelming majority of the population was dissatisfied or 'not completely satisfied' with its outcome. But nor were there any grounds for calling it a flop. The Conference's massive significance lay in the fact that the public gained an immediate opportunity to observe the clash of various political views and was able to understand the differences between one political leader and another. In short, the Party Conference raised the masses' level of political competence.

The Conference's most important decisions were unanticipated not only by the general public but also by activists in the unofficial political groups. Gorbachev's proposals to convene a Congress of People's Deputies in spring 1989 and to combine the posts of President of the Congress and First Secretary of the corresponding Party committee originated directly at the Conference and had not been discussed beforehand. To all appearances this was something of a surprise even to the delegates. On the one hand, the Conference proclaimed the principle of returning all power from the Party to elected soviets; but on the other, the proposed solutions could in no sense satisfy even comparatively moderate supporters of democratization. Direct elections to the Supreme Soviet were replaced by indirect ones. In reality, ordinary voters were deprived of the opportunity to influence directly the composition of the highest legislative body. The packed Congress of People's Deputies, unable to function, would only have to meet for a few days in order to elect at once both chambers of the Supreme Soviet. In addition, the Congress would be composed, according to Gorbachev's plan, not only of elected deputies from constituencies but also of representatives of official organizations elected at plenums and conferences (including representatives of the Party!). Everyone had already had a fine opportunity to familiarize themselves with how these 'internal' elections would proceed during the run-up to the Conference. The overwhelming majority of Popular Front supporters, therefore, adopted a sharply critical attitude to the proposed Congress. Essentially, it appeared to be a new version of the representation of estates from the Middle Ages, with popular deputies sitting alongside delegates of the nomenklatura and bureaucratic lords unelected by the people. Popular Front lawyers calculated that top officials, who were in the leading organs of several official organizations, would have the right to vote two or three times when ordinary citizens would only be able to vote once. In essence, the principle of a universal, equal electoral right had thus been overturned. It was also plain that the most unpopular figures in Party and State, who would genuinely risk being defeated in a general election, could now certainly enter the Congress and then be elected to the Supreme Soviet.

The plan to combine offices also drew severe criticism, with many seeing it as an attempt to create the semblance of a transfer of power to the soviets without genuine political reform. Only Gorbachev's proposal to hold elections to the local soviets by October 1989 gained the support of the Popular Front.

At any event, the Party Conference did not signal the end of the social upsurge. Spontaneous meetings and discussions continued on Pushkin Square and in the Arbat district of Moscow. The PF organizing committee, stronger after the cessation of internal squabbling, strove actively to utilize the remaining warm months for work on the streets. On 31 July Socialist Initiative received permission to hold a meeting at the Olympic sports complex – this in fact became the capital's first official meeting in support of the Popular Front. A fresh meeting took place in Kuibyshev on 21 July which this time had already been officially sanctioned. Representatives of the city authorities had made careful arrangements for it and mobilized 'their own people' to endorse the 'policies of the Party *obkom* and *gorkom*'. Previously prepared slogans in defence of Muravyev and his course were handed out in the enterprises. The result, however, was the complete opposite of what had been planned. The crowd of many thousands, mobilized by the authorities themselves, decisively backed the supporters of the Popular Front. In fact, they would not let Muravev and his entourage speak. 'Their speeches,' the local paper acknowledged, 'or at least those bits that could be heard, were reduced to general phrases about perestroika, criticism of the informals and appeals to the effect that "we must work".'[11] Repeating like an incantation the slogan 'democracy is impossible without discipline', they were unable to advance a single concrete proposal. The authorities' helplessness contrasted especially sharply with the organization of the masses. As the police conceded, they had practically nothing to do at the meeting.

The direct consequence of the meeting in Kuibyshev was the removal of Muravev from his post. Even hostile journalists were forced to acknowledge that this success had turned the Popular Front in Kuibyshev into a real political force: 'an obscure group has grown in three months into a solid organization with its own sections, programmatic and constitutional positions and a definite political orientation'.[12]

The number of organizing committees in the localities continued to grow like an avalanche. The local press in Yaroslavl, Kuibyshev and Kazan was no longer just criticizing the 'informals' but more and more often letting them have their say. In many cases, supporters of the Popular Front gained the opportunity not only to declare their principles in the pages of the press but also to promote their own candidates in elections. In Irkutsk, a PF candidate was elected to the local soviet. In Kazan the PF candidate, Yuri S. Kotov, became head of the nature conservation department at the local university although he was opposed by the *raikom* First Secretary, B. D. Leushin. The PF candidate received 75.7 per cent of the votes cast but was not recognized as the winner as he had not gained a majority of the overall number of those registered to vote in that electoral district (of the 11,074 registered electors, only about 6,500 had voted on polling day). However, despite the fact that 38 per cent failed to vote, the PF was able to celebrate victory as the balance in favour of its candidate was obvious. The growth in the ranks of the movement permitted one of the ideologists and leaders of the PF in Kazan, the writer Dias Valiev, to declare triumphantly that 'the time has arrived for the people's open political activity and a movement has finally arisen that is capable of seriously talking about socialism'.[13]

Nevertheless, there were no grounds for claiming that the movement was experiencing an uninterrupted rise. Throughout the country, activists were weary and the disillusionment of the masses in the results of the Party Conference was taking its toll. The PF's organizational structures, which had yet to take shape fully, could not cope with the continuously mounting volume of work. Useless information was being supplied. There was not enough money and an absence of computers and duplicating machinery; the lack of experience also had its effect. In turn, the bureaucratic circles, having recovered from the initial shock engendered by the appearance of the masses protesting in the streets, quickly began to draw up countermeasures.

The bureaucratic counter-offensive against the PF took two forms. First, administrative pressure on activists was increased. Those participating in unauthorized demonstrations began to be arrested and fined more regularly. As a matter of urgency, the Presidium of the Supreme Soviet replaced the temporary regulations on meetings and demonstrations with a corresponding decree. Henceforth local authorities had complete freedom to ban any meetings 'on legal grounds' and in accordance with the principles of a 'legal state'. Another decree gave special detachments of the internal forces, among other things, authorization to enter residential and commercial premises without the permission of the Procurator in search of 'suspicious' people. Whilst the first decree clearly seemed to be a 'muzzle' for unofficial political groups, the second could, in theory, be applied against whomever they liked. In practice, its first victims also proved to be 'informals'.

On 21 August, the Democratic Union tried to organize another unauthorized demonstration on Pushkin Square, this time devoted to the twentieth anniversary of the Soviet invasion of Czechoslovakia. The Popular Front also declared its condemnation of the invasion but decided not to participate in the demonstration – in our opinion, every political action should set itself a specific goal corresponding to today's situation. The DU's demonstrations, devoted to the anniversaries of various historical events and timetabled many months in advance, could not produce any real political results but provided ideal opportunities for all kinds of provocation. The city authorities knew in advance of the DU's planned action and prepared carefully for it. They intended on that day to teach the 'informals' a serious lesson.

Not only the regular police were involved in dispersing the DU's demonstration. Detachments of special forces had the opportunity to display themselves in all their glory. Dozens of people were beaten up and arrested. The demonstrators certainly did not expect such vicious reprisals. 'People were dragged by the hair across the tarmac', DU member Aleksandr Chuev later recalled. 'They kicked people in the head, beat them on the tarmac and punched them with lead-filled gloves. In the buses and then in the cells they beat them with truncheons.'[14] Those detained were taken to Police Station 108 where the violence continued. They took away notebooks from journalists and exposed their films. Among those arrested were passers-by and PF members who had gone just to observe the demonstration.

That evening a group of PF activists set out for Pushkin Square to obtain the release of those detained. They were met by a unit of 'special forces' who demanded that they leave immediately. In response to people's protests, one of the 'servants of law and order' asked threateningly 'Have you been reading too much Gorbachev?' When Vitaly Ponomarev together with a few comrades managed to reach Police Station 108 they encountered an ambulance and a woman doctor coming out of the station in tears repeating, 'They're bastards who did this!' Some photographers were at the scene trying to take pictures through the lighted windows of the police station of those who had been beaten up, but they were set upon by people in the grey uniforms of the 'special forces', who exposed their films and began to beat them up. When PF activists rushed to the aid of those being attacked, yet another group of 'grey angels' suddenly raced out of the station and flung themselves upon them with cries of 'Get out of here or you'll regret it!' Using truncheons, they drove people back to Pushkin Square shouting, 'Get a move on! Don't you dare come back', and so on.

Repressive actions against 'trouble-makers' were only one aspect, and not the most dangerous at that, of the new conservative strategy. Rather more menacing was the campaign which began in the press. In reality, the clashes on the streets were only a pretext for publishing numerous articles in the press against 'the irresponsible ringleaders of mass disorder'. Readers of the newspapers now gleaned information about the PF and DU primarily from the crime section in which, naturally, no serious distinction was drawn between the two organizations. Typically, the most aggressive and mendacious articles were published in precisely those organs of the press which considered themselves to be liberal.

Moskovskie Novosti carried an article by Gleb Pavlovsky entitled 'The last carriage' in which the Popular Front was accused of 'totalitarian methods'.[15] Naturally, the author did not produce a single concrete fact in support of his thesis and did not mention a single name, but the newspaper's liberal reputation seemed to serve as a guarantee of the seriousness of the accusations being levelled. It was typical that this publication, which had prided itself in giving a right to reply to Nina Andreeva's Stalinism, refused to print letters in response sent to the editors from PF activists after this and other articles of a similar nature.

In turn, *Ogonyok*, while not directly mentioning the Moscow Popular Front, came down on those 'who today dress themselves up in "left" phrases and try and take advantage of the wave of democracy and glasnost in order to rock the boat', arouse 'passions at meetings instead of work, slogans instead of deeds and supercharged emotions instead of constructive searches'.[16]

Thus, just when conservative apparatchiks were beginning swiftly and consistently to assemble a new repressive machinery, the liberal press could find nothing better to do than present the PF as a threat to democratization! Typically, many liberal commentators began not simply to attack the Left but to speak in the language of the conservatives, repeating word for word their appeals: 'don't rock the boat' and 'we must work!'. Gleb Pavlovsky's appearance as one of the chief ideologists of the new crusade against the Left was highly significant. For a few months prior to this, Pavlovsky, a participant in the August conference of unofficial groups in Moscow, was considered one of the most radical representatives of the liberal camp, a journalist who was undoubtedly close to the Left. However, by the end of summer 1988, the liberal press had accomplished a turn to the right as if under orders. How can this be explained?

It is quite clear that the spectre of the mass movement, which really made itself felt on the eve of the Party Conference, frightened many not just in the apparatus but also among the intelligentsia. If the liberal elite dreamed of a mass movement in support of perestroika, which would not advance its own demands or act independently and would not break the rules of the intra-Party struggle, then by mid-1988 it had finally become clear that there could simply be no such movement. A straightforward choice was posed: either an independent popular movement to the left of the official liberals, or no movement at all. In conditions where the liberal faction in the apparatus had been successful in achieving a compromise with the conservatives on many issues, where former radicals already occupied comfortable, bureaucratic offices, where members of the intellectual elite had gained the opportunity to travel abroad unhindered and to publish their works comparatively freely, any readiness to take political risks in these circles had rapidly subsided. In short, the second variant appeared rather more attractive than the first.

The events in Armenia became the first graphic example of the change that had taken place. The political situation there deteriorated as soon as the Party Conference finished because of the inability of the central organs to make any concessions to the popular call for the return of Nagorny Karabakh to the republic. In the meantime, the new upsurge of popular actions, strikes and demonstrations in Yerevan led the Moscow leadership to toughen its stance still further. An extremely unpleasant impression was created for television viewers as Gorbachev cut short Armenian deputies at a session of the Presidium of the USSR Supreme Soviet which was deliberating on the Karabakh question. Afterwards, activists in the Armenian movement even began to call Gorbachev a 'traitor'. But this went beyond the position of a single individual, even if that individual was the General Secretary of the CPSU. Gorbachev's hardline position regarding Armenian demands reflected the common opinion which had formed in the apparatus. Concessions to the mass movement were viewed as a sign of weakness and a threat to 'the general line'. The numerous civil initiatives of uncoordinated groups, unable to become an autonomous political factor but quite suitable for use as an additional argument in the polemic within the apparatus, of course, deserved every support – in this sense the Civil Dignity group and those like it appeared quite attractive. But then the mass socialist organizations with their base in the working class and rank-and-file intelligentsia were perceived as a threat.

It is highly revealing that the small liberal groups which split away from the PF organizing committee in June very soon abandoned the idea of founding some sort of parallel organization and began to oppose even more sharply the very notion of a Popular Front. In essence the slowing down was determined by the attitude of the masses, but this in turn presupposed a serious discussion on tactical, strategic and theoretical questions.

Liberal commentators diligently avoided discussing the strategy of perestroika. The more unclear the strategic perspective became, the more newspaper editors became fascinated with the past. They published one report after another about the crimes or even personal shortcomings of Stalin during the 1930s and 1940s; they eulogized Bukharin, who it turned out was always right about everything throughout the 1920s; and exposed the traitor Trotsky who, in the struggle with Stalin, dared to break the rules of the contest inside the apparatus and set out on the path of revolutionary action. On the other hand, today's events, the new official decisions and slogans of perestroika were stifled in the best traditions of Brezhnev's 'propaganda of success'. One could speak of obstacles on the path to change, 'the difficulties of perestroika', and of bureaucratic obstructiveness but not of the contradictions and inconsistencies of the chosen course itself. This could no longer be explained by censorship restrictions – in those cases where an editor had really tried to 'push through' controversial material he had, as a rule, succeeded. Rather, it was due to a conscious political choice: that of travelling the path of moderation, of upholding the principle of compromise decisions, and of not 'rocking the boat'. The liberals have come to realize more and more that, to use Gorbachev's expression, they are sitting in essentially the same boat as the conservatives.

Of course, the 'retrograde step' made by some liberal apparatchiks and commentators was insufficient to change the development of events. Even in the liberal-official milieu, far from everyone was inclined to moderation. On the contrary, some representatives of the intelligentsia became more radical. The organizations of the Left, which had grown stronger during the course of the hot summer of 1988, were not so easily edged out of the positions they now occupied. Many journalists consistently defended the principles of glasnost, irrespective of the vacillations in the political conjuncture. Nevertheless it must be said that, by the end of the summer of 1988, the forces of the Left were being met by a serious political challenge and a new situation for which they were unprepared. The movement was in crisis.

NOTES

1.   *Izvestiya*, 30 June 1988.
2.   *Ust'-Ilimskaya Pravda*, 3 June 1988.
3.   *Moskovskaya Pravda*.
4.   *Moskovskaya Komsomolets*, 17 June 1988.
5.   *Izvestiya*, 30 July 1988.
6.   *Komsomolskaya Iskra*, 2 September 1988.
7.   *Izvestiya*, 30 June 1988.
8.   *Izvestiya*, 1 July 1988.
9.   *Izvestiya*, 8 June 1988.
10. See *Vestnik Narodnovo Fronta Tatarii*, no. 1, 1988, p.3.
11. *Volzhsky Komsomolets*, 31 July 1988.
12. *Volzhsky Komsomolets*, 11 September 1988.
13. *Sovetskaya Tatariya*, 28 August 1988.
14. *Levyi Povorot*, no. 14, 1988, p. 37.
15. *Moskovskie Novosti*, 2 October 1988.
16. *Ogonyok*, no. 38, 1988, p. 8.

=2=

The Popular Front Movement
in Crisis?

For unofficial social and political groups across the country, August 1988 was a month of conferences. First, the combined conference of the Federation of Socialist Social Clubs (FSOK) and the All-Union Social and Political Club (VSPK) took place in Moscow. After that many of its participants once again boarded trains, not to return home, but to move to Leningrad to the conference of Popular Fronts and democratic movements.

The chief outcome of the meetings between FSOK and VSPK was the unification and some regulation of the information network. This did not, however, have any particular results as both organizations were undergoing an internal crisis and by autumn had in fact disintegrated. Participants in the meetings exchanged addresses, discussed specific questions regarding the political situation and then dispersed.

Undoubtedly, more was expected from Leningrad. While the time was not yet ripe to announce an All-Russian Popular Front, it was essential to take some decisions in preparation for a founding congress of the PF. Nevertheless, not only was no date named in Leningrad for such a congress, but an organizing committee was not even elected and the gathering ended in a clear split. A majority of those who had turned up complained about the conference's poor arrangements. The organizers had been unable to get assistance from the city authorities or receive permission to use any official premises. In moving from one flat to another someone inevitably got lost and then delegations went across the city in search of their missing members. Various claims were constantly being made to the credentials commission, especially as the deliberately broad character of the conference (not simply PF, but PF and democratic movements) gave absolutely no opportunity to determine simply who were delegates and who were guests and observers. All groups received one vote irrespective of their size and influence. At the same time decisions in the sections – when it was possible to have a vote at all – were taken by a simple majority of those present. Everyone who happened to be in the room at the time voted: observers, guests, journalists. The last two sessions took place outside the city near the ruins of a Finnish pillbox which constituted part of the Mannerheim Line during the Soviet–Finnish War in 1940. This provided the basis for some witticisms about 'the conference on the Mannerheim line'.

All the same, no one was left to spend the night at the railway station, everyone who came secured overnight accommodation, and not one of the planned activities was disrupted. Many Muscovites said not unreasonably that it would have been impossible in the capital to guarantee even this level of organization.

The conference's major problems were not, of course, provoked by organizational hiccups. Its participants were clearly divided into two groupings: one group insisted on the creation of workable structures and the adoption in the near future of programmatic documents, and stressed the movement's socialist ideals; the other did not want a unified organization, argued about the dangers of centralism and bureaucratism and made reference to general democratic principles. The first grouping centred around the delegation from the Moscow Popular Front. The second comprised some of the Leningraders, representatives of the Moscow clubs which had not joined the PF and some provincial delegates who distrusted Moscow.

The arguments were so heated that it was impossible to call them comradely discussions. The Muscovites were accused of wanting to subordinate everyone to themselves, seize power and even create a totalitarian, bureaucratic organization. In turn, one of the Muscovites spoke of sabotage, provocations and attempts to disrupt the conference. Even the report that the Presidium of the Supreme Soviet had promulgated a new decree granting virtually unlimited powers – right up to the power to enter private homes and industrial premises without permission – to special units of the internal troops, did not alter the situation. Whilst conservative forces were preparing effective means for combatting possible manifestations of social unrest, the democratic public continued to argue about the harm caused by any organization, and about the preferability of exchanging information over co-ordinated actions, which violate the 'sovereignty of individual clubs'. Voting was extremely difficult as the opponents of organization would immediately begin to protest – always on the formal grounds that neither the credentials commission nor the organizing committee had defined precisely the rights and powers of the participants, guests, and so on.

The draft programme of the Popular Front, proposed by the Moscow delegation, was approved as to its socio-political reference points and it was decided to distribute it for discussion within the groups. The conference was simply in no state, however, to go any further than this. Even the socio-political reference points were not seriously discussed. Both sides had spent so long arguing about whether the movement needed a programme at all that there was simply insufficient time to discuss its content! Not one amendment was accepted to the Moscow PF document. When the question of co-ordinating activities was reached, passions were strained to the limit and one of the Leningraders called for no vote to be taken. Some of those attending had left the premises but a vote took place all the same. As expected, the resolution proposed by the Moscow PF gained an overwhelming majority among those who remained and, considering themselves the victors, its supporters even began to sing the 'Internationale'.

However, even the opposing side were quite satisfied with the outcome, since it was now always possible to dispute the results of the voting – only slightly more than half the officially registered delegates took part in it. Many provincial delegates had left the meeting before the question of the fateful resolution arose (conference participants had this time assembled outside the city in the canteen of a tourist centre, but the session dragged on so long that delegates from other cities simply risked missing their trains). Many left fed up with the continual wranglings and chaos which reigned at the conference sessions. Some even left the conference during the first day.

When the Moscow PF representatives finally gathered for a meeting in the flat on Ligovsky Prospekt, which served as the conference head-quarters, the main problem was to ascertain the opinion of the real major-ity of delegates. Many of them, only calling in at the flat on their own business, realized there had been a split. The Sverdlovsk representative, Irina Prisekina, was only finally caught up with in Moscow. There were some amusing moments: someone had left in the headquarters flat a signature to be appended to any resolution gaining a majority of votes. Since the question of a majority had always been in dispute, it had not been possible to use the signature.

But, it was not, of course, a matter of whether or not the Moscow PF representatives had been able to stretch their number of votes. Judging by what provincial delegates had said at the flat, such a majority undoubt-edly existed, although some groupings supported the idea of a PF co-ordinating centre with serious reservations, which it had been impossible not to take into consideration. This was not, however, the most important issue. The Leningrad conference had paradoxically repeated the situation at the Second Congress of the Russian Social-Democratic and Labour Party (RSDLP) – the departure of a section of the delegates, the division into majority and minority, the dispute over who was the real victor. It should be said that the repetition of that split followed quite logically from a similar situation: the formation of a unified organization from a large number of spontaneously formed and independent clubs possessing neither tradition nor political experience, naturally presented participants in the Popular Front movement with the same problems as had confronted Russian social democrats more than eighty-five years before. The differ-ence was that this time the movement had no well-organized nucleus or unified press such as *Iskra*, founded in exile, was in 1903, nor did it have a generally recognized ideological leader like Plekhanov.

In the end, it proved impossible to create a viable co-ordinating centre, although the most active groups were able to establish and maintain links between themselves. If the leaders of the Moscow PF – of whom I was one – considered their goal to be the consolidation of initiative groups and PF organizing committees from a number of major cities on a single foundation, then overall the conference ended in serious failure, exposing the movement's contradictions and fragility.

The results of the conference are also interesting from a sociological point of view. Those who voted for co-ordinated activities were primarily delegates from new, young groups which had been formed either immediately before or immediately after the Nineteenth Party Conference and had arisen on the wave of the mass movement. The PF initiative groups from Kuibyshev and Yuzhnosakhalinsk, which were based not on clubs but on social activists, proved the Moscow PF's natural allies. Among the Leningraders it was precisely the people who had joined in the spring or summer of 1988 who were inclined to agree most often with the Muscovites. Virtually all the clubs and groups whose membership contained some workers maintained a similar stance. On the other hand, the old clubs, which had arisen in the period of liberal euphoria following the January 1987 Plenum of the CPSU Central Committee, regarded new organizational forms with apprehension. It was, however, difficult to draw straightforward conclusions since it was frequently only the leaders of groups, expressing essentially their own personal opinions, who were involved in the discussions. It was hard to tell what sort of moods existed in the groups themselves.

Nevertheless, the outcome of the conference cleared up many things. We were up against a crisis of the old organizational forms of the movement, when a discussion club – a *tusovka*, a spontaneous gathering – was the sole possible manifestation of social activity and the free word became at times more important than concrete political propositions and activity. The mass actions prior to the Party Conference revealed that such methods were exhausted. Only on the rarest occasions had old clubs been able to gain control of the new movement and reinforce it organizationally. After the Party Conference, the thousands who had attended meetings dispersed and it was discovered that democratic and left-wing groups had hardly become any stronger. They had had no organization, structures, ideas or resources for work among the masses.

It was no accident that it was in the summer of 1988 that the idea of the Popular Front spread across the country. It expressed the need for new organizational forms. The very movement for perestroika was in need of restructuring, but for many clubs and their leaders this would mean a few sacrifices.

The small organizations which had been formed were afraid of losing their identity, and their leaders their positions, in a genuinely large organization. It was no accident, therefore, that those who shouted loudest about the dangers of the movement's bureaucratization and the threat of authoritarianism were those who led their own clubs through bureau-cratic methods. For those who were 'small, but bosses' there was a very real threat – like feudal princes they feared losing their domains.

At the same time, the original groups were drained of any reserves for growth. The only solution open to the leaders of the informal clubs in such a situation was to proclaim a Popular Front in words but without a unified organization or common programme. In this way it was possible to make use of the popular slogan and authority of the mass movement while retaining the old sectarian club forms of work.

Fortunately, the Leningrad conference showed graphically that this road would lead into a blind alley. The only means of combatting authori-tarianism and bureaucratism is a democratic decision-making procedure, but it is quite impossible to safeguard this procedure from fragmentation and rivalry between small clubs and figures who lack broad support amongst activists, not to mention the support of the workers.

If the leaders of a unified democratic organization have to report back to its membership – not only to their immediate followers, but to the whole mass of the movement's participants – then the club 'feudals' will not surrender control to the base. Even if their own clubs split or repudiate the leader, they will form a new group and then intervene at various conferences under a new name to demand their share of the cake.

There is no question of founding a centralized organization in the traditional sense of the word. Those who have made such accusations have remained silent about the fact that such a task would, apart from anything else, be technically unfeasible in existing conditions. The basic organizational work has been done at a regional level and, in the co-ordinating centre being set up, a majority of members would undoubtedly represent the regions. But this does not mean that it is possible to manage without co-ordination.

The list of addresses compiled at the conference and suggested by some as a substitute for founding an organization or co-ordinating centre did not even ensure a normal circulation of information. Everyone had to send out numerous messages, which frequently didn't receive a reply not to mention any specific help. About a month after the Leningrad meeting, a majority of regional centres began to complain that it was impossible to receive any information through the 'information network'. The people on the list found it physically impossible to respond to all the letters they received. An apparatus and resources were necessary for work and neither did or could exist, for it had not been possible to create a 'bureaucracy' in Leningrad. The Leningraders themselves stuck to this method longer than anyone, trying to circulate their information to all the addresses. But, by the middle of autumn 1988, when the political situation had taken its latest turn for the worse, it proved beyond their means to continue sending out their material across the country.

As a result, all the work of maintaining links between the regions was concentrated in the hands of the Moscow PF's information centre where the corresponding conditions for a 'good' bureaucracy were created. A similar centre began to form subsequently in Leningrad but with a great delay. Essentially the effort 'not to allow centralism' only led to yet more spontaneous centralization.

For effective political actions on a regional scale, and even more so on a countrywide scale, co-ordination is essential. Either this function is carried out by democratically formed bodies or it is undertaken by behind-the-scenes manipulators from among the 'informal feudals' or even by intelligent bureaucrats. But, in any case, it is clear that the Leningrad conference was the last chaotic gathering of the 'informals'. The split had deepened and spread across the whole country – the two tendencies simply had nothing more to say to each other in noisy and pointless *tusovki*. Practical work was the order of the day and no one was going to travel from Yuzhnosakhalinsk to Leningrad just to talk to interesting people and exchange addresses (almost all of the addresses of the conference participants were already held by the Moscow PF and the Leningrad organizing committee, this list having been used to convene the conference).

In the end, the Leningrad conference proved a fateful moment of missed opportunities. The whirlpool of political events affecting local groups gave it no time for a fundamental rethink of the movement's strategy, programme and organization. August 1988 was, for supporters of the PF, the last breathing-space before a whole series of crises. This breathing-space could have been used to arrange the co-ordination of activity and form viable organs ready to defend the movement's general interests. Nothing of the sort was done. In the best Russian traditions, the delegates of the country's active left-wing groups had wasted three days at a conference simply to swap political accusations.

The results of this failure naturally told on all the subsequent stages of the political struggle. The movement continued to grow but it was possible to see at the same time a loss of support connected to a significant extent with organizational feebleness. Most of the regional centres were left to their own devices, especially as the Muscovites, who had advanced a more or less united position in Leningrad, were in reality far from always able to establish order in their own movement.

The growth of dissatisfaction at the policies of the liberal bureaucracy was inevitably drawing an ever larger number of people into the Popular Front, but, being unable to resolve its own internal problems, the PF let slip one opportunity after another. In the summer and beginning of autumn 1988 the idea of the PF was a symbol of hope in many parts of the country. The very name 'Popular Front', wrote the Kazan University newspaper, 'like a banner, serves to unite progressive social forces'.[1] Thanks to the PF the inhabitants of Yaroslavl 'are standing straight, beginning to have respect for themselves and each other and are learning to speak in a loud voice', asserted the local press.[2] Meanwhile the movement continued to suffer from numerous organizational and political disorders which retarded its growth and undermined its authority. We had won some engagements not because of our strength but rather despite our impotence, for history was on our side. But we had lost some serious battles. And very soon after the Leningrad conference the PF movement not only in Moscow but in other parts of the country suffered a number of major blows.

The bureaucracy was increasingly aware of its own interests and was formulating its strategy ever more clearly. The liberal intelligentsia, mistrustful and at times fearful of the masses, at the same time had no real strength to make the apparatus implement its will and was losing more and more of its influence. In these conditions a powerful socialist organization was needed capable of drawing behind it broad strata of workers and of beginning to fight in a revolutionary manner. We had no such organization.

NOTES

1. *Leninets* (Kazan), 12 September 1988.
2. *Severnaya Magistral'* (Yaroslavl), 19 October 1988.

Popular Front or National Front?

Everyone had been waiting for this event. The Congress of the Estonian Popular Front, scheduled for October 1988, should have become a turning-point in the development of the social movement – and not only in Estonia and the Baltic republics. For the first time in the post-Stalin era, an independent political organization in the Soviet Union was able to declare its existence openly and officially, to hold its founding congress and to appeal to society through the state-controlled mass media.

The impetuous growth of the Popular Front in Estonia had begun back in the spring when a profound struggle unfolded in this republic, as in other parts of the USSR, around the election of delegates to the Nineteenth Conference of the CPSU. However, whereas in the Russian republic it was not as a rule possible to achieve the recall of even the most unpopular deputies, in Estonia a change in the Party leadership was announced even before the Conference had begun. The local delegation set off for Moscow from a rally of a hundred thousand supporters of perestroika on Tallin's Pevcheskoe Field, which called on the republic's new leaders to fight in Moscow for radical transformations and for real independence for Estonia. The Popular Front initiative group was at the centre of these events and all hopes were pinned on it. One journalist christened this immense gathering a 'singing revolution'. And it really did seem like a a revolution with its enthusiastic masses, a change in leadership, and the formation of new mass organizations. On the streets of Tallin and other cities fluttered white, black and blue national flags, the display of which had until just recently been considered a state crime. The Moscow intelligentsia engaged in heated debate about the 'national liberation movement' in Estonia, the Western press talked about the Estonian phenomenon and Soviet papers presented the republic as a model of 'successful perestroika'.

But the Estonian phenomenon also had another side, which was at first concealed from outside observers. The rapid success of the Popular Front was engendered by the patently sympathetic attitude to it of a significant section of the local Party and managerial apparatus, which strove to gain greater autonomy from the central authorities in Moscow. Thus, the PF became the major factor in the intra-Party struggle for power; it advanced demands which had the total backing of local apparat-chiks but which for the time being they had decided not to proclaim in their own name. Finally, it could mobilize mass support, rally thousands of people around these slogans and, in effect, win for part of the local leadership the kind of mass social base that it had never had before.

Of course, the managerial apparatus in the republic was not homo-geneous. Alongside the antagonism between central and republican departments, there existed the traditional conflict between 'genuine' and 'Siberian' Estonians. Having no faith in local cadres in the 1940s, Stalin preferred to form the managerial apparatus from people who had no experience of living in the conditions of a 'bourgeois' republic. Estonian settlements in Siberia, which had existed since Tsarist times, seemed the ideal solution to this problem: on the one hand, they originated 'national cadres' (although frequently they hardly spoke Estonian) and, on the other, the local bureaucracy was freed from the legacy of the 'old society'. Not surprisingly, as 'genuine' Estonians were drawn into bureaucratic life, the rivalry between the two groups was reinforced: the 'newcomers' looked for support to Moscow, who as usual viewed them as reliable executors of their will; and the 'natives' sought a base among the intelligentsia by emphasizing their liberal and patriotic orien-tation.

The 'singing revolution' was made possible because the founders of the Popular Front quickly gained access to Estonian-language newspapers and then radio and television. The support for the PF of many high-ranking members of the Party's leadership, including the ideology secretary, I. Toome, was a secret to no one.

From the very beginning, Popular Front activists in Moscow and Leningrad were aware of the contradictory nature of the 'Estonian miracle'. Nevertheless, events in Estonia gave grounds for optimism. Although national-bureaucratic tendencies were strong, this was still a mass democratic movement, which remained part of the general process of political change in the Soviet Union. The draft programme, elaborated by Estonian PF experts, contained a whole series of radical reformist demands aimed at extending civil liberties, the formation of a legal state and securing democratic elections to the soviets. The draft stated that 'the goal of the PF is the establishment of an Estonia where all citizens will feel free and secure'. While defending the historic rights of Estonians as the indigenous nation, the authors of the draft emphasized that 'it is intolerable to infringe the democratic rights of the citizens of other nationalities'.[1]

The PF's economic programme was obviously formulated under the influence of Scandinavian social democracy. While it talked of the free development of co-operatives, personal and private property and 'constitutional guarantees' for private entrepreneurship, it also discussed the strengthening of the social security system, health-care and education, state guarantees of a living wage for all citizens and defence of the principles of social justice. According to the authors of the draft, the transition to a market economy must be accompanied by the retention of a significant role for the state and the position of the republic's leading bodies must be reinforced by transferring to them rights which previously belonged to Moscow. It was even proposed that republican departments should be left with administrative levers to intervene in the economy on prices, wages, and so on. The PF's draft programme finally spoke of the need for decentralization and the breaking-up of enterprises in the state sector. Not a word was mentioned, however, about the self-management of labour collectives or workers' participation in economic decision-making.

Although the interests of republican ministries and departments were undoubtedly one of the major factors considered in drawing up this document, it could also be said that the PF's ideologists were adhering to the tenets of democratic socialism and defending the same conception of social development as the moderate wing of the Western European Left. The Moscow PF, where the influence of Marxist ideas has been rather stronger, could not, naturally, subscribe to every point of the Estonian programme but it was prepared to support it on a whole range of positions. Thus, when a delegation of Muscovites boarded the train in readiness to take part in the Estonians' founding congress, they were in a very cheerful mood. The Estonians' impending success seemed a prologue to a more general success.

The splendour and solemnity of the Estonian congress was a genuine shock to the 'informals' from Moscow, Leningrad, Yaroslavl, Minsk and other cities, representing numerous PF organizing committees from the Slavic republics. The perfect order in the huge hall and the three and a half thousand delegates listening attentively to dozens of speakers were all strikingly different from what we were used to seeing at home; and, although the activists from Kuibyshev and Yaroslavl already had the experience of numerous meetings behind them, the Muscovites and Leningraders had not yet held one conference.

The opening speech by the Estonian PF leader, E. Savisaar, was carefully balanced. He openly alluded to the need for a transition to a multi-party system while noting that haste in this question was 'intolerable'. He called for a dialogue with the republic's Russian-speaking population, and criticized the Stalinists, nationalists and technocrats, who advised the Front 'to avoid the politics of ultimata'.[2]

Savisaar spoke very calmly, without histrionics, choosing his words carefully – in fact, to the Russians, who were used to heated and bitter discussions and meeting-room pathos, his speech might have seemed rather boring. We soon began to realize, however, that, behind the congress's peaceful flow, passions were really at boiling-point. After Savisaar, speakers advanced one demand after another, of which only a few concerned social questions. Despite appeals for a dialogue with the republic's Russian inhabitants, Front members took an uncompromising position with regard to those they contemptuously called 'migrants'.

They spoke about the possibility of forcing the Russians off the republic's territory. The various methods suggested were not distinguished by any originality. It was proposed to establish a republican citizenship, which would only be granted to individuals who had mastered the Estonian language, had lived in Estonia for no less than ten years and who were 'loyal to the republic'. The closure of the big industrial enterprises, which employed the majority of Russian workers, was discussed, and it was proposed that each departing Russian be given 10,000 roubles for 'moving expenses'. Obtaining this sum would not constitute a great hardship for the republic as 16,000 roubles are transferred to the republic's account from the central budget for every Russian worker who comes into Estonia. No compromises were permitted on the question of equal national rights: there must be only one state language – Estonian. The 40 per cent of the population who use Russian must be deprived of the right to have it recognized as a state language. It was simultaneously emphasized that 'the goal of every Estonian is an independent Estonia', and that we 'want to be the same as Finland and Sweden'.[3] But Finland does not refuse its Swedish minority the right to linguistic equal rights, while the leaders of the Estonian national movement have patently left their republic's Russian inhabitants with only two choices: either to leave or to become second-class citizens.

It was quite evident that, in this case, it was not a matter of incidental extremism unavoidable in a mass organization. The republic's official circles made it quite clear that they adhered to the same viewpoint. When a commission on language problems was established under the auspices of the Presidium of the Estonian Supreme Soviet, there were only three Russians among its twenty members. As one might have expected, the official commission's findings were barely distinguishable from the proposals expressed at the PF Congress. As *Izvestiya* acknowledged, the republican authorities had been unable to overcome their 'mistrust of the Russian-speaking population'.[4]

The policy of transferring to the Estonian language frequently had unexpected consequences. Enterprises, operating in an all-Union market, encountered numerous difficulties. A report turned up in Uzbek newspapers that, at one of the republic's enterprises, equipment had been supplied with instructions only in Estonian. In order to understand this incomprehensible text, it had been necessary to find specialist translators. In the end, the Uzbeks took revenge by starting to enclose instructions only in Uzbek with articles bound for Estonia!

The growth of Estonian nationalism provoked a reciprocal reaction among Russians and other national minorities. In Tartu, the 'International movement' (Intermovement), headed by E. Kogan, K. Kiknadze and the Siberian Estonian, Arnold Say, was formed. Intermovement's leaders declared their readiness to support the basic principles of the PF's economic and political programme but categorically opposed discrimination in any form against the Russian-speaking population. Intermovement's documents emphasized the fact that the Russian-speaking community constituted the overwhelming majority of the population in the north-east of the republic and that any policy which encroached upon the Russians' interests would paralyse the development of this region of the country. Speaking in the name of Intermovement in the pages of the republican press, Kiknadze declared that Estonia's Russian-speaking population disapproved of the law on language. 'We will accordingly continue to fight for a change in this law.' In Kiknadze's words, in cases where a majority of the Russian-speaking population do not have a command of Estonian, the only possibility for preserving equal rights for the minority to participate in political and economic life 'is the use of Russian on an equal footing with Estonian'.[5] In many respects, Intermovement's programme seemed rather more democratic than the PF's. It pushed to the forefront the idea of equal rights for citizens and for cultural and national diversity. It also suggested that Intermovement, with its democratic slogans and readiness for a dialogue with the Popular Front, should also be the 'lesser evil' for Estonians as well: if Intermovement ended in failure, the political vacuum would be filled by overtly Russian nationalists. This was directly stated in Intermovement's documents, which recognized the danger of the formation among Russians of 'chauvinist and extremist organizations'.

Despite all the formal democracy of their programme, Intermovement's leaders were perceived by public opinion as conservatives. In their declarations, there was a clearly visible anguish at the recently departed 'stability', when the rights of the non-indigenous population were ostensibly firmly guaranteed. Arnold Say, who met with the Moscow PF delegation during our visit to the Congress, gave the impression of being unquestionably honest, but indisputably conservative.

A significant section of the Russian engineering and technical intelligentsia and workers rallied, not around Intermovement, but around the United Council of Labour Collectives. The stimulus for founding this organization came from the leadership of the Tallin Motor factory. The demands in this case were very elementary: equal rights for nations and equality for the two state languages – Russian and Estonian. Under pressure from the republic's leadership and after discussions with moderate PF representatives, the Motor management were prepared to back down from their original formulations but, this time, they did not receive the backing of the workers: about 80 per cent of those employed at the factory were in favour of continuing the struggle. Both collectives and management at many other enterprises began to associate themselves with the '"Motor" declaration'. The United Council, formed in this way, acknowledged that 'the interests of the indigenous nation are paramount' whilst declaring that it would not permit 'the infringement of people's rights' and demanding the promulgation of laws to 'protect the national minorities from oppression'.[6] Behind this amazing unanimity between labour collectives and management stood not only national but also economic interests. Primarily affected were those factories under all–Union control, which worked for the Russian market and had links with dozens of suppliers and customers in all the republics. As the leaders of the enterprises themselves conceded, for them the 'Estonification' of clerical procedures could turn into a commercial catastrophe.

The situation was becoming tense and events at the Congress Sessions did nothing to calm passions. A representative of the PF organization in Kokhtla–Yarve (a predominantly Russian region of Estonia) declared from the rostrum that she 'had become terrified'. The PF's Russian activists found themselves caught between the hammer and the anvil. The Front's left wing proved another victim of the nationalist euphoria. Rem Blum, a Marxist philosopher from Tartu and one of the founders of the first PF initiative group in the republic, was not even elected to the leadership at the Congress. 'Did you notice that not one delegate has used the word "comrade" in their speeches?' he asked the confused Russian guests. 'This is very significant.' Not only was the Front's not very strong Marxist current becoming weaker, but social-democratic ideas were also losing their influence. The numerous economic proposals advanced by delegates and mechanically incorporated into the notion of 'republican self-financing' or 'the Estonian miracle' were reduced to safeguarding the Estonian economy from the all–Union market and reducing economic ties with other republics to a minimum while relying on Estonia's enormous successes in the external (Western) market. That these successes would be massive none of the Front's ideologues had the slightest doubt, although not one of them had proposed anything but the most general ideas concerning a future strategy for external trade.

In an analysis of the theory of 'independent development', defended by PF ideologues and the Estonian Party leadership, the outstanding Estonian economist, M. Bronstein, wrote:

> One has to understand the real reason for the 'Western' model. It is a reaction to the 'piracy' of all-Union departments, to the persistent shortage of good-quality production and to the impossibility of obtaining modern techniques and technology. But let us come down to earth. The West gives nothing away for free. In order to buy goods and technology from them, we must sell our goods in Western markets. But what is there to sell? ... We have tried to clarify what are our raw material, human and technological resources and who are our potential customers and competitors in both internal and external markets. The conclusions have been of little comfort: with our current production methods and the quality of our output we have, to put it mildly, very modest opportunities for competing in external markets.[7]

Taking into account the way in which the Soviet economy increasingly lags behind the West, which also affects Estonia, Bronstein wrote about the need for powerful state planning and concentration of resources in order to carry out technological renovation and bring about an independent policy of development. Meanwhile, however, the theoreticians of the Estonian PF, like a majority of liberal economists in Moscow, had no desire even to pose such questions. In the words of Vitaly Ponomarev, an economist in the Moscow PF: 'it is neither a right-wing nor a left-wing programme, it is simply incompetent'.

It was a strange congress, which staggered not only the Russian guests but also foreign journalists. Almost no one criticized the Front's leadership, there were virtually no debates on strategy or tactics and only isolated details of the programme were discussed. Candidates for the PF's governing body, who failed in the secret ballot, automatically joined (without a fresh election) the Council of Representatives, although some of them had gained very few votes. The newly elected Board and Council of Representatives came onto the stage to music and surrounded by beautiful young women in national costumes. Portraits of Savisaar and the PF's number two, Mario Lauristin, constantly figured in the pages of the PF journal, *Vestnik Narodnogo Fronta*, which appeared daily during this period. It all resembled a show with an apparently rather naive producer.

The Muscovite guests' return journey home did not, unfortunately, prove as joyous as their arrival. Differences between the Muscovite and the Estonian PF were becoming apparent not only at the level of programmatic formulations (a little bit 'to the left' or a little bit 'to the right') but also at the level of political thinking. Almost all the guests to the Estonian Congress who returned to the capital were experiencing extremely contradictory feelings. On the one hand, they had witnessed in Tallin crowded meetings, the real clash of ideas and programmes, the legal activity of several unofficial mass organizations: the 'greens', and even a small party of national independence, were also active alongside the 60,000-strong Popular Front and the 12,000-strong Intermovement. This was all evidence of a genuine democratization, which would have been inconceivable without the successes of the Popular Front. But, on the other hand, it was impossible to ignore the new dangers and anti-democratic tendencies engendered by national passions at boiling-point, and the provincialism, and at times even clumsiness, of many figures in the PF.

A similar picture emerged a few weeks later among Moscow activists who attended the Congress of the Latvian Front. On returning home, they gave a report of the trip to a gathering of the Moscow PF in which they averred that 'everything was the same as in Estonia only much worse organized'. Although radical resolutions had been passed at the Congress on social justice, civil rights and democracy, Resolution No.8 'on restricting immigration' characterized Russian settlers as 'a huge mass of badly qualified and uncultured people', who threatened the vital interests of the Latvian people. It also said in the resolution that 'only permanent residents' in the republic should be taught in Latvia's educational institutions and all PF organizations were called upon to adopt 'an intransigent attitude on this question'.

From the outset, such declarations naturally generated anxiety and then protest among Russians, especially as they were made a little more scathingly at the Congress. One of the organizers called for monuments to the pre-war dictator, Ulmanis, to be erected throughout the country and another recalled that the German occupiers had not been as bad as they are depicted. The British journalist Jonathan Steele, who was present at the founding congresses of all three Baltic national movements, stated that the situation that had taken shape in Latvia was 'potentially the most dangerous'. On the one hand, the numbers of indigenous Latvians and Russian settlers were roughly equal, and on the other, 'the Popular Front's tone is more impatient and the Communist Party more divided'.[8]

On 14 October, the organizing committee of the Latvian International Front (Interfront) was formed, which united representatives from 154 institutions and enterprises in Riga, Liepaia, Pesis and Kraslava. On 16 October, a leaflet of a certain 'Slav' society was read out on the *Labvakar* programme on Latvian TV, which appealed to Russians to take to the streets on 22 October to 'rebuff' the Latvians. The Slavs' appeal was not supported by Interfront, which appealed to its supporters to: 'carry on with your normal business on 22 October, do not organize "counter-demonstrations" and "counter-meetings" and don't give in to provocations'.[9] Set against the Slavs' inflammatory agitation, Interfront looked like a moderate and constructive movement, but a confrontation between the Latvian and Russian communities was already developing.

In such a situation, the Congress of the Lithuanian Movement for Perestroika, *Sajudis* (the local analogue of the Popular Front), was marked by the realism and moderation of its national demands. Resolution No. 7 on relations between nations was composed from the outset so as to calm the non-native population, and to stress their equal rights in the republic. It should be borne in mind that the Lithuanians had fewer grounds for uneasiness: they remained an overwhelming majority in their own country, and the Russian, Jewish and Polish communities had never constituted a single whole and thus did not have the opportunity to compete with the Lithuanians. Leaflets of an anti-Russian and anti-Polish character pasted up in Vilnius's central square were quickly torn down by Popular Front activists and condemned as 'provocative' while the Congress was in session.

Nevertheless, national enthusiasm also dominated the *Sajudis* Congress. One speaker after another mouthed poetic but quite abstract phrases about 'native Lithuania'. Before the Congress opened, the official Lithuanian leadership took the decision to reinstate the old national flag, which was raised over the ancient tower of Gediminas. Shortly after this, the newly elected Party leader, A. Brazauskas, declared, to the universal delight of *Sajudis* activists, that the old cathedral in Vilnius was being returned to the Catholic Church.

It should be said that participants in the Congress behaved in a very emotional way. They were forever jumping from their seats to chant 'Lietuva, Lietuva!'. This was all rather more reminiscent of a rally than a serious discussion. One of the delegates made the poor joke that participants in the Congress were behaving more like fans of the popular local football team, *Zhalgiris*. Not suprisingly in such an atmosphere, fine speeches meant more than constructive proposals but Brazauskas's speech, enunciated in the right tone and at the right moment, generated no less approval than the words of radical delegates who appealed to the Party 'to repent before the people'. A holiday atmosphere reigned in the city during the Congress. People walked along the streets carrying national flags and singing national songs. In the evening, there were popular street parties on Cathedral Square and fireworks over the Tower of Gediminis. The Congress was broadcast on radio and television and on the streets stood loudspeakers around which people milled, wishing to hear what was happening at the Congress. No one displayed even the slightest ill-will towards Russians and, even more important, *Sajudis* activists and Moscow representatives were able to establish very close bonds of comradeship during the Congress.

Lithuania felt that it was free. 'You can't imagine what these happenings mean to us Lithuanians', the woman who registered the Congress guests at a Vilnius hotel told us. However, raising the national flag over the capital proved rather easier than solving the world's problems. The abstract and declaratory character of *Sajudis*'s programme helped it to rally the broadest layers of the population, but this was also its weakness. The authorities, in turn, sensed the movement's vulnerability and did everything possible, while calling for dialogue and collaboration, to confine themselves to symbolic concessions. The worker activist and representative from Kaunas, K. Uoka, spoke to us with some passion about this. To the slogans of *Sajudis* the authorities responded with slogans; to calls for loyalty to the homeland – loyalty oaths to native Lithuania, to symbolic demands – they replied with symbolic gestures. However, while the leaders of *Sajudis* spoke repeatedly of their movement's socialism, they were unable to offer Congress delegates their own strategy for its development in Lithuania; in essence they conceded the initiative to the new Party leadership, which in turn was unable to offer anything concrete.

In any case the Lithuanian movement was primarily concerned with its own problems. Arvidas Uozaitis, a member of an initiative group, categorically informed the Muscovites that 'we are not interested in Russian problems'. Thus, the dreams of many Moscow activists that the Baltic Fronts might be the locomotives to pull the whole movement forward clearly did not come true. 'We can rely on no one but ourselves', the philosopher Mikhail Maliutin curtly replied in summing up a discussion of the Moscow Left. 'For all the weaknesses of the Moscow Popular Front, we have at least one advantage: we can draw conclusions from other people's mistakes.'

NOTES

1. *Vestnik Narodnogo Fronta*, no. 4, 1988.
2. *Vestnik Narodnogo Fronta*, no. 11, 1988.
3. *Vestnik Narodnogo Fronta*, no. 10, 1988.
4. *Izvestiya*, 18 October 1988.
5. *Sovetskaya Estonia*, 4 March 1989.
6. *Vpered*, 1 October 1988.
7. *EKO*, no. 12, 1988, p. 92.
8. *The Guardian*, 11 October 1988, p. 24.
9. *Sovetskaya Latvia*, 20 October 1988.

4

The Restless Borderlands

The congresses of the Popular Fronts of Estonia, Latvia and Lithuania brought the first wave of the mass movement to an unusual end. Not surprisingly, the Popular Front had formed initially in the most developed parts of the Soviet Union, where the high cultural level of the population, democratic traditions and the revolt of the local bureaucracy against the centre had combined with national unrest. Matters were rather more complicated in the Slav republics. Nevertheless, the successes of the social movement in the Baltic republics activated supporters of the PF everywhere. Things developed most quickly in Belorussia where close historical ties had been maintained with Lithuania. Belorussia is, moreover, one of the most developed areas of the Soviet Union and possesses one of the most conservative bureaucracies. As the outstanding Belorussian writer, Ales Adamovich, defined it: the republic already enjoyed 'the lamentable reputation of an anti-perestroika Vendée'.[1] In such conditions, an open clash between conservative and progressive forces became unavoidable.

Immediately after the Estonian PF Congress, members of the *Sovremennik* and *Alternativ* socialist groups, which had been joined after some wavering by activists of the *Talaka* national movement, stepped up active agitation for a Belorussian Popular Front. This collaboration between Russian-speaking socialists and Belorussian patriots could not but create anxiety in the apparatus, which had made every possible effort to set one against the other. But what provoked the bureaucracy's indignation still further was that the most authoritative representatives of the local intellectual elite, V. Bykov and Zenon Pozdnyak, were openly in favour of the immediate foundation of a Popular Front in the republic. On 15 October, the formation was announced, in Minsk, of a PF organizing committee.

The reaction of the apparatus was not slow in coming. On 18 October, the newspaper *Vechernii Minsk* published an article by the 'philosopher' V. Begun, well-known for his articles and books on the 'Zionist menace'. This time Begun refrained from arguments about Jewish misdeeds and came down exclusively on Bykov and Adamovich. The latter was accused in the pages of the newspaper of 'overstepping the mark' and of 'being distinguished by his lack of basic human decency'. All of three days later *Vechernii Minsk* published a fresh article, but this time under a collective authorship. Here Ales Adamovich was characterized as a man trying to create chaos and the leaders of *Talaka* were accused of 'bourgeois nationalism' and of attempting to revise 'the fundamental positions of Marxism–Leninism' by insinuating 'long decayed ideological rubbish' into their programmes.[2]

This article was at once reprinted in *Sovetskaya Belorossiya*, the official organ of the Belorussian Party Central Committee. If anyone had especially set themselves the aim of demonstrating the correctness of Adamovich's assessment of the local bureaucracy as an 'anti-*perestroika* Vendée', they could scarcely have received a more striking confirmation of this idea. The articles were in the same style as Nina Andreeva's lamentably famous publication in *Sovetskaya Rossiya* and contained essentially direct appeals for reprisals against those who organize 'raucous meetings' and make 'demagogic speeches'.

The next stage of the apparatus's counter-offensive turned out to be the repression of the *Sovremennik* club. On 22 October, a meeting was organized between 'Minsk public opinion' and the leadership of *Sovremennik*. 'Public opinion' was headed by members and functionaries of the Party *gorkom*, although they claimed they had come in the capacity of 'private individuals'. *Sovremennik* was accused of multifarious political sins. Anti-semitic comments were made from the hall and, in previously prepared interventions, one speaker after another 'held up the renegades to shame' for attempting to create a Popular Front in the republic and travel the 'Baltic road'. Then a resolution was adopted in which 'Minsk public opinion' called for a stop to be put to the activity of the 'informals' and for the foundation of a PF not to be permitted in the republic. Immediately afterwards, *Sovremennik* was deprived of the premises previously granted it by the authorities.

If the organizers of the 'anti-perestroika Vendée' viewed the events of 18–22 October as their victory, then it was a pyrrhic one. In the first place, they attracted the attention of the Left across the entire country to the happenings in Belorussia. In many instances, issues of *Vechernii Minsk* served as an advertisement for those being criticized. The repression of *Sovremennik* provoked sympathy towards it among the most varied circles and reinforced the collaboration between *Sovremennik* and the more left-wing *Alternativ*, which had earlier split from it. In the final analysis, the authorities' attacks only stimulated the activities of the PF's supporters.

Ultimately, the success or failure of the PF in Belorussia depended, of course, on the creation of a mass base. Articles in newspapers and discussions in conference halls only revealed the tip of the iceberg. And it was precisely the authorities' aggressive attitude which helped PF activists to understand that, without the broad support of the workers and without a mass organization, they could not achieve the realization of their goals.

The decisive test of strength occurred on 30 October. A large demonstration had been planned for that day in memory of the victims of fascism and Stalinism in Belorussia. The initiators were the 'Committee of 58', which was concerned with an investigation into Stalin's crimes in the republic, but the appeal was supported by all Popular Front groups. For their part, the authorities not only banned the demonstration but made it quite clear that the sternest measures would be taken against those disturbing the peace.

On the evening of 20 October, many of the movement's leaders were detained in their own flats. In a few cases, the authorities organized house arrest and, in the others, put the 'instigators' behind bars. Nevertheless, despite the absence of many leaders, more than ten thousand people gathered at midday at the demonstration's appointed place in Minsk's Moskovskoe cemetery. Since a large number of those arrested belonged to the *Talaka* and *Tuteishie* groups, accused by the authorities of 'nationalism', an active role in the organization of the demonstration was played by members of *Sovremennik* and *Alternativ*, the Russian-speaking socialist groups, which had escaped the attention of the authorities the previous evening.

More than a thousand police and soldiers from 'special' units were thrown in to break up the demonstration. They used dogs, clubs, water-cannon and tear gas. But the demonstration continued. The historian, Zenon Pozdnyak, a member of the PF organizing committee in Belorussia, headed the demonstration and led it to Kuropaty, where the remains of tens of thousands of people, shot under Stalin, were interred.

'What is dear is not close by, but four or five kilometres away', the Belorussian commentator, Viktor Koz'ko, later recalled.

> People went, not thinking that this was where they would be going. And the shadow of the Kuropaty tragedy fell across their faces. The procession stretched from one cemetery to the other. At a funereal pace, the escort of police and military vehicles and firemen drifted along the streets with the people. No one knew now who had been captured by whom, who was hunter and who was game. It was as though the muzzles of the water-cannon, threateningly extended and ready for battle, went unnoticed by the people. Nor were they frightened by the military vehicles, crawling alongside like eyeless cyclops. All of this technology, blended into a single column, was reminiscent of a huge caterpillar crawling spasmodically along the road, eating away the fruits and leaves from the pavement–branches.
>
> The hunt for people did not cease even while the procession was on its way to Kuropaty. After every kilometre, at every crossroads, stood lines and units of police and police cars with radios. The airwaves over Minsk were filled with the crackle of call-signs and police commands and instructions'.[3]

At Kuropaty, the bloody battles were resumed. After Pozdnyak had read out to those assembled a declaration of the formation of the Popular Front of Belorussia, the police tried to arrest him but were prevented from doing so by the crowd. This time military units were used against the demonstrators. The hunt for people continued until late evening. The overall result was that 164 were arrested, of whom 73 were members of the CPSU.

On the whole, the events of 30 October turned into a major defeat for the republic's conservative leadership. First, it had become clear that it was not possible to overcome the Popular Front through threats and even the use of force. All the basic groups only rallied more closely around each other. Second, the actions of the police provoked a wave of indignation in society at large. In the creative workers' unions, meetings were held which sharply condemned the repressions. The newspapers were forced to publish material criticizing the police. The PF activists appeared, in the eyes of the public, to be the victims of Stalinist tyranny. The defeat and confusion of the apparatchiks, who had attempted to turn the republic into a 'Vendée against perestroika', had created a qualitatively new situation in Belorussia. Minsk swiftly turned from being a bureaucratic preserve into one of the epicentres of the popular movement.

After a certain delay, material about the events at Kuropaty began to percolate through to the central press – although, in a majority of cases, it was given the interpretation least dangerous to the authorities. The newspapers reported that Stalinist-minded officials had organized the dispersal of a meeting held in memory of the victims of Stalin's repression, but they remained silent about the role of the Popular Front in these events. It seemed as if the struggle in Belorussia was a product not of the present but of the tragedies of the past.

However, thanks to the rout in Kuropaty, the Belorussian Popular Front (BPF) had achieved a popularity and recognition that not even the most painstaking propaganda could have given it. The Belorussian press continued to argue that there was no need for a PF in Belorussia as everything in the republic was just fine, but the apparatus was simultaneously forced to make concessions. Supporters of the BPF had the opportunity, if only for a certain time, to operate openly. On 19 February, a mass meeting took place at the Dinamo stadium in Minsk, which showed the movement's genuine strength. Even the official press acknowledged that this was 'an event in the public life of the republic'. Support for the Front and hostility towards the apparatus were clearly manifested in the mood of those present: 'There were howls and whistles from most of the stands when the name was called of any speaker not accepted by the BPF.'[4] The masses' irritation was understandable – after Kuropaty the local authorities had made concessions but had not in principle changed their opposition to democratization. The ever deepening mutual hostility between the ruling circles and the people did not augur well. Both sides prepared for fresh skirmishes.

The conflict between the PF and the republican authorities in Belorussia, traditionally considered the calmest of the republics, was unfolding against the background of a worsening general crisis within the empire. Something was happening in virtually all the national republics. Even during the revolutions of 1905 and 1917, the dissatisfaction of the borderlands with centralized government and the incompetence of the central apparatus in solving national problems was not displayed with such clarity as in the autumn and winter of 1988–89. The crisis in the Baltic region first died away, then it was rekindled; the struggle between Armenians and Azerbaijanis over Nagorny Karabakh was assuming the features of a confrontation between two republican governments. In defending its own interests, the national bureaucracy, in many instances, not only came into conflict with its 'class brethren' in Moscow or a neighbouring republic, but also encouraged the popular movement, at least while national demands prevailed. The central power reacted to the exacerbation of the situation with traditional administrative measures, patently failing to recognize that, by doing so, it would exacerbate the crisis still further.

Soviet republics can be divided, historically and geographically, into several groups. The Slav republics – Russia, the Ukraine and Belorussia – have always had a common history, and they existed within the framework of a single Russian state long before the establishment of the empire. The similarity of the languages, the common Orthodox religion and the Ukrainians' and Belorussians' lack of their own state has not, however, meant that the latter consider themselves Russians. Through a resident of Moscow, as a rule, gives little thought to the right of Ukrainians to self-determination and sees no great difference between Russians and Ukrainians, in Lvov the same questions are viewed differently.

The stability of the historical ties between these three peoples has made for a paradoxical situation. On the one hand, unification into a single state was patently not artificial; a significant section, if not a majority, of the populations of the Ukraine and Belorussia pushed social rather than national questions to the forefront, and activists in the democratic movement were prepared to present a united front with their co-thinkers from Russia. On the other hand, some opponents of the system, who gave priority to nationalist values, saw their task as being 'to rupture the course of history' and painfully assert their national identity, which had disappeared under the pressures of Russification and modernization. Consequently, the ends of the political spectrum in unofficial circles were a long way apart. Here one could find a powerful left-wing movement barely distinguishable from that in Moscow and Leningrad and, at the same time, nationalists rather more radical than in the Baltic republics. The consolidation of a progressive bloc was, however, somewhat facilitated by the authorities' aggressive behaviour towards any dissent. Whereas in Estonia, Party apparatchiks played a not insignificant role in founding the Popular Front, in Belorussia their attempts at repression compelled left-democratic circles to unite. In the Ukraine, the process advanced in a slower and more complicated fashion but in a similar direction.

In the republics of Central Asia a quite different situation had taken shape. These territories belonged historically to the Muslim world and, prior to the nineteenth century, had no links at all with Russia. A long-standing struggle for hegemony had existed between the peoples of this region. At the same time, in cultural, economic and religious terms, the region has proved quite homogeneous.

Economic development before the 1917 Revolution was particularly colonial and Russian settlers soon constituted the basic mass of town-dwellers, industrial workers and officials. In Kirgizia a real genocide of the native population took place before the Revolution, followed by the formation of Russian agricultural settlements, which simultaneously assumed a military function. During the Revolution and Civil War, almost all of the region's Russian-speaking inhabitants rallied around the Bolsheviks as the sole force capable of guaranteeing their interests. Here the 'dictatorship of the proletariat' became synonymous with the 'dictatorship of the Russian minority'. The Civil War was accompanied by traditional brutality towards the 'natives', a fact recognized even by Bolshevik literature of the 1920s.

The results of the subsequent period are, however, considered to be comparatively positive. Although the colonial model of development was largely retained in Central Asia, despite all the revolutionary promises, great progress both in economic and social development was undoubtedly achieved within this framework. There was a sharp increase in the population's level of education, for example. Although the demand for universal secondary education was not always met in practice, the educational system established in the 1930s was called upon to teach the children in these republics to the same level as at the 'centre'. The massive progress in health-care and higher education should not be underestimated. A serious and, on the whole, successful struggle was also conducted for the liberation of women – equal rights were not only proclaimed in theory but were also ensured by numerous governmental measures. It is thus possible to speak of this process as one of intensive social modernization. However, numerous cultural reforms were also carried out and these are not open to such a straightforward assessment. The Arab alphabet was initially replaced by the Latin and then by the Cyrillic. As a result, even the educated sector of society was deprived of access to old Islamic and pre-colonial texts and to books published outside the USSR (it should be remembered that the Tadzhik and Persian languages are virtually indistinguishable). The policy of de-Islamization has not been particularly successful, although the role of the mosque in public life has been significantly less than in a majority of neighbouring countries (in the opinion of many observers, the political and cultural role of Islam in the republics is today more closely akin to the role of Catholicism in contemporary Poland).

Industrial development, which sharply accelerated as a result of the evacuation of industrial enterprises from the western USSR during the war, has been carried out basically through the resettlement of Russian workers in Central Asia. New components have been added to the ethnic mosaic: a Jewish community formed of refugees from the western regions occupied by the fascists in 1941–42; Koreans, Crimean Tatars, Volga Germans and Meskhetian Turks deported there by Stalin. All of these new national minorities have, to some degree, suffered discrimination and have fought a struggle in defence of their rights – although their situations have been very different.

Stalin's repressions in the 1930s led to the eradication of that part of the local intelligentsia which adhered to left-wing positions. As everywhere else, the old Party cadres suffered considerably. But the greatest blow against the peoples of Central Asia was inflicted by collectivization. In Kazakhstan, a most cruel famine broke out, which was no less terrible in its consequences than in the Ukraine. The precise number of those who died has never been disclosed but the consequences of this catastrophe are felt to this day. The mass deaths during collectivization and the opening up of the virgin lands in the north of the republic, begun by Khrushchev in the 1950s, has led to Slav settlers gaining a numerical superiority over the Kazakhs. A mass flight began from the southern republics into Iran, Afghanistan and China (in Afghanistan, the descendants of Tadzhiks and Uzbeks, who had saved themselves from Stalin's collectivization, naturally found themselves in the ranks of the insurgents fighting against the Soviet forces). The actions of the government were continually met by armed resistance. The army's struggle with bands of 'basmachi', who had no desire to recognize the new decrees or the power of the 'infidels', continued into the 1940s.

In the 1970s, the development of the region, as with all the Soviet Union, was fraught with contradictions. At one and the same time, the republics' political autonomy was reinforced and their economic dependence on the centre increased. The decision that Uzbekistan should specialize in the cultivation of cotton led to catastrophic consequences. Traditional agriculture was definitively destroyed and cotton became a monoculture for whose sake everything else had to be sacrificed. The unrestrained application of chemical substances on the cotton fields not only caused damage to the environment, but became a threat to human life. Child mortality began to rise rapidly. Moscow demanded still more 'white gold', while closing its eyes to the price of fulfilling plans that were patently too ambitious. This untied completely the hands of the local bureaucracy. In the cotton fields, poisoned by various chemicals, the labour of women and children was widely employed. Instead of studying, students would be sent to the cotton fields where they would spend a significant part of their semester. The social degradation of the peasantry was striking. Children were no longer sent to school as their labour was needed in the fields, without which it was impossible to make ends meet. The population explosion, witnessed here as in other Third World areas, sharply exacerbated questions of employment. The local authorities took advantage of the obvious rural overpopulation to ensure cheap labour on the cotton plantations. In many cases, coercion was openly employed and the peasants found themselves, in effect, no better than serfs. Enquiry teams, concerned in the 1980s with investigating breaches of legality in the Uzbek republics, even uncovered local jails, built by local bosses on their own initiative for detaining malcontents and punishing the 'workshy'.

In the 1960s, the educated part of the population of Uzbekistan and Tadzhikistan took a genuine pride in the successes of their republics and gazed into the future with optimism, but by the 1980s it was a matter of 'saving the Tadzhik nation from destitution and lawlessness'.[5] Such an assessment was by no means an emotive exaggeration. According to official figures, about 12 per cent of the population of the USSR lives below the poverty line. In Tadzhikistan, however, official estimates for 1989 put the number of people without even the minimum income at 58.6 per cent with another 20 per cent on the verge of poverty. In Uzbekistan, the picture was only slightly better.

At the same time as the peasantry was being thrown ever further back into the Middle Ages, the bureaucracy was flourishing. Credit must be given to the policy of implanting 'national cadres', who had spent a prolonged period in the region, and modernization indisputably bore fruit. The educational system, formed in Stalin's times, created the opportunity to replace a portion of Russian officials by 'natives' with an outstanding grasp of both the Russian language and traditional Russian methods of bureaucratic rule. The speed in forming a national bureaucracy can be observed at all levels of government during the 1950s and 1960s. By the 1970s it was already possible to see its initial results, and it was in fact Russified Uzbeks, Tadzhiks and Kazakhs who proved the first conduits for nationalism in the bureaucratic apparatus. The principle, 'we can do no worse than the Russians', led to Russian-speaking European cadres, in some places slowly and covertly and in others quickly and blatantly, beginning to be removed from the apparatus. A section of the local Russian bureaucracy established ties with the rising new national-bureaucratic clans and adopted their way of life and principles of behaviour. Whereas the initial move was towards Russification of the educated part of the indigenous population, in the 1970s a certain 'de-Europeanization' of the local Russians themselves became evident. (This did not, however, prevent many of them from considering themselves to be 'civilizers' from a 'superior race' and from talking about 'the white man's burden'.)

It could be said that all of the processes previously experienced in the colonial world were reproduced in Central Asia. The history of India clearly demonstrates that the formation of an English-speaking bourgeoisie and bureaucracy from among the local population was the prelude to the struggle for independence. The de-Europeanization of the European colonists themselves has also been observed in many countries of the former British and French empires. But the processes unfolding in Central Asia also had their own specificity. First of all, the combination of growing bureaucratic autonomy with increasing economic dependence on the centre led to the formation of a kind of neo-feudal structure of power in the localities. Having gained a completely free hand with regard to fulfilling plan targets, the leaders of collective and state farms became semi-independent princes who began to form their own detachments of bodyguards and to exercise judgement and punishment independently. 'Private' jails were one of numerous manifestations of this fantastic feudalization which included luxurious palaces, banquets and the levying of various tributes from 'vassals'. The conflation of feudal customs and 'modern' legislation meant a rapid increase in corruption. Thousands of bribes became the norm in the apparatus. Naturally, not only 'one's own' were bought (for them it was not, as a rule, a matter of bribery but of fulfilling feudal obligations), but also Moscow bigwigs.

The peasantry's worsening situation – in tandem with luxury and corruption in the ruling circles – was evidence that the equality and progress promised by Stalinism in the country's borderlands was even less assured than at the 'centre'. But the chief source of political problems became, not the calamitous situation in the countryside, but instability in the towns. The European settlers living in Central Asia – who were already second- and sometimes even third-generation – felt their position under threat. At the same time the national bureaucracy was far from unified, being riven by clan, tribal and ancestral contradictions. The apparatus was more homogeneous in Uzbekistan, where the old tribal structure had been completely eliminated in the process of modernization and conflicts of this character were felt most severely in Kazakhstan and Tadzhikistan.

Discrimination against national minorities was practised by republican bureaucracies everywhere. Meskhetian Turks and Crimean Tatars did not have their own schools and, according to the official press, Tadzhiks living in Uzbekistan had to register themselves and their children as Uzbeks in order to gain access to educational establishments or obtain a decent job. Meanwhile, in Tadzhikistan, Uzbeks registered themselves as Tadzhiks.

The social crisis and discrimination against national minorities were supplemented by a barbaric attitude towards nature. A rapacious system of land-tenure subordinated to a single goal – the quickest achievement of the maximum cotton harvest – totally destroyed the ecology of agriculture. The children of Uzbek and Tadzhik peasants were forced to work in fields poisoned by pesticides applied in quite unbelievable quantities. An ill-conceived irrigation system did not improve the state of affairs in agriculture, leading to massive salination of the soil, the drying-up of the Aral Sea and a fall in the level of the Syr-Dar'ya and Amu-Dar'ya rivers. The region was on the threshold of an ecological catastrophe.

At first, the crisis in the countryside did not directly affect the towns, but the situation had altered by the middle of the Brezhnev era. In the 1970s, many towns, which had previously belonged entirely to European settlers and the Europeanized sector of the 'natives', began to be intensively settled by migrants from the countryside, who found themselves mostly in the position of unskilled workers. Since the majority of the population were migrants from the countryside, a body of students came into being: inhabitants of the capitals had no desire to go into the 'interior' and specialists were therefore needed. Moreover, bureaucratic quotas existed which required that a certain percentage of 'representatives of the peasantry' be compulsorily accepted into the institutes. All of these 'new' town-dwellers came into open conflict with the 'old' town-dwellers and this confrontation increasingly invigorated nationalist sentiments on both sides.

At first, the Russian-speaking majority in the towns foisted their own customs on the 'newcomers'. In Tashkent, complained *Izvestiya*, it was impossible to send a telegram or even call an ambulance in the Uzbek language. The reaction to such discrimination against the national language became the demand for 'Uzbekistanization' which, in the opinion of the central press, grew out of the 'urban sub-culture'.[8]

The unstable equilibrium of Central Asian society managed to hold until the commencement of *perestroika*, when the fight against corruption, begun in Moscow, instantaneously destabilized the situation. The anti-corruption campaign was devised by Yuri Andropov as a means of purging the system of its more obvious criminals and embezzlers and simultaneously as a major element in the tactics of his struggle for power. Having achieved the post of CPSU General Secretary, Andropov strove not only to rally around him reformist and technocratic groups in the apparatus, but also to discredit the Brezhnev group, which was wallowing in corruption, and remove the people who were a danger to him. No one, naturally, gave a thought to the long-term consequences that this campaign might have in Central Asia, where corruption had put down deep roots and become a constituent element of people's everyday existence. The crusade against corruption, begun in Uzbekistan, would have to be completed in Moscow.

Andropov's rule was shortlived, but the machine he had started continued to function even after his death. Investigations were carried out by enquiry teams sent from Russia as nobody had any faith in the law-enforcement organs of Central Asia. Mass dismissals and the arrest of local 'feudals' began. At first, the population welcomed such changes: people in the countryside, weary of feudal extortion, violence and insults, felt relieved. But very soon the situation became complicated. The energetic investigators, Tel'man Gdlyan and N. Ivanov, quickly discovered that fighting corruption in Central Asia was easier than in Russia. While they were arresting the Uzbek bosses, all problems were momentarily solved, but, once they began threatening figures in Moscow who had received 'gifts' and taken their share of feudal spoils, the investigation began to falter. At the same time, while operating in Central Asia, the Moscow investigators felt they had quite a free hand and soon learnt to fight 'barbarism' with barbaric methods. The investigation's code of conduct was continually being breached. Gdlyan's question 'what kind of legality can there be in Uzbekistan where there has been universal bribe-taking?' became popular in Tashkent.[9]

In the end, the numerous infringements of juridical procedure were used against Gdlyan himself – but this only happened when he began to point the finger at members of the Central Committee and Politburo in Moscow. At first, for a majority of the population of Central Asia, Gdlyan's activity seemed like a new colonial campaign. Uzbeks said that their republic was being forced to pay for everything.

The first political explosion, however, happened not in Uzbekistan but in Kazakhstan. Mass disturbances began in Alma-Ata after the First Secretary of the Kazakh Party, D. A. Kunaev, a loyal comrade-in-arms of Brezhnev, was removed from his post under direct pressure from Moscow, and G. V. Kolbin, who had moved from Russia, was nominated in his place. People, mainly students and unskilled young Kazakh workers, took to the streets. The unrest assumed a blatantly anti-Russian character and troops were brought into the city when the police proved unable to cope with the situation. *Pravda* wrote that 'hooligans, parasites and other anti-social elements' had come onto the streets and had 'set fire to a grocery store and private cars and had been abusive to local citizens'.[10] The central press reported that 'nationalist slogans, drawn from the murkiest depths of history' had appeared on the streets.[11] Official reports were, meanwhile, silent about the brutality and violence committed against the demonstrators by the authorities and their voluntary helpers from among the Russian population. Violence was perpetrated by both sides and no one could precisely say what they were fighting for.

When the disturbances of 17 and 18 December had been suppressed, the new leadership of the republic put ordinary participants in the events on trial while diligently avoiding conflicts with those representatives of the national bureaucracy who in reality had played no small part in organizing the disorders. Kolbin's authoritarian rule in the republic and the compromise between the 'new people' and the 'old bosses' soon showed Russian and Kazakh alike that they had been deceived. The increasingly tense struggle between ancestral clans in the apparatus was proof of the fact that the appointment of a Russian to the premier post in the republic could not alter the relations that had already formed. A year later, many Russians in Alma-Ata were saying forthrightly that 'if we'd known what Kolbin was like, we'd have united with the Kazakhs'. In the republic an anti-bureaucratic movement began to grow, drawing into its ranks representatives of both nationalities.

In Uzbekistan, events unfolded more slowly but in a highly dangerous direction for the authorities. The growing interest in Islam, and the increasing influence of radical sects, especially among the poorest section of the population, were evidence that stability was coming to an end. In the spring of 1989, a demonstration by Muslims in Tashkent led to the removal of the mufti, who were perceived as representatives of the authorities. The Islamic ecclesiastical bureaucracy did not enjoy the confidence of its congregation but Islam itself began to play an increasingly active role in the life of society. At the same time, the crisis of confidence in the official mosque led the priesthood to reinforce their own positions by distancing themselves from the authorities and trying to gain respect for religious rights.

Radical Muslims also had an influence on the burgeoning national movement, *Verlik* (Unity), which by spring 1989 had become a serious force. The liberal-national intelligentsia who headed *Verlik* had neither the apparatus nor the political experience to control the growing and increasingly radical grassroots organizations. In Khiva, it was reported that the KGB had removed large quantities of weapons from one of the mosques including an American 'Stinger' anti-aircraft rocket launcher, which had already proved its worth as a weapon against Soviet helicopters in Afghanistan. Though the 'green banner of the Prophet' did not yet flutter openly on the streets of Tashkent and Samarkand, the situation was certainly no longer under the control of the authorities. The Russified bureaucracy, as well as the European settlers, felt threatened. Relations between Tadzhiks and Uzbeks were also far from idyllic.

In May, there were mass disorders in Turkmenia, previously considered the calmest spot in Central Asia. Turkmen youth threatened co-operative shops which belonged, as a rule, to Armenians. Social discontent was thus interwoven with dissension between nations. In June, bloody inter-communal clashes flared up in Fergana, where Meskhetian Turks, deported to Central Asia by Stalin, came into conflict with the indigenous inhabitants – Uzbeks and Tadzhiks. Houses were set alight, lorries over-turned, and troops had to go onto the streets to put a stop to the bloodlet-ting. According to official figures, in two days 638 houses and 100 vehicles were set ablaze, 71 people were killed and hundreds wounded. In the course of operations to restore order, in which more than 6,000 service personnel took part, more than 1,800 firearms were seized. The authorities explained the clashes as the work of 'extremists' and 'unruly elements'.[12] Meanwhile, in the course of the disturbances, numerous social and even ecological demands were advanced and crowds of youths, mixed up in the conflicts with the Meskhetians, soon began to attack the local organs of power and threaten police stations.

On 16–17 June, similar disturbances began in the Kazakh town of Novy Uzen'. Here, as in Turkmenia, hatred towards the 'co-operative' trading bourgeoisie, which consisted mainly of Caucasians, became for the indigenous population the focus of nationalist hostility. Participants in the disturbances demanded 'the eviction from the town of all persons of Caucasian nationality and the closing of the co-operatives founded by them'.[13]

Progressive colonialism had clearly exhausted itself, but no one could propose a constructive alternative. An organized Left was virtually absent except for a few small groups connected with the Moscow Popular Front. The crisis of power was deepening in the localities at exactly the same time as the Moscow leadership, paralysed by the internal struggle for power and frightened by the growth of the mass movement in Russia, could do nothing to improve the situation.

Meanwhile, the national conflicts in the Northern Caucasus, which is part of the Russian Federation, were gradually intensifying. At the end of March 1989, a large group of Muslims seized the Palace of Culture in the village of Nizhnyi Dzhengutai and turned it into a mosque. The authorities were forced to come to terms with this. A month later, several hundred people tried to take by storm the headquarters of the Muslim Religious Administration of the Northern Caucasus in Makhachkal. There was no confidence in the official mosque and support was increasingly being enjoyed by radical Islamic sects. The mufti in the Northern Caucasus were forced to resign, and the authorities stated with alarm that 'religious fanatics have become active and have been openly vying for power in the Religious Administration'.[14] Meanwhile, the central government, not knowing what to do, could only watch the beginnings of a new crisis with growing anxiety.

Moscow proved capable of displaying its greatest activity in Transcaucasia. Of all the regions of the country, this was the least homogeneous. The Christian countries of Georgia and Armenia were traditionally part of the European world, outlying regions of the ancient Mediterranean civilization and with a thousand-year history of links with the West – with Greece, Rome and Byzantium. For these regions, Russia was simultaneously conqueror and defender from the onslaught of the 'Muslim hordes'. Azerbaijan, on the other hand, had always belonged to the Islamic world and, moreover, as in Iran, Shi'ite Muslims were dominant. Azerbaijan's urban population consisted traditionally of Europeans, and Armenians made up a significant portion of the inhabitants of the major cities.

In the nineteenth century, Armenia was divided between Turkey and Russia and during the First World War the mass extermination of Arme-

nians began on Turkish territory. Such massacres took place even in
the short period when all three Transcaucasian peoples gained their own
independent states. Border disputes between Armenia and Azerbaijan
led to bloody conflicts. By the time Armenia became part of the USSR,
it had lost a significant part of its territory and population. Not only
Nakhichevan, where Armenians constituted roughly half the population,
but also Nagorny Karabakh, where they constituted the overwhelming
majority, had passed to Azerbaijan.

Moscow's support for Azerbaijan in the territorial disputes with Armenia in the 1920s can be explained by the efforts of the centre to weaken
the Armenian republic, where the striving for independence and the
level of political activity was somewhat greater than in Azerbaijan. The
mass displacement of Armenians from Nakhichevan – which had gained
the status of an autonomous republic within Azerbaijan – was such
that, by the 1980s, they constituted only two per cent of its population – less than in Baku, the capital of Azerbaijan! Nagorny Karabakh,
however, remained predominantly Armenian but suffered constant discrimination in relation to the other regions of Azerbaijan. Here there
was a shortage of Armenian textbooks, a serious situation had developed
in the health service, it was impossible to watch Armenian television
programmes from Erevan and the police, composed in the main of Azeris,
behaved towards the inhabitants with ill-concealed hostility. All petitions
sent to Moscow with the plea to return Karabakh to Armenia went
unanswered.

It would, nevertheless, be incorrect to explain the crisis purely in
terms of national contradictions. The general social situation in Azerbaijan
underwent a steady deterioration in the late 1970s and early 1980s.
Thousands of people, unable to find work in the countryside, migrated
into the major cities: Baku, Sumgait and others. But there they encountered numerous difficulties in the search for a job and somewhere to
live. The classic Third World situation was being reproduced, the only
difference being that the 'old' town-dwellers here, as in Central Asia,
belonged to different nationalities from the 'new town-dwellers'. The
comparatively well established, traditional urban population – Armenians,
Russians, Jews and, in part, Europeanized Azeris – had skilled and well-
paid jobs. The 'new' town-dwellers – migrants from the countryside
with a poor command of Russian – retained their links with Islamic

traditions. Discontent was directed not only at the authorities, who were blamed for the origins of the crisis, but also at 'foreigners' who had 'grabbed' the best jobs in 'their' own Azerbaijani capital.

In Nagorny Karabakh, the social crisis provoked hatred for the Azerbaijani central authorities, who were responsible for the calamitous state of affairs in the territory. In an analysis of the situation, the Anglo-Pakistani journalist Tariq Ali noted that 'the slums in the capital of Nagorno-Karabakh reminded me of shanty-towns in Mexico'.[15] The interwoven national and social contradictions had created the conditions for a powerful political explosion.

Mass demonstrations and strikes, which began in Nagorny Karabakh in February 1988, soon found an echo in Armenia. The demand for the reunification of Karabakh with the Armenian republic received the support of the local bureaucracy which had also experienced the discrimination practised by Baku. The provincial soviet of Nagorny Karabakh (elected, incidentally, by far from democratic methods) formed a united front with the Party *obkom* and the demonstrators on the streets. Despite the fact that, in this case, there were differences in both the tactics and the level of radicalism in the demands being advanced, it could be said that the whole Armenian population of Karabakh had been able to unite on a national basis. The republican bureaucracy in Yerevan was reluctant to enter a struggle for the sake of the interests of Karabakh, but the pressure of the masses was so strong that it was constrained to take certain steps in support of Karabakh's demands. As a result, Moscow encountered the uncommon situation of a conflict between republics. Baku firmly insisted on the inviolability of its borders, Yerevan demanded their revision, and in Stepanakert, the capital of Karabakh, the apparatchiks declared that they were no longer subject to the republican leadership. For the first time, the Moscow leadership discovered that they were facing a confrontation not between demonstrators and the apparatus, but between two apparatuses. For its part, the Armenian popular movement was swiftly radicalizing. The bureaucracy and the liberal intelligentsia had at first been able, to a significant degree, to control it, but gradually the situation was beginning to change. The less the apparatchiks and liberals were able to obtain from Moscow, the more influence was acquired by the radicals; and the latter did not limit their demands to the reunification of Karabakh with Armenia, but were striving for profound social and political transformations in the Armenian republic itself.

In Azerbaijan too, the situation was out of control. In March 1988, crowds carried out a pogrom against the Armenian inhabitants of Sumgait with the total connivance of the local authorities. But even after the Sumgait slaughter, Moscow continued to insist on maintaining the status quo, thereby, in fact, supporting Baku's position. The central press said nothing about events in Transcaucasia, but attacked Armenian 'extremists' or spoke about the 'equal responsibility' of both sides. This provoked even greater anger among the masses in Yerevan. The Karabakh Committee, which had been organized for the struggle for national interests, was turning increasingly into a socio-political force with more and more radical positions. The liberal intellectuals, Sil'va Kaputikyan and Zorii Balayan, who were involved in the founding of the Committee, surrendered their places to young radicals, the most famous of whom became Ashot Manucharyan. The strikes in Yerevan and Stepanakert showed clearly that it was the workers who were the movement's fundamental social base.

Moscow's inability to make concessions to the Armenian movement could, perhaps, be initially explained simply by an underestimation of its strength. Maintaining the status quo was patently preferred by the apparatus, and Gorbachev hoped that the crisis would resolve itself. Consequently, as could have been anticipated, the exact opposite was achieved: every attempt to slow down the pace of events exacerbated the crisis, which gradually became the normal state of affairs in Transcaucasia. If concessions had been made to Armenian demands in February 1988, the movement would have stayed largely in the hands of the liberals and the local bureaucracy; in the winter of 1987–88, Azerbaijan still lacked a powerful mass movement. The anti-Armenian pogrom in Sumgait, whose senseless brutality had shaken the world, had clearly been organized by someone. The inability and unwillingness of the police to stop the carnage and the troops' lack of speed in arriving on the scene was undoubtedly caused by the connivance of the local apparatus and local mafia with the perpetrators of the pogrom, many of whom had been transported into Sumgait beforehand from other parts of Azerbaijan. By the summer of 1988, the situation in Baku was becoming ever more complicated, since a national movement, outside the control of the apparatus, had begun to form in the republic. By autumn, it was

clear that Islamic fundamentalists were playing a major role in this movement and, at the same time, had begun to advance anti-bureaucratic
demands. Actions against the Armenians were combined with calls for
social justice and nostalgia for the 1917 Revolution. Martial law, introduced simultaneously in Armenia and Azerbaijan, did not bring an end
to the political chaos. The bureaucracy, which had itself let the nationalist
genie out of the bottle, was totally perplexed.

Nevertheless, for Moscow, the main adversary was still the Armenian
popular movement. The first blow was struck against it in July 1988
when the use of mass pickets at a strike at Zvartnots airport served as
the formal excuse for the authorities to use force. Special troops were
hurled into Zvartnots and they used violence against the strikers and
pickets who had come to assist them from various parts of Yerevan,
also assaulting many passengers who happened to be at the airport.
Moscow television deliberately broadcast a false report across the country,
in which the victims themselves were blamed for the violence. Some
participants in the events were arrested and charged with 'group actions
connected with breaches of public order, failure to obey the lawful
demands of representatives of the state, and the consequent interruption
of the work of a state enterprise'.[16] None of the service personnel involved
in assaulting citizens in the grounds of the airport was punished.

The second blow to the Armenian national movement was delivered
a few months later, immediately after the catastrophic earthquake that
destroyed Spitak and several other of the republic's towns. The tragedy
of the people was used by the central authorities to strike a blow at
the Karabakh Committee. Ashot Manucharyan, by that time elected as
a deputy to the republic's Supreme Soviet, was arrested along with other
figures on the Committee just when they were concerned with the
organization of aid for the victims of the earthquake. For several months
Armenia was paralysed. It seemed as though the December earthquake,
the deaths of thousands of people and the arrest of popular leaders had
broken the people's will to continue the fight. The local bureaucracy
had no intention of entering into conflict with Moscow for the sake
of Karabakh, least of all for the sake of freeing the 'trouble-makers' who
had headed the mass actions. However, by the spring of 1989, the situation
was once again beginning to heat up and, in Stepanakert, there was
further strike action.

Meanwhile, the national movement in Georgia had become much stronger. The Abkhazian minority, like the inhabitants of Karabakh, demanded a change in the status of their territory and separation from Georgia which, in the opinion of Abkhazian leaders, was implementing a policy of compulsory assimilation (as in Karabakh, the mass national actions received the support of the local apparatus). At the same time, the leaders of the unofficial Georgian organizations, which had united in a Popular Front, spoke of the need to struggle for the national sovereignty of the republic and then its secession from the USSR. This time the authorities reacted even more swiftly and cruelly than in Armenia. Troops were employed against demonstrators; in Tbilisi a curfew was introduced; and on the streets blood began to be spilt.

Whilst the crisis in Transcaucasia was becoming increasingly profound and complex, it also seemed as though the situation was at a standstill. It was as if the participants in the events were trapped in a vicious circle: strikes – repression – fresh strikes – fresh repression. Neither side was willing to make concessions and there was no longer anywhere to retreat to. In the Baltic republics, on the other hand, where the national bureaucracy had displayed a quite high level of competence and the leaders of the national movement had shown themselves to be good organizers and people capable of entering a political compromise, much was changing.

Anyone visiting Estonia, Latvia or Lithuania in the winter and spring of 1989 would have been clearly convinced that a level of freedom had been achieved there, inconceivable in any other part of the country. The Popular Front movements of Belorussia, Moscow and Leningrad, which had no legal status, could publish their material there without any problems; numerous unofficial magazines and newspapers were freely printed and distributed in both Russian and the national languages. Censorship had, in reality, ceased to function and a genuine freedom for unions had been achieved. The republican authorities had discovered a valuable independence and were taking decisions without looking over their shoulder to Moscow. The question of secession from the USSR was freely discussed and elections to the Congress of People's Deputies took place quite democratically. The Party apparatus in Tallin, Riga and Vilnius had also discovered a genuine independence from the 'centre' and had implemented its own policy, playing the role essentially of an intermediary between the growing national movement and 'big brother' in Russia. This new role for the Party bureaucracy provided it with a certain authority in society, although radical supporters of the changes were not always willing to recognize the fact.

Nevertheless, the situation was far from being as pleasant as it might appear from this brief summary. The conflict between the indigenous population and the Russian-speaking community in all three republics not only remained; it intensified. Russian-speaking citizens everywhere began to form their own associations. In Estonia, all attempts to find a compromise between Intermovement and the Popular Front ended in failure. Among members of Intermovement a shift towards conservative and even Stalinist sentiments became increasingly evident. The March 1989 Congress of Intermovement took place in Tallin in an extremely tense situation, when the Russian-speaking population of the Estonian capital was agitated and anxious at the removal of the red flag from the Tall Herman tower, the symbol of Estonian statehood. Intermovement speakers accused the Popular Front of a 'creeping counter-revolution'. Any proposal contrary to the interests or opinions of the Russian-speaking minority was interpreted in the pages of *Vestnik ID* as being aimed at a 'return to bourgeois relations'. The leaders of the Estonian PF were called travellers on 'the road to anti-socialism' and the public life of the republic was condemned for its 'omnivorous pluralism'.[18]

Kiknadze and Kogan, who represented the democratic tendency in Intermovement and sympathized with many of the Estonian PF's progressive demands, retained their positions in the leading bodies but were unable to control the majority. According to Kiknadze, in spring 1989 their views were shared by about a third of the members of Intermovement. Meanwhile, Stalinist tendencies were clearly gaining strength and this complicated the search for a compromise still further.

Delegates demanded that the humble edifice of a democratic society, which had been painstakingly erected by others over the course of a whole year, and the comforts which the informal Intermovement had quietly enjoyed by holding its congress in the best hall in Tallin, should be destroyed to its foundations. Isn't this really pitiable? Even if a democracy has a certain national bias, then it has been built in a vacuum and without experience. Perhaps we could not have done anything else.[19]

The logic of confrontation, the striving to unite the Russian-speaking community at any price, has led to many democratic- and socialist-minded Russians being compelled to unite with conservatives on a purely national basis. Both movements, the Estonian PF and Intermovement, have proved extremely heterogeneous. Frequently, rank-and-file members of the PF and Intermovement would have been rather closer to each other in their political views than to certain representatives of the leadership of their own organization. This was openly stated in the pages of *Vestnik ID*:

it is precisely 'provocative and unjustified allegations' against the Russian-speaking population of the republic that have led into the ranks of Intermovement even those who, in other circumstances would have given unqualified support to the PF.[20]

National conflicts were also being exacerbated in Lithuania where, as a counterweight to *Sajudis* there arose the Russian–Polish movement 'Unity'. The situation was particularly complicated by the fact that the national demarcation was intertwined with the social. In the Baltic states, Russians are primarily workers in the big enterprises subordinated to all-Union ministries. The managerial apparatus of these enterprises is also predominantly Russian. In Lithuania, Poles constitute a significant percentage of unskilled workers situated on the bottom rung of the social ladder. Consequently, the intercommunal conflict began to assume the features of a conflict between workers and the rest of the population.

The raising of the Estonian national flag over the Tall Herman tower in Tallin was accompanied by calls for strikes in Russian-speaking enterprises and even the creation of a strike committee. It was not, however, the workers who gained a key role in this committee but representatives of the administration who, according to one participant in the events, were no less frightened of their own workers than they were of the Estonian bureaucrats against whom the actions of the Russian minority were formally being directed. On the one hand, the logic of national conflict was forcing the people of each nation to rally round their own bureaucracy and technocracy and, on the other, the Russian apparatchiks and managers were quite incapable of consistently defending the interests of the Russian workers. It was perfectly clear to the managers that a strike, instigated under purely national and even conservative slogans (the return of the old flag) could quite quickly evade their control and advance new, social demands. The upshot was that the strike, naturally, did not take place.

In Lithuania there was a wave of strikes, inspired by figures in Unity, but they had no real impact on the situation in the republic. The growth of discontent among Russian-speaking workers in the Baltic republics in the spring of 1989 forced at least some figures in the national movement to begin to think seriously about social questions, which until that time had been forgotten.

The alienation of workers from the national movement was not only caused by the fact that the workers were predominantly Russians. Among Latvian workers the ideas of the national movement also generated rather less enthusiasm than among the intelligentsia. Back at the founding congress of the Latvian PF, *Guardian* correspondent, Jonathan Steele, asserted that 'The bulk of the delegates were intellectuals in their 30s and 40s. Only a fifth were women. There were few workers.'[21] Even in Lithuania, where Lithuanians formed the basic mass of the labouring population, the movement remained predominantly intellectual.

'How do the workers relate to *Sajudis*?' wrote one of the movement's leaders, Kazimeras Uoka. 'They are interested and sympathetic. . . . Many workers come to the meetings and, I think, they even form the majority of the audience. If this can be called political activity, then the workers are displaying activity. But I wouldn't get carried away.'[22] In Uoka's opinion, the only way of gaining the genuine support of the workers is to turn *Sajudis* from a purely national problematic to a search for 'concrete social solutions', in order to avoid disillusionment and prevent meetings of *Sajudis* degenerating into 'meaningless talking-shops'. A member of the Latvian PF, S. Egorenok, criticized his own movement even more decisively in the pages of the Front's newspaper, declaring that the creative intelligentsia, which dominates the PF, 'has proved insufficiently prepared for really getting to grips with the problematic of production and its patent and manifest contradictions'.[23]

Virtually no attention was paid in the programmatic documents of the Popular Fronts of the Baltic republics to workers' self-management, the rights of workers in the enterprises, the self-organization of labour collectives and other questions of concern to worker activists. As a result, the supporters of the workers' movement within the Popular Fronts have had to stand to one side and create their own structures: 'Workers for *Sajudis*' in Lithuania and the 'Union of Workers' in Latvia. The social-democratic or left-socialist orientation of these groups should have made them attractive to that section of workers (both Balts and Russians) which was striving to avoid an escalation of the national conflicts. Egorenok directly emphasized that the task of the union founded in Latvia was to overcome the split in the workers along national lines. Social democracy in Estonia, which came into being in 1989, has adopted a similar position. However, time has already been wasted and the national division has gone too far for it to be overcome through the creation of new organizations.

The Party apparatus in the republics has been caught in a crossfire. Estonia's Intermovement openly declared that 'the leading bodies of the Estonian CP have become an appendage of the Estonian PF',[24] while the radical part of the Front has itself been increasingly inclined to undermine the Party's political monopoly by open propaganda in favour of political pluralism. In Latvia and Lithuania, the Party organs have tried to manoeuvre between the national movement and the conservatives, taking blows first from one side and then from the other. The severe conflict between the Lithuanian authorities and Unity has been accompanied by a deterioration of relations between the Party apparatus and *Sajudis*. On February 21, a Central Committee Plenum of the republic's CP decided to avoid direct confrontation with the national movement but clearly to distance itself from it. Communists active in *Sajudis* were qualified as people 'sitting in two seats'.[25] There should not, however, have been a conflict. The fact was that the local Party apparatus was undergoing a rapid restructuring and seeking a new political role for itself: that of mediator between the people of its own country and Moscow. In Estonia, Latvia and Lithuania, discussions began on the formation of an independent Communist Party, autonomous from Moscow and with its own programme and constitution (and its own system of nomenklatura appointments, allocated without interference from the centre). In the end, the role of mediator has been fulfilled quite competently by the Party apparatus in all three republics and this had led to a certain consolidation by the spring of 1989.

Events have taken shape completely differently in Moldavia. The general symptoms of national crisis were the same here as in the Baltic republics. As with the three north-western republics, Moldavia was annexed to the USSR after the signing of the 1939 Molotov–Ribbentrop Pact in Moscow, which divided spheres of influence between Hitler's Germany and Stalin's Russia. And, as in the Baltic republics, a serious conflict arose here between the indigenous population and the Slav community. The cultural situation was complicated by the fact that the Moldavian language, in reality identical to Romanian, had been transferred from the Latin to the Cyrillic alphabet. The historical and cultural links with Romania had been dismantled.

The mass Moldavian Democratic Movement, inspired by the ideas of the Baltic Popular Fronts, and receiving the support, as in the Baltic Republics, of a significant part of the local creative workers' unions, first demanded the reinstatement of the Latin alphabet and a recognition of the identity of the Moldavian and Romanian languages. This did not, however, indicate a desire to join Romania, where the Ceausescu regime was implementing a policy directed even more blatantly against the workers and the population as a whole. The Moldavians were only demanding the restoration of historical justice.

The situation was compounded by the catastrophic ecological crisis, the destruction of agriculture through the irresponsible use of chemicals, and a level of corruption that was horrendous even by Soviet standards. Mistrust of the apparatus on the one hand, and the complete inability of the apparatus to assume a new 'national' role on the other, led to events unfolding here in a quite different way to Lithuania or Estonia. The confrontation between people and apparatus, the anger not only of Moldavians, but also of Russians, Ukrainians and Jews at the incompetence and corruption of the ruling circles led to an explosion. On 12 March 1989, a mass unauthorized meeting of the Moldavian Democratic Movement took place in the republic's capital Kishinev, by the monument to the Moldavian-Romanian hero Stefan the Great. The meeting ended with the storming of the Central Committee building of the Moldavian Party. The demonstrators forced the Party First Secretary, Karen Grossu, and the Chairman of the republic's Council of Ministers to come out to them and answer questions to the accompaniment of whistles and catcalls from the crowd. In correspondence from Kishinev, *Pravda* reported that several police officers 'had received serious injuries and had been taken to hospital'.[26] Meanwhile, the local press gave a quite different interpretation of events: after the police had proved unable to disperse the crowd of many thousands – which had assembled under the slogans 'Down with the mafia!', 'The government of Moldavia: resign!' and 'We demand an extraordinary congress of the Moldavian Communist Party!' – 'servicemen from the special unit with helmets and shields in hand' were sent in to suppress the demonstration.[27] It was they who started the fighting as a result of which there were casualties on both sides.

The pattern of events in Kishinev is strikingly reminiscent of the slaughter that took place a month later in Tbilisi. Wherever the local authorities have proved incapable of competently managing the crisis and seeking a compromise, and Moscow has remained initially in the role of incompetent and passive observer, the crisis has been exacerbated and the ruling circles have found no other means at their disposal than the use of force. This official violence has, far from stabilizing the situation, only reinforced radical moods among the masses. Whereas the mass democratic and national movements at first strove to act within the framework of official legality and perceived themselves as reformist movements, the lawlessness of the authorities has brought about a transition to revolutionary methods of struggle. In a conversation with correspondents from *Vechernii Kishinev*, one of those asked the question whether he knew that the 12 March meeting was unauthorized, responded: 'The October Revolution was also unauthorized'[28].

The republican authorities in Moldavia, for their part, resorted to a silence, having no wish to enter into a dialogue with their own population. On 11 May 1989, a Central Committee Plenum of the Moldavian CP took place at which the chairman of the republic's KGB, G. I. Lavranchuk, delivered a programmatic speech. Acknowledging that the situation in the republic had assumed 'a critical and explosive character', he placed all the blame for this on the informal associations, whose ranks had been infiltrated by 'extremist', nationalist and anti-Soviet elements and even agents of the imperialist secret services. By way of an example of imperialism's activity to undermine Soviet Moldavia, he cited the trips made to Kishinev by foreign correspondents, who, in his opinion, were concerned with the gathering of 'intelligence information of a political character. They are primarily interested in the course of perestroika, socio-economic problems, the atmosphere in which the election campaign is being conducted and the activity of informal associations.'[29] Other participants in the plenum spoke in the same vein, appealing for a decisive struggle against the subversive elements. The natural outcome of such a stance has been an escalation of the crisis and the turning of Kishinev into yet another seat of tension.

By the summer of 1989, there remained hardly a single republic or region that did not have serious political problems based on nationality. On almost all occasions, Moscow has rushed from total passivity to the use of force while remaining utterly incapable of managing the crisis in a democratic manner, and of negotiating and compromising with the mass national movements. In those instances where the local Party leaders have displayed greater competence than the centre, the situation has been successfully kept under control, but, in a majority of cases, the level of political competence in the localities has been even lower than at the centre. The socio-political and national-state crises, which have been superimposed upon and intertwined with each other, have made the political situation even less controllable by reinforcing Moscow's confusion, exasperation and willingness to establish order through force. The difficulty has been, however, that the crisis has gone too far and even the use of firearms has been no guarantee of stability. The empire is in its death throes.

NOTES

1. *Ogonyok*, no. 39, 1988.
2. *Vechernii Minsk*, 21 October 1988.
3. *Yunost'*, no. 7, 1989, p. 12.
4. *Prizyv* (Domodedovo), 25 April 1989.
5. *Knizhnoe Obozrenie*, 9 June 1989, p. 2.
6. *Ekonomicheskaya Gazeta*, June 1989.
7. *Nedelya*, no. 24, 1989, p. 24.
8. *Izvestiya*, 22 July 1989.
9. *Izvestiya*, 21 May 1989.
10. *Pravda*, 19 December 1986.

11.   *Literaturnaya Gazeta*, 1 January 1987, p. 10.
12.   *Argumenty i Fakty*, no. 23, 1989.
13.   *Izvestiya*, 20 June 1989.
14.   *Izvestiya*, 22 July 1989.
15.   Tariq Ali, *Revolution from Above*, London 1988, p. 215.
16.   *Pravda*, 24 January 1988.
17.   We will return to the events of 8–9 May in Tbilisi in subsequent chapters.
18.   *Vestnik ID*, no. 4, March 1989.
19.   *Vestnik Narodnogo Fronta*, no. 17, March 1989.
20.   *Vestnik ID*, no. 4, March 1989.
21.   *The Guardian*, 10 October 1988, p. 24.
22.   *Soglasie*, no. 1, 1989, p. 2.
23.   *Atmoda*, 20 March 1989, p. 8.
24.   *Vestnik ID*, no. 4, March 1989, p. 14.
25.   *Novosti Press Agency* from Vilnius, 22 February 1989.
26.   *Pravda*, 29 February 1989.
27.   *Vechernii Kishinev*, 15 March 1989.
28.   Ibid.
29.   *Sovetskaya Moldavia*, 14 May 1989.

5

A Constitutional Crisis

While the Left in Russia was trying to resolve its organizational problems, unable to avoid a political 'slippage', and the leaders of the Baltic Popular Fronts were talking about a national rebirth, it was business as usual in the Party apparatus. The decisions of the Nineteenth Party Conference on reform of the political system needed to be fleshed out in specific documents, a national discussion of these documents had to be held and then they could be adopted. However, in conditions of mounting political tension, this planned bureaucratic procedure proved to be the detonator of a new crisis.

After the Nineteenth Conference, the basic parameters of the declared political reform were already known, so that the documents published for discussion at the end of October 1988 contained nothing new. Nevertheless, they provoked a stormy reaction across the country. Even Gorbachev subsequently admitted that such broad and widespread protests had taken him by surprise. In essence, the country was plunged into a constitutional crisis at the end of October. Not only radical political groups but also the Supreme Soviets of all the Union Republics opposed the amendments to the Constitution and the new electoral law suggested by Gorbachev and his advisers. A campaign of criticism of the government unfolded, unprecedented in scale – unlike all preceding conflicts, not only individual links of the political apparatus came under attack, but also Gorbachev himself and his course.

It was in fact easy to predict even this turn of events. Precisely because the content of the laws in preparation was known beforehand, all the fundamental political groupings had been able to make careful preparation for the developing campaign. The Moscow leadership, following traditional bureaucratic procedure in organizing a 'national discussion' of its projects, itself provided the opposition with ideal opportunities to expand the campaign.

The chief objections to the 'reform' proposed by the authorities can be summarized as follows: first, the election of the Supreme Soviet not by the electorate itself but by an intermediate body – the Congress of People's Deputies – deprived citizens of the opportunity to influence directly the composition of the highest legislative organ. Second, the leadership of the republics was extremely unhappy that henceforth the Soviet of Nationalities, which should represent their interests in the Supreme Soviet, would also be elected by the Congress in Moscow. In this way, the federal structure of the state had in fact been abolished at the level of legislative power. Such a transformation affected not only ordinary voters, but also the bureaucratic apparatus of the Union republics, depriving it of the right to direct and effectively control 'its' deputies in the Soviet of Nationalities. Thus at the same time, not only the intelligentsia and the masses, but also state officials began for the first time to worry about their political and national rights and to fight for the principles of national sovereignty.

The Left was severely critical of the 'representation of the estates': as promised at the Party Conference, the new legislation allowed official social organizations to send their deputies to the Congress according to a pre-set quota – thus bypassing the territorial election procedure. From the outset it was obvious that such 'representation' would be used to guarantee seats to political figures with no chance of being elected by the 'usual methods'. Everyone was convinced that Yegor Ligachev would be 'elected' to the Congress in this way. Naturally, this assumption was confirmed – although even at the Central Committee Plenum devoted to the election of 'deputies from the Party', a number of participants voted against his candidature. Gorbachev also preferred not to take the chance of popular elections and was among the 'Party's direct representatives'. As expected, conflicts arose among the official organizations over the number of places allocated to them at the Congress. It has remained unclear who determines this quota, and on what basis.

The law on elections, while formally granting any individual the right to nominate themselves at public meetings (on the condition that no less than five hundred people are present), simultaneously gave the electoral commissions the right to register or not register candidates at their discretion. The commissions themselves were set up according to traditional apparatus rules and no one doubted that these commissions would become obedient instruments of the regime.

In fact, there was a definite deterioration in the legislation even in comparison with the Brezhnev period. The draft was, moreover, badly prepared from a juridical point of view. It contained a vast quantity of ambiguities and contradictions which provoked endless squabbles in the course of the subsequent election campaign. All of the weak aspects of the proposed documents were, from the outset, quite obvious to specialists and were also sharply criticized by lawyers.

In the final analysis, the new legislation affected the interests of a wide range of social strata. It somehow invoked displeasure from all possible sides. How can such strange behaviour on the part of the leadership be explained, particularly at a time when the country's leaders were talking a lot about stability? Although it might seem paradoxical, the worsening of the legislation was the logical consequence of the process of democratization for Soviet society. The country had had its most democratic constitution in Stalin's time. It was another matter entirely that this constitution, like many other legal norms, had simply not been observed. After the rehabilitation of victims of Stalinism in the 1960s, when laws began to be taken more seriously, this constitution seemed too democratic, and – in its way – dangerous. It was no longer a purely propagandist document and so it began to be utilized by dissidents and participants in the movement for civil rights. As a result the constitution had to be 'amended'. The new 'fundamental law' adopted under Brezhnev was drafted in such a way as to make difficult even formal references to the Constitution by those who attempted to make use of the rights and freedoms proclaimed within it. In this regard the chief role was assigned to Article 6, which legislatively reinforced the leading role of the CPSU in Soviet society. Any action contrary to the line of the Party leadership was deemed illegal. The Brezhnev Constitution was effectively the legislative conversion of the CPSU from a political party into part of the administrative mechanism of the state. Although this process had in reality been completed rather earlier, at the end of the 1920s, the juridical registration of the indissoluble marriage between Party and state only took place under Brezhnev.

Gorbachev's constitutional reform did not at all encroach upon the preceding period's highly dubious 'innovations'. On the contrary, it developed and strengthened them. Article 6 of the USSR Constitution, while guaranteeing the CPSU the status of 'the leading force in society', did not envisage a specific mechanism for the realization of this principle. The absence of a mechanism for implementing declared rights was a notorious characteristic of all Soviet constitutions dating back to the 1920s. Paradoxically, under perestroika it was not individual protesting citizens who came up against this problem, but the CPSU itself.

In pre-perestroika times, the problem was simply resolved: by denying the country's citizens the opportunity to exercise their constitutional rights, the ruling élite thereby automatically protected its own. It was not forbidden to nominate alternative candidates – there simply couldn't be any. If it entered anybody's head to propose an opposition candidate, they would inevitably end up in an asylum. And indeed, to imagine such a thing was possible one would have to be eccentric.

Thanks to perestroika the situation radically changed. The Party could no longer use repressive methods to prevent citizens from exercising their rights. But the Party leadership was confronted with the question of how to defend its interests in a legislative manner. The 1988 constitutional reform was necessary to bring the legislation closer to reality, and legitimize the power already residing in the hands of the Party apparatus. The principle of a law-governed state was understood by the creators of the new legislation in a novel fashion. Everything that had previously been done unlawfully could henceforth be done on the basis of specific legislation.

At the same time, a press campaign was launched to enhance the concept of a 'law-governed state' in the consciousness of the masses. Eminent jurists and political figures explained that the formation of a law-governed state depended on the masses, on 'the population's legal culture', and that if we want a law-governed state tomorrow then we must learn to respect laws – any laws – today.

In essence, under the slogan of the struggle for a law-governed state, work was going on for the legalization of bureaucratic tyranny. The public was called upon to respect patently undemocratic laws and to implement decrees restricting citizens' rights and liberties. But despite all the propaganda, the official draft of the reform provoked universal dissatisfaction. Hundreds of thousands of letters, deeply critical of the draft, were received by newspaper and magazine editors, television and the Supreme Soviet. Criticism began in the press where, despite increased censorship, a place could still be found for articles expressing the viewpoint of the discontented.

The Baltic newspapers were, naturally, rather more candid than the central press. 'In order to comprehend the essence of Gorbachev's reform,' wrote *Renaissance*, the organ of the Lithuanian *Sajudis* movement,

> one has to answer the question: who needs this reform? It is evident that a conscious and active people has no need of such a reform, since, under the conditions of glasnost and democracy, the former electoral system has been less of a fetter on the possibilities for the electorate to nominate and elect its deputies. This means that the reform's major innovations will serve the country's ruling party and bureaucratic system of government. Now, it is only these forces which can create the all-powerful district electoral commissions, which in turn are devoted to the organization of the all-powerful electoral assemblies.[1]

It should be borne in mind that independent candidates were almost invariably successful in elections held under the old legislation in the conditions of perestroika. In Irkutsk, Kazan and Apatity, candidates nominated by social initiative groups or the Popular Front had already been able to outstrip their official opponents in elections to the local soviets. The only salvation for the authorities was the requirement of the old law that the victor gain more than 50 per cent, not of the votes cast, but of those registered to vote in the electoral district. Consequently, in Kazan for example, citizens had to vote several times (although there was a turn-out of more than 60 per cent, a quite acceptable proportion by Western European or American standards). The newspapers complained of the 'passivity' of the population through which the election results had proved unclear.[2] However, in reality, it was not the electors who were to blame but the legislation. In fact, the elimination of the point about the obligatory 50 per cent of the registered electorate was the sole positive aspect of the new legislation, but it was quite inadequate to reconcile the legislation with public opinion.

In the Baltic republics – where, as we have seen, there was already a certain de facto autonomy – the protest against the constitutional reform was supported not only by the Popular Fronts but also by the apparatus. In Estonia, they did not confine themselves just to criticism of the draft law, and the republic's Supreme Soviet adopted a 'Declaration on Sovereignty'. Typically, despite the tense relations between the Russian-speaking community and the Estonians, the demands for sovereignty were this time backed not only by the indigenous population but also by a significant section of the republic's non-indigenous inhabitants. According to *Vestnik Narodnogo Fronta*, this declaration was 'accepted rather more calmly than the less radical but more concrete decrees like the Law on Language' by even those Russians who did not support demands for republican sovereignty.[3]

From this point onwards, the republican authorities severely restricted central interference in its affairs, and declared the state enterprises, the mineral wealth and resources on its territory to be the property of Estonia. Such demands were quite logical – as was the anger of the Moscow apparatus at such blatant insubordination 'in the provinces'.

The crisis was rapidly exacerbated. The Estonian declaration generated mass enthusiasm in Latvia and Lithuania, although the national apparatus was not prepared to act so decisively as in Estonia. This came as an unwelcome surprise to the Estonian Popular Front, which placed its hopes not only in the solidarity of the workers but also in the solidarity of the republican bureaucracy. It was the restraint of the national apparatchiks in the other republics which probably forced the Tallin leadership of the Estonian PF to turn its attention to the weak Moscow PF. Unfortunately, the Moscow movement could do little at this time to help the Baltic republics. In Vilnius, Tallin and Riga, mass demonstrations took place against the constitutional reform. In Moscow, we were only able to hold a press conference at which we declared our solidarity with the Baltic republics.

The unwillingness or inability of the Baltic Popular Fronts to do something to develop the movement in Russia rebounded against them. At the moment when support in Moscow was crucial, the Left's opportunities were extremely limited. The Moscow PF continued to suffer from an information blackout, with no possibility of utilizing the official press even simply to talk about itself or make its existence known. The Russian-language publications of the Baltic PFs had a tiny circulation and paid almost no attention to events occurring outside the Baltic republics.

In the end, the crisis 'resolved itself'. As expected, the Supreme Soviet adopted all the basic points of the new law on elections and amendments to the Constitution without any changes. The decrees on meetings and demonstrations and the special forces had been ratified even earlier. The Estonian Declaration on sovereignty was repudiated as being contrary to the USSR Constitution. Not one of these decisions provoked the catastrophic consequences predicted at meetings. Estonia did not begin to detach itself from the USSR although many were afraid that the conflict between Tallin and Moscow would seriously strengthen the striving for independence. The leadership in Tallin did not simply submit itself to Moscow's decision: the refusal of the USSR Supreme Soviet to recognize the Estonian Declaration was 'acknowledged' in Estonia but no one revoked the Declaration. The 1988 constitutional crisis revealed a stale-mate situation: the republics were still incapable of forcing Moscow to consider their demands, and Moscow was no longer capable of forcing the republics to carry out its instructions.

The only way of 'unblocking' the situation and providing an opportunity for a transition to genuine federalism, or to the union of independent states of which the ideologues of the national movement in the Baltic republics had spoken, would have been a considerable strengthening of the forces of the Left in Russia itself and a successful democratization in Moscow itself. In practice, the situation was taking a quite different shape. Here also a distinct 'stalemate' had arisen. The leadership had clearly lost its taste for liberal reforms, though it did not want to use repression or change the official course in any serious way, but the mass movement was not yet able to throw down a challenge to the authorities.

This democracy of inertia gave progressive forces no opportunity to seize the initiative. The Moscow Popular Front remained in its own political ghetto. The élite intelligentsia, united in Moscow Tribune, unsuccessfully attempted to form a liberal lobby at the very moment when the authorities were less and less inclined to listen to liberal speeches and the masses were adopting an increasingly sceptical attitude to their promises. The radicalization of the masses was obvious but, at the same time, events were unfolding slowly: the democracy of inertia corresponded to the creeping radicalization of a significant part of the population.

The Left itself had, to a large extent, not yet shaken off its liberal illusions. As before, many placed their hopes on a market reform of the economy, which, it was supposed, would naturally further political democratization. They gave no thought to the fact that the advocates of economic freedom for managers and privileged layers were not at all striving to grant political freedom to 'lower' strata, who would not automatically gain anything from such a reform.

In essence, the country was emerging from one crisis and falling slowly into another. Problems were accumulating and finding no solution. Perestroika, which had begun triumphantly in 1986 with a promise to grant everything to everyone, was, while glorified in the pages of 'quality' Western publications, turning into a permanent crisis.

NOTES

1. *Vozrozhdenie (Atginimas)*, 13 January 1989.
2. *Sovetskaya Tartariya*, 27 September 1988.
3. *Vestnik Narodnogo Fronta*, no. 18, April 1989.

Election Fever

'It is possible that there will be more important elections in our history, but more cheerful – never.' With these words philosopher Mikhail Maliutin began his speech to the electorate as Moscow Popular Front candidate for the Congress of People's Deputies. It was conceivable that he could be among the number of comparatively successful candidates: he had not been impeded by the authorities and his supporters had been able to distribute leaflets freely and to organize meetings. The Popular Front had provided several dozen activists for Maliutin's campaign and even a certain amount of money. Nevertheless, the speaker's subsequent irony and irritation were fully understandable: participants in the electoral struggle had to expend considerable efforts just to get themselves on the list of election candidates, and many were unsuccessful.

For independent candidates, the electoral campaign turned into a peculiar obstacle race. First, one had to apply to the constituency electoral commission for permission to organize a public gathering, which had to be attended by no less than 500 inhabitants of that constituency. If the assembly is 'unofficial', if errors are discovered in the registration or if official representatives of the authorities are not present, the results are immediately annulled. Moreover, as Yuri Rantalov, the head of an oppositional Komsomol grouping, has acknowledged, the Central Electoral Commission acted 'in a totally anti-democratic fashion by proposing all manner of procedural rules not stipulated in the Law on Elections'.[1]

It was far from easy to obtain permission to organize a gathering. The situation varied in different cities in the country – from Saratov, where on the whole everything happened according to the old procedures with one candidate for one seat, or Stavropol where the local Popular Front initiative group was at once put under pressure, to Tallin, where the Popular Front was in fact master of the situation. Even within Moscow serious differences between various regions of the city came to light. In the Cheremushkinsky or Sevastopolsky districts of the capital, initiative groups organized by the PF encountered no obstacles of any kind in calling meetings and even the anti-communist, pro-American Democratic Union could try to promote their own candidate. But, in contrast, in Perovsky and a few other districts, the meeting's initiators were informed that, first of all, they would have to undertake a preliminary election among members of the public. Each of the 500 participants in the gathering would have to represent no less than 175 of the district's inhabitants. Consequently, in order to call the meeting no less than 87,500 people would have to be questioned! Activists in the Moscow PF, however, accepted this challenge, since they thus gained the opportunity to hold dozens of agitational meetings in the area. In the Kirovsky district of Moscow, the authorities acted rather more radically. They simply refused the PF initiative group the right to hold meetings by saying it was 'pointless' to put up the proposed candidates in that area.

However, even where permission was gained without any great difficulty, it was still necessary to surmount a vast number of obstacles. The initiative group had to assemble the agreed number of people in the hall granted to it. Achieving this was not a simple matter, given the problems of disseminating information. Although the constituency electoral commission was obliged by law to convene the meeting, in practice everything had to be done by the initiative group. They had to notify people somehow of the impending meeting, while having no access to printing equipment, radio, television or the press. Electoral leaflets often had to be reproduced in secret by an activist using computers and duplicating facilities at work. Sometimes this had to be paid for at 'black market' prices.

Having almost no experience, many initiative groups missed the opportunities presented to them. At a meeting in the Leningradsky district of Moscow, there were fewer than a hundred people present; on other occasions, gatherings were just a few dozen short of the magical figure of 500. In such circumstances, the representatives of the district electoral commission would announce that the meeting could not take place and would ask people to go home. As a rule the public would refuse to comply, shouting would start and spontaneous meetings would take place, sometimes lasting for several hours. The representatives of the authorities would criticize the initiative group for badly organizing the gathering and the other side would blame the authorities for 'sabotaging democratization' and for an unwillingness to keep workers informed about the course of the electoral struggle. In the general clamour it was at times difficult to make anything out. The crowd almost always sided with the meeting's organizers and the local authorities would be criticized for numerous errors and mistakes that had nothing to do with the meetings.

Wherever a quorum was successfully secured, the meeting would usually vote for the candidate nominated by the initiative group but this still did not signify a decisive victory: in accordance with the new laws the district electoral commission had the right to vet the candidates. To this end district assemblies would be convened, the majority of those taking part being selected by the commission itself. But even if a candidate managed to survive all of these experiences, became registered and, finally, was victorious at the polls, there was absolutely no guarantee of successful entry into the Supreme Soviet. There sit only those chosen by the Congress of People's Deputies from among its number. According to the new laws, not only deputies elected from traditional territorial and national-territorial constituencies can participate in the Congress, but also representatives of the Party, Komsomol and numerous official organizations for whom a quota of seats has been reserved beforehand. In accordance with this electoral law, the 190 people who participated in the session of the Presidium of the Academy of Sciences on 18 January 1989, were able, for example, to choose 23 candidates for deputies – giving them a voting power equivalent to five million votes of the electors in territorial constituencies. Such a difference (1 vote = 25,000 ordinary votes) signified, in reality, the total eradication of an equal electoral law and blatant discrimination against the masses. The medieval principle of representation according to estate was triumphant.

A sharp conflict arose in the Academy of Sciences between the Presidium and the basic mass of research workers. Candidates who had received wide support in the academic institutes had been eliminated by the Presidium. Among those rejected was academician Andrei Sakharov, who had been nominated by fifty-five institutes. Workers at the institutes refused to accept the Presidium's decision, sent a complaint to the Central Electoral Commission and declared their intention to hold a demonstration – the first in the entire history of the Academy of Sciences.

On 2 February, more than two thousand people from fifty of Moscow's research institutes assembled at the Presidium of the Academy of Sciences. Professors and academicians had taken to the streets for the first time in their lives to proclaim their demands. Placards with radical slogans were raised in the crowd and clearly expressed the new mood. The Academy's Vice-President, V. I. Kudryavtsev, attempted to address the gathering, but was met with cries of 'Get him off!' and 'Shame!' In this sense, the crowd, a good half of which was composed of Doctors of Science and academicians, was barely distinguishable from any other aggressive crowd. Kudryavtsev was dismayed, promised to tender his resignation and then left the microphone. (He did not however keep his promise.) Meanwhile, the crisis in the Academy of Sciences had clearly gone beyond the initial conflict over the elections. Of the five resolutions adopted by the meeting, only two were connected with the elections (an appeal for the deputies officially elected from the Academy to withdraw their candidatures and an appeal to boycott the voting at the electoral conference, which should have confirmed the Presidium's decision). The remainder concerned a vote of confidence, a call for the immediate resignation of the Presidium, and a voicing of the need to form a democratic union of scholars. The organizers of the meeting had established a link with the Co-ordinating Council of the Moscow PF. In this way, the struggle within the Academy generated by the contradictions between scholars and administrators began to assume a political character. About two weeks after the meeting, it was announced that Andrei Sakharov and R. Z. Sogdeev were withdrawing their candidatures from various territorial districts and would seek nomination only from the Academy. Thus the situation was exacerbated still further.

A no less complex struggle was also going on in the creative unions, where the criteria for selecting candidates frequently had nothing to do with their political views. The philosopher Valentin Tolstykh, Secretary of the Executive of the USSR Cinematographers' Union declared that, in the elections, members of the Union had been influenced by such qualities in a candidate as 'honesty, modesty and principles'.[2] In the Union of Theatre Workers, as participants themselves have admitted, the executive plenum, which was selecting the candidates, turned into a veritable farce. Voting had to take place four times, as virtually none of the candidates could command a sufficient number of votes. Only the leaders of the Union – actors K. Lavrov and M. Ulyanov, producer O. Efremov and theatrical composer R. Pauls – went through on the first ballot. Someone demanded that musical theatre should also be represented and someone else disputed the candidates' creative successes, claiming it was intolerable to elect poor producers as deputies to the Congress. Representatives of the national republics demanded that they should be allocated a certain number of places but that was still not enough for all the republics. It was eventually decided to nominate eight 'extra' candidates and grant a special conference of the Union the right to the final decision. The State Institute of Theatrical Art supported the candidature of V. Vasiliev on the grounds that he was one of the best dancers in the history of Russian ballet. In the Writers' Union, there was a clash between the traditional literary groupings of 'national conservatives' and 'liberal Westernizers'. Only in a few instances was the candidates' political platform discussed, and then only in very general terms.

Meetings in enterprises, scientific institutions and places of residence also took place under the slogan 'Elect good, principled people'. The candidates' political platforms proved so secondary that at times the gathering was prepared to support simultaneously two candidates, representing quite different positions. In this situation, those who combined personal authority with definite political influence proved the most successful. The symbolic figures of Boris Yeltsin and Andrei Sakharov were guaranteed success, being nominated many times in such diverse districts that the picture often became still more confused. It should be borne in mind that most initiative groups were acting in the dark, with no knowledge of who was being nominated in neighbouring districts.

The unofficial groupings needed very significant organizational and monetary resources to gain any influence in this chaotic process. The liberal Democratic Union, which looked to the capitalist model of development and had been able to draw attention to itself through noisy demonstrations in the summer of 1988, was this time almost unable to participate in events. Smaller left-wing and right-wing groups went virtually unmentioned. Only the Popular Front was able to run its own campaign. Even where PF supporters failed to hold a meeting and achieve the magical 500, they could still claim some success: in all electoral districts there emerged local branches of the Popular Front, which began to grow very quickly. The official press conceded that the Moscow PF had managed to engage in 'purposeful electoral activity' and had shown 'serious intentions and not a little organizational potential'.[3] The PF's activities and leaflets provoked enormous interest – the Party organization in the Union of Cinematographers declared its support for the movement and Front candidates managed to address workers' collectives. In the end, all four PF candidates – the philosopher Mikhail Maliutin, the historian Sergei Stankevich, the lawyers Rimma Goncharenko and Sergei Druganov – successfully negotiated the first stage of the campaign. The Popular Front's electoral machine, despite numerous individual defects, the complete lack of experience and blatant pessimism of its candidates, did its job.

PF organizations also achieved a distinct success in the Russian provinces. In Kuibyshev and Yaroslavl they managed to nominate their own candidates despite the authorities' strenuous opposition. In Stavropol, the persecution meted out to the local PF Organizing Committee after it had tried to intervene in the running of the elections at least served to publicize it.

The exception was the attitude of the Sverdlovsk (Urals) Popular Front, which declared a boycott of the elections. Although this unwillingness to participate in what was patently a lost cause was totally understandable, such a decision scarcely strengthened the PF's position in the city. As Maliutin noted, an organization that declines to make use of the opportunity of an electoral campaign 'automatically reduces itself to a political zero'.[4] The Sverdlovsk position, based on traditional Bolshevik schemas, was nonetheless an exception. (Subsequently, in the course of the electoral struggle, the Urals PF revised its position.) In a majority of cases, PF activists tended rather towards the over-optimistic delusion that the Congress of People's Deputies might become a genuinely democratic body.

The electoral campaign once again confirmed the old truth that it is impossible to have serious politics without a mass organization. The more chaotic the nomination of candidates became, the greater was the need for serious organizational groundwork. The Popular Front's success contrasted particularly with the blatant feebleness of the liberal intelligentsia, which was quite incapable of achieving any sort of results outside the framework of the official structures. The scandal which broke on 9 January 1989, following the unsuccessful attempt to promote the candidature of Vitaly Korotich, editor of the popular liberal magazine *Ogonyok*, might serve as an instructive example. Although, on this occasion, the meeting organizers would have been quite capable of assembling a sufficient number of people, they preferred not to display any special activism. When representatives of the Popular Front, who supported Korotich's candidature, proposed to send their people to agitate among local residents and maintain order at the meeting, they were met with a flat refusal. Korotich's entourage were confident of success and had no intention of encouraging the 'overly radical' activists of the PF. The consequences of this decision were immediate: instead of the obligatory 500, only 373 electors were recorded. The gathering decided to turn itself into a public meeting with Korotich. The representatives of the authorities, who were usually very strict with initiative groups, this time exercized leniency. But at that moment something very unexpected happened. The *Izvestiya* correspondent reported that

> Suddenly, a command was heard from above and home-made placards were brought into the hall from the balcony, among which 'Korotich is chief of the scum of perestroika' and 'The vanguard has no faith in the yellow press' were the least offensive.
> The microphones which had been set up in the hall were surrounded by groups of people whose unity was underlined by badges with the image of Georgii Pobedonosets. They shouted throughout the hall:
> 'The people don't need Korotich!'
> 'Expose the opportunist!'[5]

The hall had been taken over by supporters of the fascist movement *Pamyat'* (Memory), and it was the followers of Igor Sychev – whom the official press portrayed as the 'moderate' and even 'healthy' wing of the movement – who were running amok here.

With difficulty, Korotich managed to avoid being beaten up. He was shielded by Aleksandr Feodorovsky, a member of the Co-ordinating Council of the Moscow Popular Front. A few days later an article about the *Pamyat'* riot appeared in the pages of *Ogonyok*; its author claimed that these events were caused by the 'disorganization' of 'decent people'. 'We are not welded into teams, committees, organizations, groups', moaned the journalist. Precisely because of this, 'a small but cohesive unit' of fascist youths 'can do what it likes'.[6] In reality, *Pamyat'*'s success in the 'Korotich affair' can in no way be explained by the inability of 'progressive people' to unite; rather, it was due to the unwillingness or fear of the *Ogonyok* leaders to accept organizational assistance from the Left. The following day, when PF activists began to distribute leaflets on the streets, describing what had happened and calling for unity to repulse *Pamyat'*, representatives of *Ogonyok* even demanded that these activities should cease. A letter from Maliutin and Feodorovsky, which set out the Front's position, was published in the magazine only after all references to the PF were withdrawn. Thus the 'Korotich affair' once again displayed the contradictions which had been characteristic of the Moscow intellectual elite over the course of several months. On the one hand, the liberal public bemoaned their own disunity and lack of organization and spoke with rapture about the Baltic republics and Poland with their powerful democratic movements; but, on the other hand, they fled in terror from any attempt to found a strong mass organization.

In essence, the first stage of the electoral campaign revealed not only the weak aspects of the new legislation but also the extremely low level of society's political culture. Yuri Raptanov pessimistically stated: 'Our emotions have overflowed: the opportunity to elect, propose, speak freely at meetings! But what is really the case? Everything is just as it was. The apparatus decides.'[7] In a majority of cases, electors were faced with a random collection of candidates, who frequently had no political profile of their own. These were in the main good people, conscientious professionals, but in no sense politicians. But, at the same time, public interest in politics was growing rapidly. The elections had activated tens of thousands of people, who were, perhaps, unable to find their bearings in the political situation but did not wish to remain passive. Empty shelves and the bosses' unfulfilled promises were generating increasing discontent and a profound need for change.

NOTES

1. *Komsomol'skaya Iskra*, 1 February 1989.
2. *Literaturnaya Gazeta*, 1 February 1989.
3. *Sovetskaya Molodezh'*, 10 February 1989.
4. *Molodezhnaya Tribuna*, no. 1, 1989, p. 9.
5. *Izvestiya*, 18 January 1989.
6. *Ogonyok*, no. 3, 1989, p. 31.
7. *Komsomol'skaya Iskra*, 1 February 1989.

A Difficult Hegemony

In June 1988, when meetings calling for the creation of a Popular Front were taking place all across the country, few of us in the movement realized just how difficult the task of establishing a mass democratic organization would prove to be. The lack of political experience even among the leaders of the movement, a shortage of information, a pathological fear of even the most democratic forms of centralized leadership (which led at times to a complete incapacity for collective action), the clash of personal ambitions – all of these combined to obstruct the development of the Popular Front from the very outset. But an even greater barrier was the fragility of the Popular Front itself. The upsurge which began in summer 1988 had already given way to a slump by August and September. A new revival became evident in mid-autumn under the influence of the Baltic Popular Fronts and the constitutional crisis provoked by the official attempt at political reform. In the spring of 1989, the pre-election campaign sparked the next round of mass activism. All these fluctuations were invariably reflected in the situation within the Popular Front, and not just in Moscow. A sturdy organization could withstand short-term shifts in the political climate without any particular trouble. But the Front's fragility as a movement hindered its organizational development.

A Leningrad conference of the organizing committees of the Popular Fronts of Russia, the Ukraine, and Belorussia brought the obvious crisis of the movement out into the open. Although the Moscow organizing committee was quite unified in expressing its views at the conference, one should not be deceived into thinking that all these problems have finally been resolved in the capital. After the demonstrations in Pushkin Square and the withdrawal of the anarchists and the liberals from the organizing committees, the main body of the groups was able to consolidate itself around the positions of democratic socialism, and recognize the need for unity. However, the Popular Front of the capital lacked an effective organizational structure, a common programme, and an elected leadership. A dual responsibility rested on the socialist groups at the core of the organizing committee of the Moscow PF: to consolidate the movement both organizationally and ideologically, and to preserve the broad character of the movement.

The hegemony of the socialists in the PF was preordained by past events. The pro-capitalist groups of a liberal persuasion joined the Democratic Union. The 'Patriotic Tendency' represented mainly by Evgenii Dergunov and his supporters in the Popular Front had to distance themselves demonstratively from the anti-semitic Black Hundreds in *Pamyat'*, but many supporters of the movement still continued to regard it with suspicion. In addition to this, nobody besides the socialists possessed their own cadres of professional social scientists and a more-or-less coherent socio-economic conception. Finally, the activists of the socialist groups demonstrated their capacity for solidarity and effective resolute action.

A socialist programme facilitated the joining together of ecologists, Marxists, supporters of local self-management, student activists, and radical democrats. Now we had to make this alliance of left forces a going concern.

The first step on the path to the establishment of an effective organization was the selection of a Co-ordinating Council (CC) in autumn 1988. This CC was charged with initiating preparations for a founding conference of the Moscow PF as well as conducting the current activity of the Front. In distinction from the organizing committee consisting of group representatives, the CC was elected on a personal basis. Elected to the CC were Oleg Ananian, Andrei Babushkin, Mikhail Maliutin, Anatolii Medvedev, Sergei Stankevich, Mikhail Shneider, Aleksandr Feodorovsky, Andrei Danilov and myself. Danilov never began work in the CC. After the Leningrad conference where he tried to scream the necessary resolutions through ratification, Danilov – until a few months before one of the leaders of the Popular Front – rapidly began to lose his standing within the movement, and in fact has left its ranks. Thus the working Co-ordinating Council was composed of eight individuals – characteristically, all of them belonged to socialist groups, and four were members of the CPSU.

The selection of the CC greatly improved the situation within the movement. Organizational work was undertaken which very quickly made itself felt in the course of pre-election activity. The PF's financial affairs were set in order, and the establishment of an information centre maintaining links with other organizing committees was begun. The first issue of the bulletin *News of the Popular Front* appeared. The old club structure had given way to a new structure based on a technical division of labour and political solidarity.

In such conditions, the most important task of the CC was not merely to prepare documents for the founding conference but also to establish a close link between the organization and its mass social base. The clubs had a tendency to withdraw into themselves, as a rule never encompassing more than sixty people. Now we had to 'go to the people' in the nine-teenth-century Populist manner and test out on a mass audience ideas formulated in the period of internal club discussions. The supporters of the PF – mainly the lower strata of the intelligentsia and some skilled workers and students who respond enthusiastically to radical ideas – had to find in the Moscow PF a capable defender of their social interests.

Successful work in the course of the pre-election campaign led to a rapid growth in the movement's ranks. An ever-increasing number of people became familiar with the activity of the PF in Moscow. District groups set up in the course of the elections were consolidated. Residents of the capital who had earlier come to hear of the Moscow PF mainly through mendacious articles published in *Vechernyaya Moskva* and *Moskovskaya Pravda*, discovered that the movement's participants were by no means the bloodthirsty extremists depicted in the newspapers.

Meanwhile this success paradoxically heightened the internal difficulties of the organization. Most new members of the Front lacked political experience, had little understanding of the balance of power, and knew practically nothing about the disputes between the activists of the left groups on the eve of the Party Conference. In order to keep the situation under control and consolidate a constantly growing movement, it was urgently necessary to ratify at least a provisional programme and constitution (in effect until the 'official' founding conference).

The situation was complicated by the unexpected appearance of a new actor on the political scene. In December 1988, a small group of people led by Valerii Skurlatov suddenly proclaimed itself the Russian Popular Front, and demanded that subordinate regional organizations from Moscow, Leningrad, Sverdlovsk, and so on, subject themselves to its authority. Although Skurlatov had not participated in the Popular Front movement until that time, he was far from a complete unknown to those with a knowledge of the course of public life in our country. As early as 1965, when he was working in the Moscow City Committee of the Komsomol, Skurlatov wrote a document entitled 'A Charter of Morals'. In this he demanded the universal militarization of youth, the restoration of corporal punishment in the schools, the stiffening of criminal legislation on the principle 'two eyes for an eye', and the restoration of patriarchal customs to preserve 'maidenly honour': 'smearing the gates with tar', 'public display of the sheet after the wedding night', and so on. The Charter proposed corporal punishment and even sterilization for women who slept with foreigners.[1] This document caused a scandal, and Skurlatov was forced to transfer to another job. Subsequently, he maintained close contacts with the leaders of the anti-Semitic movement which eventually became *Pamyat'*, but he later broke with them. Thus the establishment of the Russian Front was Skurlatov's third appearance on the political scene.

The system of political work chosen by Skurlatov and his friends proved to be simple in the extreme. They spent several days writing a programme and constitution which they then and there declared to be final. The document in question represents a capricious blend of the programmatic demands of the Democratic Union and *Pamyat'*. On the one hand, the document firmly emphasizes the need for Russian patriotism, a return to national roots, and so on. On the other, the economic programme envisages an orientation towards the development of private enterprise, joint stock companies, and the elimination of state participation in the economy. The authors of the programme paid particular attention to the extension of the rights of foreign capital on Soviet territory – this from the lips of 'principled patriots'! However, they also proposed the resurrection of the old Flag of Saint Andrew (the flag of the imperial family before the revolution) with the 'golden bird of rebirth' in the centre as a means of satisfying the national pride of ethnic Russians.

All this would be laughable if the Skurlatov initiative had not gained official support from the outset. After Skurlatov and his supporters held a 'constituent assembly' on 15 December 1988, TASS issued a nationwide report on the establishment of the Russian PF. This report was immediately published in *Sovetskaya Rossiya* – the same newspaper which had earlier become famous for its publication of Nina Andreeva's notorious letter in defence of Stalin. The newly established organization immediately obtained office space, and set about distributing a circular letter across the country which stated that Skurlatov and his friends were the sole genuine Popular Front. An instruction booklet for the Popular Front activist was prepared and mimeographed in which it was proposed that citizens supporting the Russian PF gather information about 'anti-perestroika behaviour' and report it to the proper authorities.

The whole episode seriously disrupted the activities of the Popular Front organizing committees in the provinces while greatly complicating discussions with the authorities in Moscow. After this incident the city bureaucrats could always say: 'Let the two Popular Fronts first work it out among themselves and then we will speak with them.' An analogous situation in Kuibyshev arose almost simultaneously with the 'Skurlatov initiative' in Moscow.

However, this was not the main problem. The efforts of the Skurlatov group, without activists or a mass base to compete with the Co-ordinating Council of the Moscow PF, were futile. Precisely for this reason, an attempt was made from the very beginning to split the Moscow Popular Front itself. The Skurlatov group became the pole of attraction for all those individuals and clubs dissatisfied with the Co-ordinating Council. By pitting one group against another, the Front would either be torn apart, or deprived of its well-defined political orientation and transformed into a loose coalition of disparate groups. Formally, only two small organizations joined the Russian PF – the Club of Social Innovators led by V. Rozanov and the Federation of Social Union (FSU) of Evgenii Dergunov. Moreover, the actions of its leader caused serious discontent within the FSU. Tamara Ziborova, editor of the FSU bulletin *Moskovskii Vestnik*, refused to carry out Dergunov's demand and publish *Pamyat'* documents without commentary. As a result of this incident, she was forced to leave the bulletin. The meetings of the representatives of the two groups turned into total bedlam. At each of them, Rozanov and the other 'social innovators' delivered endless attacks on the CC, accusing it of usurping power, incompetence, and so on. By February, the work of the organizing council had become completely paralysed by the incessant wrangling between the supporters of the CC and the 'opposition'. A conference had to be convened as soon as possible to ratify some sort of common resolutions and clarify the real mood of the majority of the members of the Moscow PF.

Meanwhile, discussions with the authorities on the legally recognized convening of the conference proceeded with extreme difficulty. No response was forthcoming to the first claims lodged with the Moscow City Soviet in conformity with the legislation in force. Most likely, this delay was connected not with the deliberate resistance of the authorities to the development of the movement, but with the indecision and opposition of various tendencies within the apparatus itself. In these conditions, *any* decision requested by the Moscow PF was a difficult matter for the bureaucrats of the Moscow City Soviet. The conference was repeatedly postponed due to the lack of official permission, difficulty in obtaining a hall, or the slow work of the credentials commission. Only at the beginning of March was the organization able to arrange the two-day rental of the Pavilion of Animal Husbandry at the Exhibition Hall of National Economic Achievements of the USSR. Without giving written permission, the Moscow City Soviet stated that it did not see any obstacles to the convening of the conference.

The city authorities' readiness to agree to compromise decisions was bolstered by the fact that the city again began to be inundated by a wave of unsanctioned meetings and demonstrations which were even more well-attended than the previous summer. The Democratic Union, taking advantage of the spring warmth, had decided to open its next season of meetings and demonstrations – scheduled at least six months before – and this boded ill for the authorities. Also, the crisis in the Academy of Sciences continued to deepen, the ecological movement was reviving, and the voters openly expressed their discontent with the decisions of every official organ in charge of the course of the elections. Against this background, a conference of the Moscow PF appeared to be the lesser evil.

The conference opened on 2 March 1989. According to the credentials commission, 78 voting delegates participated in the conference, representing 34 support groups of the Moscow Popular Front (specifically 21 informal associations and 13 district organizations of the MPF). Several groups did not manage to register their membership officially in the Front and conduct elections, thus losing voting status. There were 175 individuals registered as guests or delegates with a consultative vote. The Co-ordinating Council also decided to deny voting status to its own members, who could all speak at the conference but not vote.

A poll conducted among voting delegates revealed that 39 per cent of them had participated in the movement for less than three months, and more than 50 per cent for less than six months. In addition, the majority of delegates entering the Popular Front at the end of 1988 or early 1989 had never before taken part in other informal movements, and lacked any direct experience of political struggle.

The first day of the conference seemingly confirmed the worst fears. The delegates needed ninety minutes to resolve procedural questions and then took hours to choose a working presidium, although little depended on this organ. As could be expected, the delegates proved extremely susceptible to demagoguery. Nevertheless, the constant personal attacks on the members of the Co-ordinating Council quickly began to cause consternation in the hall and the situation changed.

I was assigned to open discussion on the draft programme. In contrast to the alternative variants sprouting up at the last moment, the draft programme endorsed by the CC was very well known to the delegates. And, as paradoxical as it may seem, this was also the vulnerable point of the draft: its shortcomings were also well-known to all. In this situation, it seemed expedient not to reiterate or defend the draft but merely to focus delegates' attention on the key items of the discussion.

First of all, I emphasized the shifts which had taken place in the movement itself. Previously, we had simply urged that reform be implemented more resolutely, consistently and quickly, but now we needed to come to grips with the question of precisely what sort of reforms we required. The experience of four years of perestroika had demonstrated that we should not support all elite reforms because they frequently involve only a struggle for the redistribution of power and privilege within the framework of the old power structure and traditional system. On the other hand, the movement should define its own strategic priorities and elaborate a concept of the sort of society we are striving towards. We need democratic reforms, not political reforms. Precisely for this reason, we should not support the new electoral legislation, which does not bring us the least bit closer to democratic popular sovereignty. We should fight for a transition to democratic methods of decision-making, a reorientation of the economy to human needs, promotion of ecological priorities and the preservation of social guarantees. I also spoke about the fact that our movement was established on a foundation of socialist traditions which we should not repudiate under any circumstances. The socialist orientation of the Popular Front enabled its organizational and political consolidation without at the same time preventing its promotion of common democratic demands. Among the questions around the draft programme was that of a multi-party system. The authors came out in favour, but this slogan would only acquire real sense when new parties emerged within society. The central problem was not the number of parties, but the lack of viable democratic institutions. I also cautioned against an abstract absorption in political questions – a characteristic of the intelligentsia – and an obliviousness to social problems, which cannot be addressed without a well-defined programme. This returned us to the question of socialism.

The only serious alternative to the CC's programme was the proposals of Evgenii Dergunov. His speech was emotional and well prepared, and although Dergunov mostly based his remarks on Skurlatov's programme, he tried to avoid the extremism and obvious contradictions characteristic of the latter. Having begun with a sharp criticism of the official leadership of the CPSU, Dergunov proposed replacing the call for co-operation with the progressive wing of the leadership by a policy of an alliance with rank-and-file communists. This appeal found some support even among leftists. Paradoxically, Dergunov repeated almost verbatim the old Comintern resolution of the 1920s on relations with social democracy (a policy which, incidentally, facilitated the accession of the fascists to power in Germany). Having criticized the Western orientation of the Democratic Union, Dergunov simultaneously declared that the 'DU was 80 per cent correct', and called on us to encourage the emergence of a private sector in the country even though this, in his own words, also ran counter to 'our traditions'. Finally, he spoke about the Popular Front's underestimation of the 'national factor' and Russian patriotism. In his opinion, the same underestimation of the national factor by the Left led to the triumph of fascism in Germany. Dergunov declared that his position had nothing in common with *Pamyat'*; that Jews, Tatars, and representatives of other national minorities could also become honorary Russian patriots (but not genuine ethnic Russians). As for those who do not want to be patriots – let them leave and good riddance to them. According to Dergunov, the majority of workers and peasants share this patriotic ideal.

This position brought intense criticism from the floor, but the most vulnerable points were not even touched upon. It is totally incomprehensible how 'Russian patriots' intend to create an efficient private sector without a bourgeoisie. Only the mafia or the most corrupt segment of the bureaucracy could serve as capital investors, and neither of these are distinguished by any great economic and entrepreneurial culture. And the compulsory nature of Russian patriotism (whoever is not a patriot – let them leave) naturally undermines trust in the democratic rhetoric of the patriots. Dergunov was obviously trying to occupy the middle ground between the socialist majority of the Popular Front and right-wing nationalists, but he was not able to pull it off. Despite the positive reaction of the hall to many of his statements, the conference as a whole did not support his stance. Evidently, 'Russian patriots', if they wish to remain within the framework of a democratic and left-wing organization, must seriously rethink their positions and somehow extricate themselves from the most patent contradictions. Declarations of love for the motherland have obviously become insufficient, and a cogent socio-economic programme responding to the interests of the country is needed.

The turnabout in the mood of the delegates in favour of the CC was plainly expressed at the end of the day in the unanimous support for Mikhail Maliutin's resolution proposing that the conference charge the editorial commission to ratify a precisely formulated decision on the programme and constitution. The delegates understood perfectly that we could no longer go on without a programme and constitution. The majority did not want to leave the conference empty-handed and they needed results. Fruitless discussions and demagoguery no longer interested anybody.

Disputes about the constitution proceeded much more quietly. Not everybody found the notion of introducing individual membership into the Moscow PF acceptable. But the discontented groups were mollified by the creation of a new status of 'associated collective members'. The latter would not pay membership dues, and would neither share all of the provisions of the programme and constitution, nor have the right to nominate their own people to the leading bodies of the Popular Front. The conference speeches of the leader of the Committee of Social Self-Management of Moscow's Brateevo sub-district, S. Druganov, and the Moscow PF's election candidate, Sergei Stankevich, proved enormous successes. In the editorial commission elected by the conference, the overwhelming majority supported the Co-ordinating Council. Those critics who did not want to tear the movement apart (like Dergunov) accepted a compromise. Those who kept up attacks on the line of the majority revealed themselves ever more clearly as disruptive elements. Out-of-town guests present at the conference passed a resolution condemning the Skurlatov tendency. In brief, the situation changed rapidly for the better.

Over these two days, the delegates received a good lesson in political discussion, and to their credit, they quickly grasped what was going on. In comparison with the conferences of the Baltic Popular Fronts, everything was much more poorly organized – and ours was a much less important event – but the conference did prove to be much more democratic. Every tendency had a chance to make their views known. In the final analysis, Dergunov's group just could not get on with the Moscow PF's socialist majority. Shortly after the March conference, Dergunov and a few other 'patriots' left the Popular Front and joined up with Skurlatov, but they couldn't get on with him either. Skurlatov's organization soon split and Dergunov was once again forced to leave. All this splendidly demonstrates that the ideology of 'Russian patriotism' cannot form the basis for the consolidation of a serious political project.

The work of the conference was completed by the passing of a resolution endorsing the decision of the editorial commission made on the basis of the Co-ordinating Council's draft programme, and endorsing the CC's proposal on the constitution. Then by an overwhelming majority, the CC's term of office was extended right up to the official founding conference. In place of the retiring Feodorovsky, Lieutenant-Colonel

V. Urazhtsev was elected to the CC. This caused the chief sensation at the conference because Urazhtsev had joined the Popular Front only a few weeks before. He was one of the delegates who constituted the real majority at the conference and assured its success in the final reckoning.

The enrolment of new people confirmed the success of that policy which the socialist groups had implemented from the Popular Front's very inception in the capital. This was even more evident against the backdrop of the crisis gripping other unofficial organizations in the course of the elections. The Moscow PF not only grew rapidly during this period of stagnation in other organizations, but it managed simultaneously to consolidate itself organizationally and politically – a supremely difficult task. The movement acquired its own character and established its own political tradition. In fact, the conference capped the course of events begun in the summer of 1988. The founding period had come to a close. We still awaited the official founding conference, but the organization had already arisen and could function.

As is so often the case, the last word belongs to Mikhail Maliutin: 'Whatever happens, now nobody can say that a Popular Front does not exist in Moscow'.

NOTES

1. See *News of the Popular Front*, no. 1, 1988.

8

The Spring Whirlpool: The Elections,
Yeltsin and the Popular Front

In any country elections are the culmination of a political struggle. For Soviet society, the chance to elect deputies from several candidates for the first time in approximately sixty years was in itself unique. To the authorities, the elections were proof of the reality of democratization, and to the liberal intelligentsia they were a test of the civil maturity of the people. Although the elections were held in accordance with an extremely muddled and patently undemocratic electoral law, they opened up significant opportunities for unofficial political groups to make themselves known. They put to the test both those official candidates – representatives of the Party or managerial bureaucracy – who risked proposing themselves to the electors, and representatives of unofficial political groupings and currents who had to demonstrate their capacity for practical work with the masses, competence and flexibility. The latter, who had striven over the previous two years to speak in the name of society (as, indeed, had the Party-state bureaucracy) now had to subject themselves to a serious examination: did society, or at least part of it, indeed have confidence in them and see them as a viable alternative?

Meanwhile, events did not initially evolve too dramatically. After the Moscow PF and the movement for a Popular Front in some other cities had been able, despite the mass of legal restrictions, to nominate their own candidates, the time for district electoral assemblies arrived. No one had any doubts that this superfluous stage between the nomination

111

of candidates and the elections was designed as a filter for undesirable candidates. Sergei Stankevich, nominated by the Moscow PF for the Cheremushkinsky electoral district, equated this procedure with a journey through the Minotaur's labyrinth. According to his gloomy prognosis, few representatives of left-wing and democratic currents would survive. Nevertheless, Stankevich himself managed to survive, although the district assemblies did in fact sift out many representatives of the liberal intelligentsia and supporters of the Popular Front.

Even the official organs subsequently had to acknowledge this fact. In the words of the weekly *Argumenty i Fakty*, the district assemblies 'were distinctive traps for deputies unwelcome to the apparatus'.[2] For example, the lawyer Sergei Druganov, a participant in the Moscow PF movement, was nominated at an assembly of 2,000 representatives of the 47,000 inhabitants of the sub-district of Brateevo. But he was 'sifted' by a district assembly of 810 people mobilized by the apparatus. Later, after repeated elections in the Proletarsko-Tagansky district, the district assembly sifted out all of the unofficial candidates on the grounds that they were not resident in the given area. 'None of them was allowed to say even a single word', wrote *Sovetskaya Kul'tura*, 'although such a right is specifically accorded them in the relevant article of the law on elections. The rights of thousands of the district's residents, who had placed their trust in them, were also flagrantly violated'.[3]

In some cases, however, district assemblies passed off comparatively democratically. There seemed to be no sort of logic or system; the situation developed differently in each region of Moscow. Much depended on how well prepared the candidates and their agents were for the assembly. Mark Zakharov, delegated from the Union of Theatre Workers to the Congress of People's Deputies and simultaneously an agent for one of his colleagues, compared these assemblies with a bad stage show.

> Here I happened to watch for twelve hours running as a variety of procedural experiments were carried out under the guidance of unseen and frightened 'directors', who were, however, occasionally glimpsed in the wings. Their fussing behind the scenes was visible to the naked eye throughout the entire twelve hours. Confusion reigned in the packed hall at the general and obvious 'directorial' clumsiness.[4]

Frequently the question of whether one candidate or another should be added to the list was decided by a majority of only a few votes – Maliutin fell short of being registered by all of twenty votes. Meanwhile not a single instance has been recorded where an assembly filtered out a big economic manager or Party apparatchik. As the press conceded, these candidates 'were as a rule subject to the most favourable procedures on the part of the electoral commissions'.[5]

As a result of the system of 'filters', about a third of the electoral districts across the country were left with a single candidate, and in many cases the electors were presented with a choice between two people who both defended the interests of the apparatus. Among the candidates there turned out to be a massive number of enterprise directors, decorated workers who rarely showed up in their own labour collectives, and high-ranking officials. Some of them chose for themselves a 'safer' district, preferring not to be balloted in the major industrial centres. Others found themselves without any serious rivals. All the same, there were among the candidates people with radical political views. For example, in the Oktyabr'sky district of Moscow, after the Popular Front had been unable get its own candidate past the electoral commission, Moscow PF activists rallied behind Ilya Zaslavsky, the candidate of the Society of Invalids. This man who, on the eve of the election campaign had, in his own words, an extremely hazy notion of what the Popular Front was about, had a few months later become one of the movement's leaders in both the district and the city. Analogous situations arose with other candidates. The rapid politicization of the masses was opening up new opportunities for strengthening the forces of the Left.

The electoral campaign slowly gathered pace. Up to the middle of March, an impartial observer, walking along the streets of Moscow, could hardly have guessed that an electoral campaign was going on in the capital. At first official posters with pictures of the candidates did not attract much attention and there was considerable delay in their appearance on the walls of buildings. It was possible to find posters and leaflets of initiative groups in support of every conceivable candidate, although not without difficulty, as the activists of unofficial organizations initially had no money for the production of agitational material on a mass scale and didn't know where and how to get it printed. And the posters of numerous bureaucratic grandees were so poorly produced that they simply did not attract any attention.

However, after 10 March, things began to warm up. An increasingly bitter struggle was going on between the candidates and the various sides resorted to more and more dirty tactics. Flinging mud at rivals, slandering them and drawing attention to their physical shortcomings or nationality all became part of the typical methods of this election campaign. Such smear tactics were evidence of not only the masses' but also the candidates' low level of political culture.

The Second Secretary of the Moscow Party *gorkom*, Yuri Prokofiev, contrived to be both a candidate and a member of the Central Electoral Commission at the same time. When, at a public meeting with this candidate at the Ural cinema on 11 March, a member of the audience tried publicly to protest at this state of affairs, the trouble-maker was removed from the hall by the stewards and beaten up. The victim immediately gave a statement to the prosecutor's office but was still waiting for the case to be examined when the elections finished.

By mid-March the papers were already writing about a genuine poster war. A *Moskovskaya Pravda* correspondent, describing the course of the electoral struggle in the capital, recounted that he had met on the street an old woman carrying a placard bearing an abusive attack on one of the candidates. When asked the reasons for such savage hatred of this person, the old woman replied that she did not know the candidate at all but simply that 'two youths gave me a rouble and asked me to stand around for a while'. The article concluded with an appeal by the journalist that 'We won't abuse pictures of our rivals! We won't engage in mud-slinging!'[6] Alas, these exhortations had no effect. Defaced portraits could be found at every turn. Old people, who had a poor grasp of the meaning of the elections, were cultivated very intensively. Supporters of all candidates employed a Dickensian array of methods from bribing to intimidating the electors. Somehow we seemed to have managed to borrow all of the negative features of nineteenth-century bourgeois elections without adopting any of the positive ones.

Fortunately, such a conclusion proved to be premature. During the nomination of candidates it was obvious that a sharp struggle was developing around the figure of Boris Yeltsin, who had come forward as a candidate for the Moscow constituency. By being nominated as a candidate for the entire capital, Yeltsin was in fact proposing to Muscovites that they submit the city Party organization – and, to a significant extent, the CPSU Central Committee, which had removed him from his post as Moscow's Party leader in November 1987 – to a vote of no confidence. Attempts to prevent Yeltsin's nomination or to compel him to be balloted in another district were a total failure. From the very outset, the mass support for the disgraced leader was so strong that his victory was guaranteed – even the district electoral assembly, a majority of whom had been selected by the city authorities, gave Yeltsin's opponents no chance to 'filter' him.

In order to understand the 'Yeltsin phenomenon' it is first necessary to look at why the apparatchiks have such a profound hatred of him. It is precisely this hatred, manifested at every step, which has aroused the broad masses' no less profound love of him. Russian culture has traditionally adopted a sympathetic attitude towards the victim, a readiness to support whoever engages in an unequal battle and suffers unjust persecution. Yeltsin, on his own admission, was unable to achieve great success while governing the capital although he made titanic efforts to improve the situation. Nevertheless, to the public at large, he was not so much a former leader of the Party apparatus as a victim of that apparatus. For the apparatchiks, however, Yeltsin was first and foremost a conscious breaker of the rules. It was not just that his demands were radical – many of his declarations and actions were barely distinguishable from those of other political figures, including Gorbachev, who were rather more successful in the apparatus. Yeltsin was accused of shuffling cadres, of dismissing old bureaucrats and of unrestrained criticism. But in 1986–87, all representatives of the new perestroika leadership were involved in that, including even such a generally recognized conservative as Yegor Ligachev. Nor did Yeltsin's calls for democratization and his speeches in support of social justice in and of themselves go beyond the bounds of what was permitted. But from the very beginning of his term in Moscow, Yeltsin came into conflict with a majority of the apparatus. His opponents, moreover, turned out to include not only the conservatives but also many well-known liberals.

The reason for Yeltsin's incompatibility with the apparatus is quite simple. The Minister of Foreign Affairs and eminent representative of the liberal current, Eduard Shevardnadze, spoke quite candidly about it during the bureaucratic reprisals against Yeltsin in autumn 1987. Yeltsin tried to 'impose his style on the Party'. This 'style' consisted in rejecting attempts to implement his line through behind-the-scenes compromises and alliances, through merely reshuffling the apparatus. Instead, the former Urals engineer, having become the hero of Moscow, attempted honestly and openly to discuss all current differences, to inform the public of the struggle going on in the apparatus and in fact to appeal to the masses in the role of the final arbiter in intra-Party disputes. Such a position was as unacceptable to the liberals and even the 'radicals' within the apparatus as it was to the conservatives – the blow was not inflicted by one faction alone. The very sovereignty of the apparatus – its right, with or without glasnost, to be the sole determinant of the country's fate – had been placed in doubt. Specific decisions were not in dispute, but the very decision-making mechanism, so dear to many 'progressives' who argue that the 'conservative and idle masses' should not be allowed access to real power, had been called into question.

It is unclear whether Yeltsin himself was conscious of the political gravity of his mutiny but, in any case, both the apparatus and the masses instinctively sensed its significance. The hatred of the apparatus for Yeltsin cannot be explained by tactical considerations; rather, it was the instinctive hatred for a 'traitor'. While the capital's disgraced leader strove to conduct his election campaign in the most moderate style possible by avoiding confrontations, attacks on him by the apparatchiks were constantly on the increase.

A speech by the First Secretary of the Moscow *gorkom*, Lev Zaikov, in which it was clearly stated that perestroika was threatened by danger 'from the left', served as a signal for the anti-Yeltsin campaign to commence. In Zaikov's opinion, all of the city's and the country's problems could be blamed on 'vanguardists' disseminating 'leftist-utopian sentiments' and arousing 'a fair amount of ambition and adventurism'.[8] It was obvious to anyone even remotely familiar with the style of bureaucratic speeches that he was talking primarily about Yeltsin and his supporters. The wrath of the capital's bureaucracy was simultaneously directed against the informal organizations. Taking advantage of an unauthorized demonstration by the liberal Democratic Union, *Moskovskaya Pravda* sharply criticized the Moscow police for not being prepared to employ sufficiently tough measures against those breaching public order (this was a blatant lie: both the DU and the Moscow Popular Front had been repeatedly subjected to persecution).

On 15–16 March 1989, the long-planned Plenum of the CPSU Central Committee on agriculture took place. As intended, this gathering of the top Party leadership adopted the latest package of proposals for developing leasehold relations in the countryside. These decisions, regarded by the Western press as a decisive agrarian reform, failed to provoke much public interest. Even the official press overtly characterized them as a compromise both half-hearted and transitional. All the same, the March 1989 Plenum was destined to go down in history. Despite the expectations of many Kremlinologists, the major event of these two days proved not to be the debate on the agrarian question but the heated discussion of the 'Yeltsin affair'. A Central Committee commission was formed to examine and assess those of Yeltsin's actions which 'are contrary to Central Committee directives, Party ethics and the constitutional norms of the CPSU'.[9]

For millions of Muscovites and tens of millions across the country, the import of these events was quite plain: they wanted to sacrifice Yeltsin again. A punishment was being prepared. On 19 March in *Moskovskaya Pravda*, there appeared a verbose article signed by a member of the Central Committee, the 'metal-worker' V. Tikhomirov, which depicted Yeltsin as a demagogue 'bringing the Party into disrepute'. In the capital a crisis exploded.

At midday on 19 March, a crowd of roughly three thousand people gathered in Gorky Park to try and express their solidarity with the disgraced leader. Leaflets distributed by Skurlatov's Russian Popular Front had called for this meeting but the authors of the leaflet could not bring themselves to take charge of the assembled crowd. The thousands of people, left to their own devices, spontaneously organized a march to the Kremlin. The crowd had grown to fifteen thousand by the time it was finally stopped by special police and turned in the direction of Gorky Street. On Soviet Square, in front of the Moscow Soviet building, there was a spontaneous rally calling for an immediate end to the persecution of Yeltsin in the press, the granting to him of a right of reply and the disbandment of the Central Committee commission. Those assembled decided to return to the same place for an answer on Wednesday, 22 March and elected from among their number an initiative group to hold negotiations with the Moscow Soviet. Since this all took place beneath the equestrian statue of Yuri Dolgoruky, the founder of Moscow, the gathering became known to Muscovites as 'the first rally under the hoof'.

The events of 19 March proved to be an unpleasant surprise not only for the Moscow Soviet and the Party gorkom; most of the informal political groups were also quite unprepared for it. 'Democratic Perestroika', the club of left-liberal academic opinion, only joined the movement on the eve of the elections. Nor was there any sign of DU activists on the streets. This organization, which calls meetings to mark any historical date, kept away from the real political crisis. Moreover, for the anti-communists of the DU, there was no difference whatsoever between Yeltsin and his persecutors. Even Moscow Tribune, which unites representatives of the liberal intellectual elite, did not react to events. Its leaders did not address meetings or even adopt any sort of common declaration about the Yeltsin crisis.

The Russian Popular Front displayed some initial activism and continually strove to agitate among the crowd, especially at the concluding stage of the crisis. However, the Russian PF's nationalist slogans and calls for the restoration of private ownership did not generate any particular enthusiasm among participants in the mass movement.

The initiative group of 'the first rally under the hoof' was in no state to control the situation. It did not possess its own apparatus, communications or resources. Grasping this fact, the Moscow Soviet flatly refused to allow it to hold a rally. Furthermore, it was reported in the press that members of the initiative group themselves rejected a repeat meeting (although the same members of the group later categorically repudiated this report). The trouble was that the initiative group was in no position to cancel the meeting as it could not have organized it anyway. It was perfectly clear that, irrespective of reports in the papers, a crowd would gather on the Square at the appointed time. This was also understood by the authorities. Police general, P. S. Bogdanov, responsible for the maintenance of order in the city, acknowledged that a 'tense situation' prevailed in the capital. He warned the public that 'anarchy and permissiveness' would not be allowed and that 'the strictest measures' would be taken against those breaching public order.[10] It was quite obvious that the authorities were still pinning their hopes on force.

In this situation, the Moscow Popular Front (MPF) proved to be the only organization capable of drawing the mass movement behind it and of preventing clashes between Yeltsin's more passionate supporters and the police. MPF representatives went to the Moscow Soviet to declare their readiness to ensure order during the rally if the authorities gave them official permission and provided a public-address system. As anticipated, the delegation met with a refusal although it was obvious that the Moscow leadership was wavering.

On the evening of 21 March, preparations for the rally began among all the Moscow PF's district groups. It was decided that, in the event that Soviet Square was sealed off by the police, the columns of demonstrators would be directed to Trubnaya Square and the rally would be held there. It was on Trubnaya Square in November 1987 that activists of the Federation of Socialist Clubs (FSOK) had tried to hold the first meeting in support of Yeltsin. Leaflets with information on the unfolding situation were printed and handed out by activists. A large meeting in support of Yeltsin had been organized earlier by the MPF group at Moscow University – in fact, by 20 March, they had already assumed the co-ordinating functions in the mass movement.

A major role was played by Sergei Stankevich who, together with other candidates close to the MPF – Murashev and Zaslavsky – had sent a telegram to the CPSU Central Committee in protest at the setting up of the CC commission. Another twelve candidates endorsed this telegram. For the first time during the elections something like a unified electoral bloc was beginning to take shape. It was not simply a question of support for Yeltsin but of forming a genuine left-wing initiative. In turn, MPF agitators called not only for the election of Yeltsin and Stankevich but also for decisive support for the progressive bloc and the 'radical threesome' (Zaslavsky, Stankevich and Murashev). The unity achieved during this period between the electoral struggle and the mass movement 'on the streets' had always been a key idea in the MPF's strategy. The Popular Front movement in the capital had now gained its historical opportunity.

The 22 March rally started neither quite as planned by the MPF organizing committee nor quite as expected by the police. The crowd had already begun to gather by five o'clock. Yeltsin and his entourage, who had dissociated themselves from the 19 March rally, had this time not taken any position at all. At 4.45 p.m. I arrived at Yeltsin's electoral headquarters on Pushkin Street. There was nobody there. The doors were locked, the telephones disconnected. In a way this was the correct thing to do: the candidate and his agents were afraid of provocations. However, it also meant that complete control of the situation could only be gained through the MPF organizing committee, with which participants in the action could be in constant contact.

The police, who had planned to cordon off the Square by 7 p.m., were taken by surprise. By six o'clock, a rally of ten thousand people was already underway in the Square. When the police finally cordoned off the Square, small groups of people began to try and break through from side streets. Roughly five hundred people were able to do so from the Moscow Soviet end and they rushed towards the Dolgoruky monument across Gorky Street where the traffic had not yet been brought to a halt. At that moment a history student, Yaroslav Leontiev, one of the MPF's most popular activists, stormed up to the leaders of the police cordon and demanded that the amplifier set up behind police lines be handed over to representatives of the Front. The demand was immediately met, since it had become clear even to the guardians of law and order that this was the only way of averting a battle. A fresh cordon was formed at once around the bus with the public address system – by members of the Front. The rally began to assume an organized character.

When members of the Popular Front went straight after these events to the Moscow Soviet to announce a new rally, they were not met by a refusal. The fact was that the 'second rally under the hoof' had concluded with not only a unanimous decision to support the bloc of progressive candidates but also with a call to hold a final all-Moscow demonstration on 25 March on the parade ground by the stadium at Luzhniki. People were quite determined to go there with or without the city authorities' permission. The crisis was reaching its peak.

On 25 March, according to police figures, 35,000 people were present at Luzhniki. The rally concluded with a resolution in support of the bloc of progressive candidates. The crowd dispersed singing the 'Internationale'.

The elections which took place the following day turned out to be a real defeat for the apparatus, and not only in Moscow. People everywhere voted against Party functionaries, state officials and high-ranking managers. 'Worker-candidates' were also usually defeated as their own 'class brothers' saw them as puppets of the Party bureaucracy. Among the losers were also many representatives of the 'liberal faction' in the apparatus, for example, the First Secretary of the Sevastopolsky *raikom* of Moscow, Bryachikhin. The electors displayed little interest in the fine distinctions between bureaucratic factions: they simply voted against 'the bosses'. This was openly acknowledged in the pages of *Izvestiya* by the First Secretary of the Khabarovsk Party *raikom*, V. S. Pasternak, who, like many of his colleagues, had suffered defeat in the elections:

> People were fed up with commands and bellowing, they were tired of diktats from the apparatus and they loathed workers who placed private and frequently mercenary interests above the political interests of the Party. It is at times very difficult for me as leader of a regional Party organization, and I've been in this post all of six months, to establish normal contact with people. There is suspicion, mistrust and even hostility: you're all tarred, they say, with the same brush.'[11]

The Party–state apparatus suffered its most serious defeat in Leningrad. The sensation was caused by the failure of a number of candidates, who had no rivals at all – being, in time-honoured fashion, the only ones on the list – to achieve enough votes for selection. In the Baltic republics, the Popular Fronts of Latvia and Estonia gained an overwhelming majority of votes and seats. The *Sajudis* movement – the Lithuanian Popular Front – received virtually all the votes and the republic's Party leadership only appeared among the deputies at all because *Sajudis* presented it with two districts by withdrawing its own candidates.

The election of representatives of the social organizations also brought some unpleasant surprises for the apparatus. Among the deputies from the creative unions, many people well known for their radical views were selected. In the course of the struggle, the liberal intelligentsia itself moved markedly to the left and began to display a readiness to collaborate with the MPF and the Yeltsinists. In the Academy of Sciences, representatives of the research institutes, who were attending the common conference, defeated a majority of the Presidium's candidates and gained re-run elections in which Andrei Sakharov joined the ranks of the deputies. Participants in academic elections were frequently guided by the scientific merits of the candidates and not by their political platform. Thus

S. Averintsev, the most outstanding specialist on classical literature, was elected a deputy. Also among the deputies were the economists, G. Lisichkin, N. Shmelev, N. Petrakov and P. Bunich, advocates of the ideology of the 'free market' and very popular among the liberal elite.

In the end, liberal figures were able to form a quite significant group at the Congress. However, they were not in the main elected by the people in territorial constituencies but were delegated from social organizations (although this principle of 'direct representation' had been universally condemned as anti-democratic). The fact that the liberals had been able to achieve success even through one of the least democratic mechanisms provided for by the law speaks for itself. The contradictory nature of the liberal elite's position lay in their demanding greater freedom while at the same time not being prepared for a real democratic struggle alongside the mass movement, or to take the workers' interests into account in their own political project.

The elections gave the technocracy important opportunities to strengthen its influence. The number of top figures from the governmental apparatus in the ranks of people's deputies diminished, while the number of representatives of the intermediate tier (enterprise directors, and so on) sharply increased. According to sociologists' data, this group was 'one of the most significant' at the Congress.[12] This is explained not so much by the popularity of directors and technocrats as by the fact that they often proved the only acceptable candidate to the masses once the district assembly had filtered out all the radicals and liberals.

Yeltsin's success exceeded all expectations. In gaining 90 per cent of the votes, he unquestionably became even more of a danger to his adversaries in the apparatus. Nevertheless, the election results did not engender enormous optimism in the leading circles of the Moscow Popular Front. The bureaucracy had suffered above all a moral defeat. The great majority of delegates, both those elected from territorial constituencies and those delegated from social organizations, was in no sense especially radical. Even among those who sided with the progressive bloc there were some who vacillated between liberal and left-wing positions. The authorities preserved their monopoly on information, even trying to stop the countrywide dissemination of reports about what had happened in Moscow and Leningrad. The mass meetings of 22 and 25 March were mentioned in *Moskovskaya Pravda* and even assessed positively, but readers learnt nothing about their organizers nor about the demands being put forward. TASS distributed a report throughout the country in which it was stated that those taking part in the meeting were concerned with eulogizing the wisdom of the authorities and the electoral law which was 'undoubtedly progressive'.[13] Just as before, the Left had no access to the mass media.

In a number of Moscow districts, the electoral campaign continued, as none of the candidates had been able to win a majority of votes. In other districts where the single candidate had failed to reach the requisite level of support or the electors had boycotted the elections, everything had to begin again from the beginning. Once again, the nomination of candidates was accompanied by the difficulties which had characterized the first phase of the electoral struggle. A bitter struggle flared up during the second round of elections in Moscow's Cheremushkinsky district. The official candidates had been defeated in the first round and this time opposing each other were Sergei Stankevich, who had received 49 per cent of the votes in the first round, and Mikhail Lemeshev, who had received the support of nationalist Russian groups and had gained 32 per cent of the votes on 26 March. In fact, the election turned into a direct confrontation between left and right, with the struggle on the streets unfolding primarily between the MPF and *Pamyat'*, in the course of which, anti-semitic agitation was carried out. In the Party *raikom*, the question of the communist Stankevich's breach of Party discipline was examined and the withdrawal of his candidature demanded. Rightwing dissidents called for a vote against 'red' Stankevich and the Moscow Popular Front which was full of 'communist agents'. Nevertheless, the overwhelming majority of the area's residents supported the MPF candidate. On 8 April, a repeat meeting of the Front took place on the parade ground at Luzhniki attended by about eight thousand people from various parts of the capital. They enthusiastically greeted Stankevich and Ilya Zaslavsky, who had already been elected as a deputy for the Oktyabr'sky district with MPF support. On 9 April, having won 56 per cent of the vote, Stankevich became a deputy.

For the MPF the election results signified the transition to a qualitatively new stage of activity. For the first time, a leader of an unofficial political organization had been elected to the country's highest organ of power. The balance of forces among opposition groups had thus been determined.

If it had been possible, back in February, to treat the MPF as just one of many informal organizations – albeit bigger – now it must be reckoned a serious political force. The deputies, Zaslavsky and Murashev, whose groups had united with Front activists during the electoral campaign, joined the MPF. In some parts of Moscow regional Front committees began to be formed. Support groups sprang up in enterprises and academic institutes. At Moscow University a sharp radicalization began not only of ordinary students but also of a section of the basic Komsomol apparatus which actually united with Moscow PF activists. Thanks to this, the university, in the best traditions of the revolutionary movement, began to turn into a major stronghold of the Left.

In many districts across the country, where elections were re-run, the general tendency to move to the left was displayed even more strongly. In Leningrad, both the election campaign itself and its final results were proof of the serious progress made by the Popular Front and other democratic or opposition groups. 'The struggle was hard, perhaps even brutal', Leningraders E. Zelinsky and V. Monakhov related in the pages of the Estonian PF's bulletin:

> At one electoral meeting, one of the speakers died right at the rostrum. Three days later, one of the candidates, Yuri Boldyrev, spoke at the funeral service. The other candidate, the First Secretary of the CPSU *gorkom* did not deign to turn up to the funeral'.[14]

The most popular candidate proved to be the investigator, N. Ivanov, who had taken part in the struggle to expose corruption in the highest echelons of power. In this case, the leaders of the Leningrad PF, primarily M. Sal'e, committed a serious error, not only by putting up their own candidate against Ivanov but also by initiating an energetic campaign against him. They accused him of not following the letter of the law in the fight against corruption. A participant in the movement recalls that at Popular Front meetings

> Ivanov was criticized both verbally and in the 'coarse language of placards', and leaflets directed against him were given out in great quantities to those present. The results of the election are well known to everyone: the agitation at the meeting had no tangible results'.[15]

The vast majority of the people of Leningrad cast their vote for the Muscovite Ivanov, who became the representative of the whole city in a 'national-territorial' constituency. This fact is even more significant in that the inhabitants of the former northern capital are in general highly jealous and mistrustful of Muscovites. In essence, the vote for Ivanov was on a par with the vote for Yeltsin in Moscow but, unlike the Moscow PF, the Leningrad Front not only did not gain from the mass populist movement, but actually lost by standing in opposition to it. Among the Front activists themselves, however, including many members of the leadership, Ivanov's activity provoked clear sympathy. At the demand of the majority, the Leningrad PF's founding congress in June adopted a resolution in solidarity with Ivanov's supporters – a belated acknowledgement of the mistake made during the course of the elections.

In a certain sense the dissident movement was as much a loser during the elections as was the apparatus. The inability of the DU, 'Glasnost' and Civil Dignity to have any serious influence on the masses was quite clearly revealed. The only group to achieve a certain success turned out to be the nationalist Russian Popular Front, although it was still in no position seriously to challenge the Left.

In Yaroslavl, the PF candidate I. B. Shamshev was victorious.

Infringements and manipulation abounded during the elections. Frequently, voters coming out towards evening discovered that someone had already voted for them. Some people had the sense to complain to the PF and the district electoral commission. After the elections in this district were declared null-and-void, a recount of the votes showed that Shamshev had received 50.087 per cent. Victory!'[16]

In Moscow, the most bitter struggle unfolded in the Kuntsevo district, where a number of liberal public figures were on the ballot paper along with the 'hero' of the war in Afghanistan, Colonel A. Rutskoy. Rutskoy's campaign rallied all reactionary forces from Stalinists to monarchists into a single bloc. The whole area was plastered with his leaflets which called for an end to the 'domination' of the intelligentsia and anarchy. Rutskoy's supporters would remind people that the Metropolitan had blessed him, a member of 'a hereditary military dynasty since the fourteenth century', for 'the heroic deed of deputyship'; they would yell out anti-semitic slogans and, at the same time as attacking the Left, would not forget to declare that they were ready to defend our country from the pillage of transnational corporations, fight corruption and take care to reinforce the army. In brief, all this smacked very much of the traditional collection of fascist propaganda clichés.

The Moscow Popular Front took a decision to support the candidature of dramatist Mikhail Shatrov, who in turn declared his solidarity with their basic demands. The key point in Shatrov's programme was the call for the renovation of the Party while simultaneously recognizing the necessity of a multi-party system. Apart from this, Shatrov tried to draw voters' attention to the need for a serious discussion about democratic socialism. On the whole, however, it was a limp campaign; Shatrov himself sustained its intensity with difficulty and the MPF group in Kuntsevo, although it grew during the course of the election campaign, remained embryonic.

Rutskoy proved to be the victor on the first round with about 30 per cent of the votes. In second place came the deputy chief editor of *Moskovskaya Pravda*, V. Logunov, famous for the fact that, during the crisis days of 24–25 March, he had distanced himself from his own paper and supported Yeltsin. On the second round, all left-wing and democratic groups united, not only for the sake of a Logunov victory, but first and foremost so as not to let Rutskoy become deputy. The MPF began to send into Kuntsevo its own activists from other areas. Spontaneous meetings sprang up everywhere and virtually every bus stop was plastered with leaflets. *Pamyat'* supporters also arrived in Kuntsevo in fairly large numbers. Opponents' leaflets were torn down, slashed with razor blades or burnt. In the end, Logunov emerged as victor, having gained more than 60 per cent of the vote.

The elections in Kuntsevo and Cheremushki showed the precise relationship of forces between *Pamyat'* and the Left. Even if the Black Hundreds of *Pamyat'* and their co-thinkers in the Party *raikoms* had been able to mount a strong campaign, they would never have been able to emerge as victors, and in fact they kept at a level of between 30 and 37 per cent of the votes. On the other hand, a unified left-progressive bloc proved able to gain 50–60 per cent. All the same, the very fact that tens of thousands of people voted for Rutskoy cannot but make one sit up and take notice. In Kuntsevo, where a large part of the population consists of unskilled or semi-skilled workers, the choice could only be between the left-wing populist Logunov, leaning for support on the authority of Yeltsin, and the extreme right-wing populist, Rutskoy. The populist wave left no room for the liberals and severely restricted the possibilities for socialists. The difference between the former and the latter consisted in the fact that the socialists were able to work effectively with populist currents.

Unquestionably, the prime victor in the elections was Boris Yeltsin. His triumph in Moscow raised him to the stature of a national leader. On 25–26 March, people came from all over the country, having removed their names from the electoral register at home in order to have the opportunity to vote for Yeltsin. The vote on 25 March was essentially a vote of no confidence in the Moscow City Party and, not surprisingly, straight after the elections, rank-and-file communists began to demand an extraordinary conference of the City Party to elect a new leadership. This demand very soon grew into a call for an extraordinary Party Congress.

The elections, in fact, clearly revealed the total lack of unity between the Party apparatus and rank-and-file members of the CPSU, who had voted unanimously together with the rest of the workers against the bureaucracy. The results of the elections were interpreted by some observers as a massive defeat for the Party as its functionaries had not received the support of the masses and by others as a success for the CPSU because Party members constituted about 87 per cent of Congress deputies, more than in the previous Supreme Soviet. In fact, however, the elections only showed once again that the CPSU is by no means a political party in the usual sense of the word. The fact that a candidate belonged to the CPSU was of absolutely no interest to the electorate. Party members often flung mud at each other in their campaigns – this was no surprise to anyone and was certainly not seen as a sign of a split or a crisis. It was another matter when apparatchik candidates clashed with communists who, like Stankevich, were standing on democratic positions.

The divide in the Party did not occur between factions of liberals and conservatives, but was on a social and 'class' basis between the top and the bottom. In such a situation, the call for an extraordinary Party Congress became genuinely explosive, especially as the CPSU constitution allows for the possibility in such circumstances of creating an organizing committee independent of the Central Committee, and this could in fact signify the foundation of a new Communist Party. Maliutin and other CPSU members, participating in the MPF, were speaking of the need for an extraordinary Congress even before the Nineteenth Party Conference, but it was only now that this idea began to take hold of the masses: the situation was maturing.

Meanwhile, Yeltsin was clearly in no hurry to play the trump cards in his hand. Immediately after his success at the polls he left Moscow for a holiday. Nothing had been done to build on the success that had been achieved. In this instance, the peculiarities of Yeltsin's movement, which was accustomed to conducting primarily defensive battles, had a telling effect.

Despite Yeltsin's massive success in the elections, all the weaknesses of 'Yeltsinism' were revealed with absolute clarity in the spring of 1989. Yeltsin's programme remained as broad as possible, attractive to the vast majority of workers, undoubtedly radical but also quite vague. Most prominent were demands for amending and democratizing the electoral law, decentralizing the system of management, ensuring democratic elections in the appropriate organs of power, devoting more attention to the social sphere, curtailing capital investment in industrial construction and decreasing the number of ministries. These positions coincided completely with the MPF programme. But there was a serious difference: the latter was striving to elaborate an all-embracing strategy of struggle for democratic socialism while Yeltsin had at the forefront topical and, moreover, unspecific slogans (what sort of new electoral law? how would a change in priorities be secured? and so on). In the final analysis, the transition from defence to attack required serious work on the programme.

The mass Yeltsinist movement remained highly heterogeneous in its social composition. During the electoral campaign, the Yeltsinists were able to organize and create their own structures in many districts of the capital but they possessed no political 'middle' cadres. Leaders of the Yeltsinist movement in various parts of the city barely knew each other and were frequently not even in touch with each other while they strove independently to establish communications with their leader or his immediate circle. Routine horizontal co-ordination on a city-wide scale was realized, as before, through the Popular Front.

The populist movement which had formed around Yeltsin proved extremely dependent on the personality of its leader, in many cases taking the form of a leadership cult. At Yeltsin's rallies, a few excited women would carry placards announcing, in the spirit of the old Stalinist practices, that Yeltsin is the 'Lenin of today'. Paradoxically, Yeltsinism was able to revive old ideological clichés and stereotypes and turn them against the system. Just as the ruling elite, having led the country into a blind-alley, was seeking a way out in 'ideological revisionism', it encountered the democratic revolt of the masses who retained their loyalty to traditional notions. It was easily ascertained in the course of discussions that the workers would quickly support the idea of a multi-party system, but certainly had no wish to accept the new official course of struggling against 'wage-levelling' (*uravnilovka*), of reinforcing social differentiation and of encouraging foreign or private and co-operative enterprise. All these moods were clearly embodied in Yeltsinism, but the democratic revolt was still no guarantee of the success of revolutionary renewal. Furthermore, the transition from the 'politics of revolt' to revolutionary renewal was proving unbelievably difficult.

The social base of the MPF was not homogeneous either. Nevertheless, a majority of activists and supporters belonged to the lower echelon of the technical, engineering and scientific intelligentsia: the new proletariat. The Popular Front gained strongholds at the University and other higher educational establishments. During the course of the electoral campaign, the number of workers among the activists began to grow, but they were primarily skilled workers. The MPF found itself in a very strong position in Cheremushki thanks to the large concentration of modern enterprises. The Yeltsinists, on the other hand, enjoyed the support of semi- and un-skilled workers. On the whole, their position was quite strong in the factories, but they were unclear how to act further and what to do with the factory groups. It could be said, therefore, that the Yeltsinists and the MPF needed each other. If the Yeltsinist movement was unable to seize the strategic initiative and was frequently lacking in political culture, then the Front suffered from a distinct narrowness in its social base. A rapprochement between these two forces opened up the prospect of a genuinely serious offensive strategy.

The apparatus was, in its turn however, preparing a counter-offensive. The chief lesson of the elections for those who had lost was that the time had come to halt the process of democratization. If liberal games in the press did not, in and of themselves, hold any special terrors, then the masses coming on to the streets were seen as a direct threat. The first blows were aimed precisely against the 'streets' and the mass opposition movements.

The bureaucracy's counter-attack began in the borderlands of the empire. The PF movement in the Baltic republics had become too strong to confront directly and was evaluated by the local Party authorities as being comparatively moderate; however, in Belorussia and Georgia, where mass actions had just begun and the slogans being advanced were rather more radical, the authorities were determined to put a stop to the 'descent into anarchy'. On 31 March 1989, the Belorussian Supreme Soviet adopted a decree on administrative offences. Article 167, paragraph 2 of this decree – 'The unlawful use of flags and pennants, the making, distribution or carrying of placards, emblems and symbols' – forbade the utilization of the Belorussian national red and white flag and also the emblem of the Belorussian PF as this might cause harm to 'state and public order and citizens' rights and lawful interests'. Article 172 – 'The illegal distribution of printed publications' – was directed not just against Belorussian or Moscow samizdat but also against the importation into the republic of the Russian-language publications of the Baltic PFs.

On the night of 24–25 March, the premises of the Belorussian PF at the Writers' House in Minsk were raided. The police declared that they were looking for explosives. Naturally, they did not discover any dynamite or bombs but they did remove all of the movement's documents and publications. Editions of unofficial Belorussian publications, printed in Vilnius, began to be intercepted.

On 10 April, a new decree was promulgated in Moscow on state crimes which stipulated severe punishments for calls for 'the overthrow or alteration' of the social or state system. Article 11 of the decree provided the potential for people to be imprisoned for 'discrediting' official social organizations. In fact, this document could be used to justify any political repression. The decree was sanctioned by none other than Gorbachev in his capacity as President of the Presidium of the USSR Supreme Soviet. The culmination of these events was 'Bloody Sunday' on 9 April 1989 in Tbilisi. According to figures from the procurator's office, in 1988–89,

59 peaceful meetings had been held in Tbilisi, only four of which were authorized. This time a peaceful demonstration near Government House was halted with unprecedented brutality by the armed forces and special units of the MVD (Ministry of Internal Affairs). Newly-elected people's deputies, M. Belikov, B. Vasiliev, A. Gel'man, D. Lun'kov, E. Shengelaya and Ye. Yakovlev, who arrived in the Georgian capital immediately after the tragedy, stated:

> Everything that happened here was inhumane. This is already clear today even though a careful investigation into the guilt of the military and Party-state leaders has not yet been completed. The demonstrators were not dispersed but beaten after the exits from the square had been sealed off. Those who did manage to break out were pursued and continued to be beaten. Why were entrenching tools widely used? Why were lachrymatory and as yet unknown chemical agents employed? Why has this all been denied until now despite the evidence and why has there been no willingness even to tell doctors in Tbilisi the precise composition of the 'chemicals' used so as to facilitate the effective treatment of the victims? Did no one give any thought as to how this would all fail to change attitudes towards the army and the Soviet soldier for the better? They did not even manage to announce the curfew in a normal way, in good time, but did it just a few minutes before its introduction, as a result of which hundreds of people were arrested and one person was killed, shot, at the wheel of a car, when he failed to stop at the demand of a patrol.[17]

The general result of the slaughter was that, in one night, 16 were killed, 14 of whom were women. The eldest was seventy and there were two youths of sixteen. One pregnant woman was killed. About 40 people were 'missing'. People were still dying days later. On the square there lay more than 1,000 pairs of shoes, about 350 handbags, children's clothing, textbooks, notes; 4,038 people suffering from poisoning came to the hospitals, of whom 543 were detained. The day after the events, victims continued to turn up at the hospitals as the area had not been cleaned up and people were still being poisoned, including children from schools located next to the scene of events. The Georgian Deputy Minister of Health, I. Menagrishvili, said angrily: 'No one even thought that such a thing was possible. We have given aid to the victims, with no idea that, at the same time, the population was being slowly poisoned in the area next to Government House.'[18] All these facts subsequently were known not only to the press, but also to the rostrum at the Congress of People's Deputies. However, General Rodionov, who had been in charge of the operation, and who, to the outrage of Georgians, was seated at the Congress as a deputy from their republic, continued to deny everything.

The massacre in Tbilisi was well organized; the operation was carefully prepared and executed according to all the rules of the military art – with the surrounding and pursuit of unarmed 'adversaries'. It would be naive to try and explain all this as an accident or as due to the disorganization of the forces of law and order, especially as the local military leadership vacillated and refused to give the order to use the army without express instructions from Moscow. The insulting disinformation published in the central and republican newspapers straight after the tragedy – *Pravda* and *Zarya Vostoka* wrote that the people died 'as a result of the crush that had arisen' – was also no accident.[19] In Tbilisi, the people were taught a lesson. The bureaucracy reminded the people that it would not tolerate 'the power of the streets'. Irrespective of any elections or congresses of deputies, the real levers of control remained in the hands of the apparatus and the Georgians had been granted the opportunity to experience this at first hand.

The Tbilisi events induced horror and indignation among Moscow's liberal intelligentsia. Numerous resolutions condemning the massacre of unarmed demonstrators began to be passed. The club of the intellectual elite, Moscow Tribune, even decided to hold a demonstration in front of the Georgian republic's delegation in Moscow. About three hundred people, a large number of whom were observers and sympathizers with no relationship to Tribune, gathered in the Arbat but were quite quickly dispersed by the police. The personal popularity and academic titles of the club's leading figures were of no help to them in this case. The writers' committee 'April' devoted virtually an entire day to condemning the Georgian tragedy. People with tears in their eyes gave speeches, each more radical than the last, but the only concrete proposal came from representatives of the Moscow Popular Front – to begin collecting money for a monument to the victims of Tbilisi's 'Bloody Sunday'.

The Tbilisi tragedy clearly exposed the total helplessness of traditional Moscow liberalism in the face of a serious political crisis: Liberal intellectuals were capable of influencing events only while they were still being listened to. The degree of their political influence was directly proportional to the degree of patience and goodwill on the part of the authorities. When it came to a real political struggle, they had at their disposal no organizational resources, no precise strategy or tactics, and could only utter angry words. The decision of members of Moscow Tribune to hold a demonstration was proof of their complete indignation at the actions of the authorities – members of this respectable organization preferred to meet in the comfortable hall of the House of Scholars. However, even now, the streets were still an alien and comfortless place – they belonged to the extremists of the MPF and in certain instances to the 'subversive elements' of the DU. After the numerous meetings of the election campaign, Tribune's demonstration in the Arbat simply went unnoticed. The press, usually rather more attentive to the utterances of the 'spiritual leaders' of perestroika than to the ideas and declarations of the 'radicals', on this occasion turned a blind eye and Tribune's resolution was published by no one.

For the Democratic Union, the events in Tbilisi were in their own way beneficial. Having lost the initiative during the election campaign, the DU could now draw attention to itself through demonstrations in support of Georgia. A demonstration was called for 23 April and, as always, was widely publicized in the official press. *Moskovskaya Pravda* even reported on the imminent demonstration beforehand, thus summoning people from all over the city to the scene of events. At the same time, it was also reported that homemade explosive devices, the origin of which had not been established, had been discovered on the Moscow Underground. The bombs had been defused at once, but the Underground was plastered with leaflets signed by the KGB appealing to passengers to be on their guard. Similar communications were broadcast constantly over the Underground's radio network. The KGB leaflets outwardly bore a sinister resemblance to DU leaflets, but they were in fact homemade, somehow printed on a computer and stuck to the windows of the carriages in exactly the same way as MPF activists did in Cheremushki during the election campaign. It was natural, therefore, that attention was drawn to the KGB communications and passengers read them attentively. The mysterious terrorists, however, continued to evade justice.

An analysis of the situation made by the MPF Co-ordinating Council revealed several crucial features. Back at the beginning of the election campaign, Maliutin had publicly warned about the possibility, after the elections, of bloodletting and all kinds of provocation. The increase in tension had patently not been accidental. The apparatus's counter-offensive could not develop in conditions of political equilibrium – it had been necessary to exacerbate the situation still further so as to gain the opportunity to 'normalize' it.

The broad publicity organized by the authorities for the Democratic Union, in contrast with the complete silence (wherever possible) about the activities of the Popular Front and spontaneous mass actions, also served as propagandist tactics. The DU was perceived by the authorities as a troublesome but not especially dangerous organization, since, during its year of existence, the DU had shown a total incapacity to broaden its social base. 'Lumpen-intellectuals', who had not only broken with the system but had broken loose from their own professional milieu, dominated the DU. Attempts to seek support in the private and co-operative sector had not met with success, since despite the theories of DU ideologues, millionaires felt quite at home within the system; and, even if political or economic problems arose for them, these patriotic businessmen preferred to resolve them through behind-the-scenes understandings with the authorities and not through the support of the DU. Certain social groups were genuinely striving for the maximum utilization of capitalist methods as a way out of the crisis (in this category belonged not only millionaire 'co-operators' but also a significant section of the managerial apparatus) but it was precisely these groups who were the least interested in a democratization which could bring into question their new privileges and give room for the activities of radical left-wing forces. These circles essentially constituted the mainstay of supporters of the 'strong hand' outside of the apparatus.

The Popular Front, on the other hand, with its endeavours to strengthen its organizations in the localities, to create a network of cells in the enterprises and simultaneously to avoid confrontations wherever possible, appeared rather more dangerous and at the same time less vulnerable. This was why the official press did everything possible to draw attention to the DU, as a counterweight to the MPF. According to the calculations of the MPF information centre, by mid-May 1989, there had been, for every member of the DU living in the capital, 2.5 articles about their organization published in the central or Moscow press, and more than five for every member of *Pamyat'*. The public could only have found out about the MPF, which was roughly four-and-a-half to five times bigger than the Moscow DU, from a small article by Mikhail Maliutin published in the magazine *Gorizont*.

The tactics of the conservative counter-offensive were to provoke unofficial organizations constantly into various acts of protest, which could then serve as an excuse for new repression and 'turning the screw'. It was quite natural that the DU, which had had only one means of political struggle – the street demonstration – at its disposal during the entire period of its existence, ideally fitted into this scenario. When, on 23 April, the leaders of the DU appealed to Moscovite public opinion to demonstrate against the massacre in Georgia, neither the liberals from Moscow Tribune nor the MPF Co-ordinating Council joined in the call, afraid that such a demonstration on the eve of the CPSU Central Committee Plenum set for the 25th might do more harm than good. Nevertheless, a significant portion of MPF activists went on to the streets and took part in the protest actions. When a large number of the demonstration's organizers from the DU were arrested by the police, it was MPF members who marched in the front ranks of the demonstration which headed from Pushkin Square to the Arbat towards the Georgian Cultural Centre. Georgii Gusev, a member of the MPF organizing council, was met with cries of displeasure when he tried to appeal to the crowd to disperse. At the following meeting of the organizing council, many activists began to demand his immediate expulsion from the Front.

All this was evidence of the fact that bureaucratic provocations were forcing people who supported the Left to adopt positions similar to those of the Democratic Union. For the MPF Co-ordinating Council, 23 April provided a serious lesson. Although the Council had not taken a special decision against participating in the demonstration, it had not only failed to support the DU but, more importantly, it had failed to propose an alternative of its own. Systematic work in the labour collectives and the struggle of MPF activists within the CPSU for an early Party Congress could not give rapid results and the situation was quickly deteriorating.

As a result there was no alternative to actions on the streets.

The CPSU Central Committee Plenum, which opened on 25 April, gave the public a clear indication of the mood of the majority of the Party apparatus. The Plenum's major and well prepared sensation was the retirement of a whole group of former high-ranking functionaries who still remained members of the Central Committee. Once the pensioners had left the highest organ of power, the Plenum essentially had nothing to do, although it did discuss the outcome of the elections. It was quite clear from the speeches of Committee members that the apparatus saw the elections not simply as a failure but as almost a catastrophe. In reality, there was not much difference between the speeches of the 'veterans of stagnation' who had gone into retirement and the 'new people'. All unanimously appealed for the closing of ranks and for a battle against the unofficial organizations and, in effect, a battle against the people who had had the effrontery to vote incorrectly. The chief danger to the country was the 'extremists' from the 'so-called Popular Fronts' and, naturally, the Democratic Union. The dissemination of samizdat was likened to 'a kind of ideological Aids' and complaints were heard that the electorate had fallen 'under the influence of informal associations and their leaders, who interpret the concepts of "democratization" and "*glasnost*" too freely'.[20]

The speech of V. K. Mesyats, First Secretary of the Moscow *obkom* of the CPSU, proved to be a programmatic intervention. Declaring that 'we cannot retreat, comrades' any further, he called for the adoption of 'immediate measures against these informal organizations'. The April Decree on state crimes, seen as being very necessary but late in being adopted, was due to become the chief means for such a struggle. The second point of the programme for political normalization expressed at the Plenum was an open call not to permit free or even semi-free elections to the local organs of power and the Supreme Soviets of the Union republics. The First Secretary of the Komi *obkom* of the CPSU, V. I. Mel′nikov, appealed to those present:

> Comrades! We are facing new elections. Today at this gathering, the secretaries of the city and regional committees declare that they will not go into these elections under such circumstances because there is a 100 per cent guarantee that they won't be elected'.[21]

It should be recognized that, here, Gorbachev displayed his political flexibility. It was in him that dismayed apparatchiks saw, although without sufficient justification, the cause of all their troubles. The April Decree calmed their anger somewhat but did not eliminate the tension. At the same time, the General Secretary was clearly endeavouring to maintain his liberal political appearance both in the West and inside the country. Consequently, his concluding speech contained an obscure reference to extremists and demagogues, who are harming perestroika, but it was, at the same time, in sharp contrast to the calls voiced at the Plenum for a pogrom. The decision – unprecedented in modern Soviet history – to publish all of the Plenum proceedings in the press, gave Gorbachev a particular advantage. Even if public opinion had disapproved of his specific actions or speeches, the leader would still compare favourably with his colleagues at the CPSU Central Committee.

Many observers, anticipating the worst, evaluated the Plenum as a victory for the liberal forces. In actual fact, it merely served as the apparatus's last warning to the people and to Gorbachev himself. Pressure on unofficial organizations continued after the Plenum. The police undertook a whole series of actions to curtail the activity of illegal publications – state equipment, which had previously been utilized for these purposes, was placed under strict control.

A new scandal broke in mid-May when deputy Tel'man Gdlyan came under criticism. To the electorate, Gdlyan's name was associated with the fight against corruption and the exposure of bribery and embezzlement in the highest echelons of power. At the same time, Gdlyan was renowned for rather hard and not always correct methods of conducting his investigations. In the USSR Supreme Court there had been a five-year struggle for a review of the case of Estonian inventor Johannes Hint, who had died in jail while awaiting rehabilitation. Hint had been accused of multifarious intrigues but the investigation team, headed in its final stages by Gdlyan, working for the USSR Prosecutor's Office, had been unable to gather convincing evidence. And so final rehabilitation, already posthumous, had been awaited for a very long time. The Supreme Court's final decision not only referred to Hint's innocence but also directly condemned Gdlyan who was dismissed from his job with the Prosecutor's Office immediately afterwards. A number of employees of the Prosecutor's Office from Gdlyan and Ivanov's team were dismissed from their jobs and left without any means of subsistence. The press launched a campaign against Gdlyan, and this campaign was joined by journalists who had gained firm reputations as liberals. 'Essentially', wrote O. Chaikovskaya in *Literaturnaya Gazeta*,

> we have a case of an attempted right-wing putsch and an attempted restoration of extra-judicial punishment. And the amazing thing is that now, when there is so much talk about creating a legal state, this 'Gdlyanite movement' also fell, it turns out, on fertile soil and has already spread across the country!

Chaikovskaya declared that some of the real material for the cases on corruption had been 'deliberately concealed by the investigation and it's not difficult to prove it'.[22] Evidence was not, however, forthcoming.

Gdlyan's electors interpreted this as an attempt to put an end to the struggle against the mafia. Irrespective of who was right in this case from a juridical point of view, it looked quite suspicious that the Supreme Court, which had been unable to rehabilitate Hint over the course of a number of years, should suddenly act with such decisiveness.

In mentioning 'the talk about a legal state', Chaikovskaya had unwittingly exposed the essence of the problem. Despite all the talk about law, the vast majority of people knew from their own experience that they were living in a far from legal state and the masses, having no respect for the official law, were prepared to support fighters for justice even if they did not stick particularly strictly to the letter of the law. The liberals, for their part, insisted that the precise observance of all laws (including Stalin's and Brezhnev's!) was the shortest route to the cultivation of a consciousness of the law and the formation of a legal state. Clearly, this could not convince the masses, to whom these laws were quite alien.

In Moscow, meetings and demonstrations began once again. More and more often Gorbachev found himself the subject of criticism. On the eve of the opening of the Congress of People's Deputies the situation was deteriorating still further.

Gorbachev's meeting with Muscovite deputies showed this group's complete uncontrollability. The deputies were often unable to propose and implement their own alternative but they were resolutely determined to ruin the initial scenario elaborated by the Party apparatus for the holding of the Congress. In these circumstances, the MPF initiated an active campaign in support of the proposals advanced by Sergei Stankevich. Its aim was to prevent the Congress from being reduced to elections for the USSR Supreme Soviet. At the next MPF meeting at Luzhniki on 13 May, a resolution was adopted demanding that the Congress revise the electoral law and constitution. It was hoped to turn the Congress into a kind of constituent assembly.

Whether the Congress could take such radical decisions remained an open question. A significant section of delegates – from Siberia and the major Russian industrial centres, not to mention the Baltic republics – were in a decisive mood; but it was impossible to underestimate the apparatus 'faction' and the numerous delegates from the Russian hinterland, Central Asia and, in part, Transcaucasia. The vacillations of the liberal figures and their fear of the masses notably increased during the course of the Yeltsin crisis, and the stubborn silence of Yeltsin himself, who was patently playing a waiting game, all made the situation extremely muddled and unclear. In the last analysis, much depended, not on the Congress itself, but on what happened on the streets.

The mobilization of the masses and their capacity once again, as at the peak of the Yeltsin crisis, to organize themselves and advance precise political demands should, in the end, have determined the outcome of the struggle in the Kremlin. In turn, the Popular Front movement in Moscow, Leningrad and the big industrial centres of Russia had to take a decisive political action. Only within the PF movement could the street activity be turned into a genuine alternative to the lobbies of the apparatus. The Popular Front approached the moment in its brief history for which it had been originally created. By organizing the spontaneous mass protest, it needed to turn it into constructive political action.

The MPF's founding conference, scheduled for 20–21 May, had to become not only a decisive step in the movement's registration and legalization, but also had to reveal the extent of its readiness to undertake its tasks. As before the March programmatic conference within the MPF, the activism of people and groups unhappy with the policy of the Co-ordinating Council sharply increased. On the one hand, the question was raised once again of whether the PF should be a 'purely democratic' or socialist movement. In the draft programme prepared for the founding conference, the MPF's socialist orientation was clearly demonstrated. At the same time, general democratic demands were formulated in an extraordinarily precise form: a multi-party system, free trade unions, equal rights for nations, and the abrogation of constitutional positions assigning a leading role to the CPSU. The economic section of the draft spoke about the self-management of labour collectives in the state sector, the combination of plan and market on the basis of democratically formulated priorities and social guarantees and also defence of the environment. This document did not provoke any serious objections in essence but the demand was voiced for the word 'socialism' to be everywhere deleted. On the other hand, the representatives of the old clubs which were frequently in decline and losing influence, attacked the Co-ordinating Council for striving to create a unified organization 'of a party type'.

In essence, the May 1989 discussion was a rehearsal of what had already taken place both in June and August 1988 during the formation of the MPF organizing committee and at the Leningrad Conference, and in the March programmatic conference of the MPF. The movement's amazing capacity to mark time on programmatic and ideological questions may be explained, paradoxically, by its successes during the election campaign. The movement's rapid growth was evident, but the number of Front activists in the capital increased more rapidly than it was possible to resolve the movement's internal problems, and as a result proved a mixed blessing. The Co-ordinating Council had constantly to struggle against the threat of erosion of the MPF's newly forming political profile.

The greatest crisis took shape in precisely those districts of Moscow where the biggest successes had been registered during the election campaign. A large number of people poured into the ranks of the MPF, attracted by the effectiveness of our activity rather than by our ideology. This time the organization had to pay for dallying over the elaboration of a programme. The group which had formed in Cheremushki around Stankevich's election campaign split almost equally into 'socialists' and 'democrats'. Analogous divisions occurred in the Oktyabr'sky and Timiryazevsky districts. Meanwhile, the new groups which had formed in the enterprises and scientific research institutes were clearly oriented towards the original conception of a socialist front. Such a distinction is not accidental: in the course of the electoral campaign, broad coalitions naturally emerged on the basis of the most general democratic slogans. The patchwork of MPF territorial groups, which had grown up through electoral work, reflected this situation. At the same time the groups in the enterprises were constructed primarily as associations of like-minded people, drawn to the MPF by its ideology and with an interest in systematic work on social questions – hence a clear interest in the socialist component of the MPF's programme of self-management, social justice, and so on.

As anticipated, the founding conference turned into an arena for heated arguments between supporters of the Co-ordinating Council and the 'democratic faction'. After the decisions made in March, when the pro-gramme's fundamental theses had been ratified by the overwhelming majority of group representatives, it was easy to predict the result of these discussions. The draft programme, prepared by the Co-ordinating Council, was adopted by a massive majority. The 'democratic faction' received about 10–12 per cent of the vote and, in the elections to the new Co-ordinating Council, one place out of 13. All of the old members of the Co-ordinating Council were re-elected.

On the whole, the conference left a double impression. In comparison with the founding congresses of the Baltic Fronts or the Democratic Union, it appeared remarkably democratic: the minority was given the opportunity to speak rather more frequently than the majority; members of the Co-ordinating Council did not vote at all; a large number of amendments were introduced into the text of both the programme and the constitution. However, the discussion was conducted chaotically and endless arguments were needed to resolve even the most elementary procedural questions. To everyone's surprise, the participants in the con-ference were able to resolve all questions in one day. By the evening of 20 May 1989, the Moscow Popular Front was able to declare itself founded.

Although the democratic faction asserted that the word 'socialism' would frighten away people used to its association with the traditional Soviet system, none of its supporters left the organization. The resolution on 'democratic socialism' adopted at the conference not only reinforced the MPF's socialist orientation but also provided a precise definition of this term; and an analogous resolution was adopted by the Leningrad PF at roughly the same time. The documents of the Popular Fronts spoke of democratic socialism as a society in which the workers would gain the opportunity to participate in making productive, economic and social decisions; in which there would be social guarantees for all citizens, and unlimited democracy. Quite clearly, despite the misgivings of the democratic faction, such a vision of socialism was comprehended and supported in the most diverse strata of society.

It was not, however, just a question of terminology. The democratic faction found support among comparatively successful representatives of the scientific intelligentsia and radical youth detached from the everyday problems of the population and attracted to 'pure' politics. Not surprisingly, these social groups tended to favour liberal market reform projects in the economy without giving much thought to what such a reform might entail for the majority of the population. There was little to distinguish the political and economic ideals of the democratic faction from those of Valeriya Novodvorskaya and other leaders of the DU – as representatives of the democratic faction declared, it was the tactics of the DU that did not suit them.

All the same, the socialist majority could in no way boast that it was capable of providing a clear programme for the country's way out of the crisis or that it was ready to propose solutions aimed at an effective defence of the interests of a majority of workers. In many ways, the slogans of the MPF's socialist majority remained just as abstract as those of the democratic faction. Moreover, even after its founding conference, the MPF was totally unable to overcome its chronically ingrained organizational difficulties. The need to create a more disciplined, centralized and unified organization with a clear and detailed programme was reinforced among activists. This demand had already assumed a more precise character in May when a group of young members of Socialist Initiative had declared the necessity of founding a Socialist Party. At the same time, the need to overcome the Front's traditionally intellectual character also became clearer. Although workers were joining the movement in increasing numbers, participating in meetings and from time to time reading MPF materials, the movement as a whole was very distant from their real problems and immediate interests. In this sense there was little to distinguish the MPF from the Baltic Fronts despite all the ideological differences between them.

The events which unfolded around the Congress of People's Deputies clearly showed the strong and weak sides of the MPF and simultaneously demonstrated the real balance of power and possibilities between the various tendencies of the 'progressive' camp.

NOTES

1. *Novosti NF*, no. 1, 1989.
2. *Argumenty i Fakty*, no. 19, 1989, p. 2.
3. *Sovetskaya Kul'tura*, 25 April 1989.
4. *Ogonyok*, no. 16, 1989, p. 3.
5. *Izvestiya*, 6 May 1989.
6. *Moskovskaya Pravda*, 19 March 1989.
7. *Izvestiya TsK KPSS*, no. 2, 1989.
8. *Moskovskaya Pravda*, 11 March 1989.
9. *Pravda*, 17 March 1989.
10. *Moskovskaya Pravda*, 21 March 1989.
11. *Izvestiya*, 6 April 1989.
12. *Izvestiya*, 6 May 1989.
13. *Moskovskaya Pravda*, 26 March 1989.
14. *Vestnik Narodnogo Fronta* (Tallin), no. 19, April 1989.
15. *Severo-Zapad*, no. 10, 1989, p. 2.
16. *Vesti iz Yaroslavlya*, no. 2, 1989.
17. *Moskovskie Novosti*, 23 April 1989.
18. *Argumenty i Fakty*, no. 21, 1989, p. 7.
19. See *Zarya Vostoka*, 11 April 1989. According to the original version, published by the Georgian Party leadership and supported by the CPSU Central Committee, 'extremists and irresponsible elements' were blamed for everything.
20. *Pravda*, 27 April 1989.
21. Ibid.
22. *Literaturnaya Gazeta*, 24 May 1989, p. 13.

9

The Congress and
Around the Congress

During the last few days before the Congress of People's Deputies opened in Moscow the whole country lived in impatient anticipation. Even those who were sceptical about the potential of this forum were caught up in the general mood. Meetings were held in Moscow at which deputies were called upon to make the Congress a real political force, to take power into their hands, and even to turn the Congress of Deputies into a constituent assembly as the Estates General had done in France exactly two hundred years before. At these meetings there were for the first time not only calls for the establishment of a multi-party system but also overt criticism of Gorbachev. This criticism did not come from Muscovite intellectual circles; on the contrary, such a radicalization of the masses had taken liberal circles by surprise and, as always, frightened them considerably.

The largest pre-Congress meeting took place on 21 May near the stadium at Luzhniki. The official press initially estimated the number taking part to be as much as a hundred thousand, but then spoke about 'a crowd of more than seventy thousand'.[1] For the first time representatives of all democratic and opposition groups stood together on the platform at Luzhniki: the Moscow Popular Front, the Democratic Union, the organization 'Communists for Perestroika', the Confederation of Anarcho-Syndicalists, Boris Yeltsin and Andrei Sakharov. But the tone was set and the meeting conducted by representatives of the Moscow Tribune club of the liberal elite.

Opening the meeting, one of is club's leaders, L.M. Batkin, clearly set out the basic political line of the group which constituted a majority of the 'bloc of progressive deputies' which had emerged during the elections. Batkin categorically distanced himself from the anti-Gorbachev feelings which were becoming increasingly prevalent among the lower orders. 'While maintaining independence of opinion with regard to Gorbachev himself', he declared, 'we must support him against the Right. At this political moment we cannot do without him. But neither can he do without us!'[2].

The first two days of the Congress's work vividly showed the penalties of such reasoning. Gorbachev was quite able to manage without the support of the deputies from the liberal Moscow group – in fact he had absolutely no need of them. The liberals' tactics, which assumed that Gorbachev would try to balance in the centre between the progressive ('left-wing', as they put it) and conservative deputies, were based on an elementary failure to understand the laws by which the apparatus operates. The logic of apparatus politics excludes the possibility of public opposition to the leadership even if the official line generates no enthusiasm. It is not surprising therefore that, from the very start, the conservative apparatchiks with their habitual bureaucratic discipline should have become Gorbachev's chief prop during such a public event as the Congress of People's Deputies. The General Secretary's other support came from the Central Asian deputies, as a rule elected under the old system of 'one candidate for one seat' and accustomed to listening to the bosses. Both these groups attentively followed the behaviour of the leader and, as if on command, supported everything he demanded. It was actually the liberals who, in endeavouring to express their discontent and defend their opinions at every turn, proved the major hindrance to the Congress's normal functioning. Despite persistent public declarations of their sincere love for Gorbachev, it was they who constantly came into conflict with him.

Clashes over procedural questions, which began from day one, went on against a background of total organizational confusion. Even the official press acknowledged that they were

> shaken by the Congress's 'abysmally low' level of organization: hordes of deputies in the aisles waiting to speak, constant to-ing and fro-ing;

endless questions; lack of clarity; the appearance of chairs, solemnly brought
in for the 'queue' for the rostrum; the absence of microphones (in the
hall the sound system was 'one-way', the stalls were fitted only with
headphones – you could listen but you could not speak or be heard);
the failure to publish a list of deputies – which went on for days! – so
that even simple lapel badges, indicating the deputy's name, became a
problem.[3]

Some episodes have become anecdotal. The Congress began to vote
with no counting arrangement and no agreement on the voting procedure
– as a result of which the task of counting the votes fell on Gorbachev
himself. The compilers of the official stenographic record, not daring
to lose a single word falling from the lips of 'the leader of perestroika',
preserved for posterity the following utterance by the General Secretary:
'One, two, three, four, five ...' Twenty-one lines of the official protocol
published in *Izvestiya* were filled with the counting of numbers.

Various procedural and technical failures dogged the heels of the Congress organizers. In the middle of the first session Deputy A. V. Levashev
from Leningrad unexpectedly remembered that, according to the Constitution, Gorbachev did not have the right to conduct the Congress and
the session would have to start afresh. So much the worse for the Constitution: the delegates decided there and then to abolish the offending article.
In the second half of the Congress, however, there were fewer false
starts. Somehow Deputy Chemodanov, who should have been elected
to the Supreme Soviet, was dropped from the voting record. A petty
constitutional crisis continued throughout the session with Chemodanov,
not helping the Congress leadership, declaring his intention to withdraw.

In establishing order, Gorbachev time and again intervened with such
profound sentences as 'Don't worry, I know what to do', or 'In this
case no count is necessary. This is by way of a question and has no
such significance. We won't take a count'.[4] It is clear that neither Gorbachev nor his entourage had taken account of the difference between
a Party conference and a parliamentary session, but this was not the only
cause of the numerous small crises settled during the course of events
by Gorbachev himself. Some delegates suspected the malicious intent
of the apparatus, and the public, glued to their televisions, surmised that
they weren't issuing permanent credentials probably because they wanted

Gdlyan and Ivanov to give up being delegates. In reality, the disorder in the Congress reflected the general disorder in the country and the growing crisis of the apparatus which was incapable of dealing with even its most elementary and traditional tasks in the new situation. It was not, however, just a matter of bad organization.

From its very inception, the project of a Congress was ambiguous and contradictory. Its tasks were vaguely defined. Paradoxically, what Gorbachev needed was not so much a parliament as elections. The electoral struggle should have proved that the new organ of power was legitimate in the eyes of Western public opinion, and to a significant degree in the eyes of Soviet society itself, and that, consequently, Gorbachev was the legitimately elected president. True, he avoided the electoral procedure himself and was nominated to the Congress as a representative of the CPSU on the slate of the 'social organizations'. This procedure incidentally eliminated any chances of the General Secretary gaining independence from the elite of the Party apparatus even if he had wanted to. Gorbachev needed a Congress of electors. The liberals, on the other hand, strove to attach greater political significance to the Congress but decided not to fight to turn the Congress into a genuine centre of alternative power. The 'Decree on Power', proposed by Andrei Sakharov, would have broadened the Congress's powers beyond Gorbachev's intentions, but in no way aspired to limit the totality of executive power which resided in the hands of Gorbachev and the Party apparatus. In conditions where, despite all the debate about a legal state, only executive power had any real meaning in the country, the liberals hoped essentially to replace the Congress of electors with an executive organ under a 'progressive' autocrat. The maximum they aspired to was the role played by the Duma in the final years of Russian Tsarism. But, alas, the Congress was unable to play this role.

For the people following the Congress on television and radio, the Congress was first and foremost a brilliant political spectacle. There was enormous interest in the Congress and it is difficult to overestimate its role in the development of society's political culture. Deputies' tongues had been loosened. The very procedure of the Congress provoked inevitable conflict between Gorbachev and deputies. In this strained atmosphere, the consideration of candidates for the Presidency could not take place without critical speeches directed at the leader. For the first time a broad public watched as the acting General Secretary was forced to respond to public criticism of himself.

> Well, you tell us, who could have guessed even a short while ago that, before the eyes of the whole country, one of the leaders of Moscow's informals, the young Deputy S. V. Stankevich, would be able to dispute the opinion of Deputy . . . M. S. Gorbachev

wrote *Izvestiya* correspondents in some dismay.[5] Stankevich's speech concerning the voting procedure was, however, far from being the most unpleasant for Gorbachev. It was even more difficult for him to reply to questions on how it was that he knew nothing about the slaughter in Tbilisi, or with what funds his luxurious dacha in the Crimea was being built (the leader of perestroika had to admit that it was with state funds).

Skirmishes like these made the Congress a wonderful sight for the millions of people following it on radio and television. The demand for live transmission of the Congress had been advanced by liberal circles immediately after the March elections and this was perhaps the only one of their demands which had been realized. It should be acknowledged that the public's interest in the programmes from the Palace of Congresses proved completely justified: the show surpassed all expectations. The popular satirist Mikhail Zhvanetsky wrote:

> Broadcasts of the Congress are like reports from an underwater world. Only in colour. Rooted to the spot, we, the hordes of naive and foolish people on this side of the screen, have watched with delight AS IT HAPPENS . . .
> As it happens!!!
> Who said we are incapable of anything? Rubbish! This is far above the world level. Intrigues, preparations, procurements, closing ranks and splitting them . . . Brilliant![6]

In the meantime, everything went according to the initial scenario. Gorbachev endeavoured to bring the Congress to an early close, have himself elected President of the Supreme Soviet, form the Supreme Soviet, confirm Ryzhkov as Prime Minister and, having thus fulfilled the original plan, set off for West Germany for a prearranged official visit. The liberals, on the other hand, who had immediately begun to identify closely with the Moscow deputies, insisted that the work of Congress should, from the very outset, be conducted according to all the rules of parliamentary debate; they said it should be prolonged, thus giving an opportunity for factions to form and for the elections to be held on an alternative basis.

From the point of view of normal parliamentary logic, the liberal group was undoubtedly right, but the Congress was in no sense a parliament on the Western model. Gorbachev naturally made use of the powerful majority behind him to defeat one liberal proposal after another. Such a turn of events at first caused despair and dismay among representatives of the liberal group. Gorbachev was synonymous at the Congress with the leader of the conservatives! In turn the apparatchiks, united around Gorbachev and sensing his support even on secondary questions, behaved even more aggressively. Both liberals and conservatives knew beforehand that the outcome of the elections for the highest offices of state had been preordained. If this had not been the case it is quite possible the Congress would not have taken place at all. But for the progressive bloc the results of the voting for the Supreme Soviet came as a total surprise: the majority had unanimously 'sifted' all the representatives of liberal circles about whom they knew even a little, on the basis of public pronouncements or declarations made during the course of the Congress.

This was all too much even for Gorbachev's loyal admirers. The mood of discontent was expressed best of all by Yuri Afanasyev when he declared on 27 May that the work of the Congress was creating a 'dispiriting impression' on him. The Congress was dominated by 'an aggressively obedient majority and you, Mikhail Sergeevich [Gorbachev], have either been paying close attention to this majority or have been skilfully influencing it'. In fact, even such well-known representatives of the progressive intelligentsia as the writer Sergei Zalygin, who had made a name for himself in the struggle against the ecologically damaging policies of the Ministry of Water, and Roy Medvedev, associated with this majority. As a result, Afanasyev declared 'we have formed a Stalinist–Brezhnevite Supreme Soviet'[7].

At the same time, the liberals were unable to propose any countertactics. With hindsight Andrei Sakharov conceded that 'the "liberal" minority really is a minority; it is split. It has no internal clarity or unanimity'. Sakharov complained that 'nothing has been learned tactically and there has arisen a kind of confrontation between the majority and the "Moscow group", which was in itself democratic'. In his opinion the Muscovites 'spoke a lot instead of sharing the burden of interventions with co-thinkers from other places. This created the impression of exclusiveness'.[8] This irritated not only deputies from the Russian provinces but also representatives of the Baltic Republics, who agreed with the Muscovites on many questions. The Estonian deputy, A. Khaug, declared: 'in relations with the "Moscow group" you feel that they consider themselves cleverer than the rest'. The Muscovites, for their part, having relied on the total support of the Baltic deputies showed their exasperation and this heated the situation still further and led the Baltic deputies to the conclusion that 'an imperial consciousness is now manifesting itself' in Moscow.[9]

But even this was not the major problem. Such errors were quickly learnt from and the Muscovites spent the whole of the second half of the Congress winning round deputies from other cities. The real weakness of the liberals consisted in the fact that, while demanding alternative elections, the liberal group could not, and did not really want to, advance an alternative programme. Each representative of the 'Moscow fraction' and its provincial allies who criticized Gorbachev was forever emphasizing that these were personal disagreements and that their loyalty to the leader remained unshakeable. It should not be forgotten that provision for Gorbachev's nomination as the sole candidate for the post of President of the Supreme Soviet had been made in the decisions of the Nineteenth Party Conference, in which many of the future deputies of the 'Moscow group' (including Yuri Afanasyev) had participated, and they had not once publicly voiced their opposition to these decisions prior to the Congress.

Boris Yeltsin, who had gathered 90 per cent of the votes in Moscow and had turned into a genuinely popular leader thanks to the struggle that had unfolded around his name, was the most serious alternative candidate; in the event of direct Presidential elections he would have had a chance of victory at least in some regions of the country. During the meeting at Luzhniki on 21 May the crowd began chanting – quite unexpectedly for the representatives of Moscow Tribune – 'Yeltsin for President!' This was all quite familiar to liberal deputies who had been present at these events, but they continued obstinately to insist that there was no realistic alternative candidate while insisting 'on principle' that alternative elections be held. This was all too reminiscent of the theatre of the absurd.

The decisions of the CPSU Central Committee Plenum, which were adopted immediately before the Congress and envisaged the election of Gorbachev as President, placed Yeltsin in a difficult position. During the course of the intra-Party discussion both Gorbachev and his immediate circle referred on several occasions with undisguised hostility to the 'crowd' at Luzhniki, which had proposed its own candidate for the post of President. It should be recognized, however, that, in terms of fear and loathing of the 'crowd', the liberal deputies conceded nothing to the General Secretary. To them, Yeltsin was associated with this 'crowd' and to support it meant to open the way for 'populism' – a term liberal circles had for some time used for any mass movement.

All the same, Yeltsin's candidature was advanced by provincial deputies, but the disgraced Moscow leader refused to stand, deferring to the Central Committee decision. Both official and unofficial public opinion polls indicated an immediate drop in his popularity. As had already happened several times before, Yeltsin avoided direct confrontation with the apparatus despite the fact that this time he had behind him the support of millions of people.

It should be acknowledged, however, that Yeltsin's retreat was provoked not so much by fear of the apparatus as by the total absence of support in the Moscow group. After the numerous declarations by liberal ideologists that they intended firmly to support Gorbachev (despite the General Secretary's patently scornful attitude to many of the liberals' speeches and the loutish behaviour of the majority under his control, who disrupted the speeches of liberal Frondeurs with shouts and noise), Yeltsin had nothing to hope for at this Congress.

It was obvious, however, that the matter could not be reduced to the personality of the President. The demand for alternative elections without a consistent alternative strategy was quite impossible, as people from Gorbachev's entourage rushed to point out to the Congress. The opposition, concerned in the main with petty wranglings with the majority over procedural questions, might have aroused the sympathy of television viewers but could not present itself as a credible alternative to the powers that be. The speeches of the Moscow economist, Gavriil Popov, who at first called for the open declaration of an opposition fraction and then retracted his statement, clearly demonstrated the ambivalence and inconsistency of the liberal position.

The liberals' own programme began to be outlined somewhat later during a discussion of Gorbachev and Ryzhkov's reports on the government's proposals. There was nothing sensational in these reports themselves except for Gorbachev's direct admission that the economic reforms being implemented by official circles inflicted a blow against the interests of the working class. The whole of Ryzhkov's report was devoted essentially to finding ways to preserve as much as possible of the old administrative system of management alongside new market methods.

The liberals' proposals were, in their turn, concerned with how the transition to a capitalist system could be made more resolutely. This time the orientation to capitalism was talked about quite openly. Gavriil Popov declared:

> The experience of the advanced capitalist countries shows that the economically developed countries have a state sector of roughly 30–40 per cent. I think it would be sufficient, taking into account our traditions and social interests, to leave 50 per cent of the economy in the hands of the state. The remaining 50 per cent should be transferred into the hands of the co-operative, private and individual sector.

It was proposed that agriculture be transferred in its entirety into private hands: 'The whole experience of all prosperous countries indicates that there the basis of agriculture is peasant family agriculture: farmers.'[10]

The trouble with all such reasoning was not so much its ideological overtones as that it was completely divorced from the real problems and potential of Soviet society. References to the 'prosperous West' have no bearing on the question of how to regulate our own crisis. This has been pointed out in the pages of *Nedelya* by academician Leonid Abalkin: 'Let us avoid making easy judgements. We say: land to the peasants! But we are not thinking: we no longer have peasants or the desire to take over the land.'[11]

The liberal economists' chief weakness was their complete lack of a concrete programme for a way out of the crisis. A few specific proposals were reduced to appeals to devote more resources to the debt with the West or to curtail capital investment in certain branches of the economy. Even Yeltsin spoke in the same vein, demanding a 40 per cent cut to investment in construction without explaining how he arrived at this figure and how the cuts would be spread among specific building projects. It was evidently assumed that these questions would, in time-honoured bureaucratic fashion, be resolved by the 'centre'. Amazingly, the economists, calling for a reduction in the state sector, reasoned in exactly the same way. No one explained which enterprises or branches would be transferred into private hands and on the basis of what criteria. The question was not even posed as to who would be the new owners and shareholders although it was quite clear that, apart from foreign capital, only representatives of the old bureaucracy and mafia could have the financial means to buy state property.

Nor was any evidence adduced that the selling-off of state property would lead to the increased efficiency of the economy, if references to the 'pioneering experience' of the West are discounted. Also forgotten was the fact that the Western economy, significantly more developed and incomparably more balanced, does not in general encounter the many problems to be resolved in the USSR, and that attempts to implement a liberal economic course close to the spirit of Shmelev and Popov have frequently led to catastrophic consequences in less developed countries. No one has paid any attention even to the experience of 'fraternal countries' like Hungary and Yugoslavia, which have been experiencing increasing difficulties in the process of a liberal economic reform.

In the final analysis, the programme of the liberal 'opposition' differed from the official one only in its lack of specificity and the patent incapacity of its authors to acknowledge the scale of the difficulties confronting the Soviet economy. The tendency to give 'simple answers' in the form of slogans distinguished the ideologists of liberalism from the practical people in the apparatus – to the disadvantage of the former. They both aimed for the same thing, but the ideologists, having replaced the old slogans with new ones, were less capable of breaking out of the traditional sloganizing mentality.

While the liberals were calling for the renunciation of wage-levelling and for an orientation to the experience of 'the advanced capitalist countries', the masses were striving for greater social equality and had absolutely no desire to pay the price of the reforms. At the same time, the Moscow group of liberal deputies was, for vast numbers of people in the country, associated with free-thinking and independence, and remained the sole real opposition known to the public at large. If the supporters of the General Secretary had demonstrated that there was no alternative to his candidature at the Congress, then for the people the streets were no alternative, at least initially, to support for the liberal minority, irrespective of how far the liberals' profound intentions coincided with the masses' genuine aspirations.

On the first day of the Congress a spontaneous rally began on Pushkin Square. By the end of the session Stankevich had turned up to address those assembled. A short while afterwards Andrei Sakharov appeared with a few more deputies. Dispersal of unauthorized meetings in such circumstances would have proved a difficult affair: beating up demonstrators in the presence of deputies was clearly improper. Both the Moscow police and the city authorities had learnt much from the experience of the Yeltsin crisis in March and now tried to avoid confrontations with the crowd. Some police officers had already become used to the demonstrators and treated them without their former hostility.

Although the decree on meetings and demonstrations was still in force and the efforts of the 'Moscow group' to have it repealed or at least temporarily suspended during the Congress had failed, the decree's operation in the capital was in effect paralysed. Stormy debates unfolded at the Congress during which it was announced that the holding of meetings at Luzhniki over the period of the Congress would be permitted without the need for special authorization. True, the Congress did not in reality play the decisive role in this. On the very eve of that discussion, representatives of the Moscow PF came to an agreement with the Moscow Soviet on allowing meetings at Luzhniki. This small incident was significant in itself: Congress deputies became engaged in heated arguments over issues which had already been resolved and whose resolution depended not on the balance of votes in the hall of the Kremlin Palace of Congresses but on the real balance of forces in the capital and society.

One way or another, for three weeks Moscow enjoyed the freedom to hold meetings. This applied not only to the Popular Front, which held meetings jointly with the Memorial society at Luzhniki, but also to the Democratic Union, which continued to assemble unhindered on Pushkin Square. On different days, meetings at Luzhniki, however, typically drew between 100,000 and 200,000 people, while Pushkin Square attracted no more than 3,000 even on the days of the greatest upsurge. The contrast was so obvious that even DU members could not ignore it. In fact, during the days of the Moscow meetings, the social-democratic faction of the DU, headed by Aleksandr Lukashev, broke with Valeriya Novodvorskaya and worked together with the Moscow Popular Front. As during the days of the Yeltsin crisis, smaller political groupings were not seen on the streets – with the exception of Skurlatov's group, which would appear at meetings with a huge naval flag of the Russian empire but had absolutely no impact on their outcome.

As always the press reported on the Moscow meetings in a vague and incomprehensible fashion. True to itself, *Moskovskaya Pravda* exploded with an indignant article in which it was stated that the meetings lacked any genuine pluralism of opinions and no opportunity was given to speakers whose views were at variance with the ideas of the Popular Front. In reality, even representatives of the apparatus were allowed to speak but the crowd did not want to hear them. However, the thousands of people who came to Luzhniki from all corners of the city displayed no less patience towards speakers than did the Congress majority, which drove those who were unwelcome from the rostrum with slow hand-claps and shouting. 'The Congress is like a meeting. A meeting is like the Congress', journalists asserted.[12]

On the whole, the meetings conveyed to the impartial observer the impression of good organization and this favourably distinguished them from the chaos in the Palace of Congresses. However, such organization was achieved only with difficulty. Every day there were several times more people on the speakers' list than would be able to speak. Bursting to get to the rostrum were some quite unbelievable characters – some patently drunk or mad. The stewards, appointed by the Moscow PF to keep order, averted chaos with considerable difficulty. At the end of a meeting many demanded a march from Luzhniki to the Rossiya Hotel where the deputies were staying in order to demand apologies from the Central Asian representatives for their shocking behaviour – they had persistently spoken in opposition to the Muscovites. It is difficult to predict how this might have turned out.

The discontent on the streets was turning increasingly against Gorbachev, who was continually exposed to the attacks of speakers at the meetings. The size of the meeting on 21 May was soon surpassed. During the Congress the police reported that 150,000 and in the end even 200,000 were gathered at Luzhniki. Leaders of the Moscow PF now had the opportunity to address crowds of many thousands. Calls for strike action were heard and the crowd enthusiastically greeted those who spoke of the need for a transition to a multi-party system and the foundation of a Socialist Party.

The majority of speakers appealed formally for solidarity with the progressive deputies of the 'Moscow group' but the 'Luzhniki alternative' was clearly different from the proposals of even the most radical deputies of the 'Moscow group'. Luzhniki reacted to the election of the new Supreme Soviet with a resolution refusing to recognize the power of the new organ, since it did not reflect the real balance of political forces in the country or in the Congress. The exclusion of Yeltsin from the Supreme Soviet despite his five million votes, caused deep shock. Participants in the meetings not only declared their unwillingness to submit to the decisions of the new Supreme Soviet and the government that would be formed by it but also demanded immediate preparations for the fresh, direct and free election of the Supreme Soviet, the immediate abolition of direct representation for social organizations and – a demand typical of participants in meetings of communists – the immediate summoning of an extraordinary CPSU Congress.

A critical situation arose on 27 and 28 May. The thousands of people at Luzhniki, incensed by the outcome of the elections to the Supreme Soviet, passed a resolution declaring 30 May a 'day of action'. It was proposed that, on that day, meetings, demonstrations and, most important, protest strikes would take place not only in Moscow but in other parts of the country. After representatives of the Zelenograd labour collective, who had already held a one-hour warning strike prior to the Congress in support of Gdlyan and Ivanov, had spoken at the meeting at Luzhniki, it became clear that these were not just idle threats. The following day, when I had to meet representatives of the Moscow Soviet apparatus on Popular Front business, it was obvious they were in no mood for a joke.

The voice of the crowd was also heard in the Kremlin Palace of Congresses. Ales Adamovich recalls that

> Delegates began to receive thousands of letters and telegrams and the tele-
> phone was forever ringing; in Luzhniki a meeting of 100,000 had gathered.
> Crowds of Muscovites met delegates on their way out of the Kremlin.
> This profoundly influenced the work of the Congress. So profoundly that
> on Monday 29 May the atmosphere at the Congress suddenly and radically
> changed'.[13]

A solution to the crisis was found, however, in the spirit of vulgar
vaudeville. Gavriil Popov unexpectedly informed the Congress that a
certain deputy, Kazannik, intended to stand down from the Supreme
Soviet in favour of Yeltsin. The comedy and absurdity of this situation
lay in the fact that, for some reason, Kazannik was unable immediately
to make the declaration himself and moreover waited two days to
announce his decision, and in the fact that Popov himself had never
been distinguished by his sympathy for Yeltsin (in particular, it was he
who had attacked the Moscow Party leader in the pages of *Moskovskie
Novosti* after Yeltsin had been disgraced). Straight after Popov and Kazannik's declarations, childish squabbling began over procedural matters.
Kazannik said that he would only withdraw his candidature if it was
decided beforehand that he would be replaced by Yeltsin, whereas others
said that it was first necessary to accept Kazannik's resignation and only
then to decide the question of Yeltsin. Gorbachev calmed everyone down
by meeting Kazannik's demand that Yeltsin be automatically nominated
for the available place.

Yeltsin's election to the Supreme Soviet quickly relieved the tension,
but on the whole his political reputation suffered as a result of these
events. The fact that he had forced his way into the highest organ of
state power through this comic stage-management did him few favours.
Yeltsin's radical interventions at the Supreme Soviet only partially com-
pensated for his loss of authority. Neither did collaboration with the
Congress's liberal fraction reinforce his position. Feeling no sympathy
whatsoever towards Yeltsin, the liberals cynically used him and left him
to the whim of providence whenever it suited them. On the one hand,
Yeltsin made agreed declarations in the name of the 'Moscow group'
of deputies, and served as the lure at meetings where the 'stars' from

Moscow Tribune entered the limelight. On the other hand, in the press and in private conversations, the liberal public was forever distancing itself from the Yeltsinists and criticizing their 'populism' and 'illusions' of social justice. In their turn, the masses, who had supported Yeltsin, began to lose their former faith in him.

Yeltsin's authority remained comparatively high but the popularity of Gdlyan and Ivanov was growing rapidly. These two figures, who occupied a position close to Yeltsin – the struggle against corruption, calls for social equality, attacks on the apparatus, and so on – were rather more overtly in conflict with the liberals and did not make such concessions with regard to the Gorbachev group, with whom Yeltsin still avoided direct confrontation. As a result, Gdlyan and Ivanov found themselves the centre of attraction for the millions of Muscovites and Leningraders disillusioned by the Congress. The creation of a commission at the Congress to investigate the Gdlyan and Ivanov affair which was joined by many liberal figures, including Roy Medvedev, only fuelled the flames. The electors decisively declared that they would support these uncompromising investigators. The liberals' references to numerous breaches of legal procedures by these two figures changed nothing since the masses knew there was no possibility of fighting corruption by strictly legal methods – and the laws themselves induced no respect at all.

The dividing line between the liberals and the radically minded masses was becoming more and more evident. For the liberal deputies the growth of mass dissatisfaction with the Congress signified above all, not a chance to take control of the course of events, but only an opportunity for a behind-the-scenes deal with Gorbachev's group. Yuri Karyakin, in a clear expression of the majority of the liberal group's point of view, publicly distanced himself from the deputy chosen by Moscow PF forces, Yuri Vlasov, who had begun to speak about the possibility of limiting Gorbachev's power and creating a constitutional procedure for removing the President. In Karyakin's opinion, criticism directed at the leader of perestroika represented a 'dangerous tendency'.[14] Henceforth, the struggle with this and other such 'dangers' became a more and more important task for the liberal elite.

The radicals had meanwhile found themselves for some time out of the game. The Left's tactic of providing 'critical support' for the liberal bloc had deprived them of the opportunity for independent action.

Stankevich, who had intervened effectively at the Congress in its first days, was completely subordinated to 'bloc discipline' and in fact relin-quished it in order to play some sort of independent role at the Congress. Other deputies who were close to the Popular Front movement were patently lacking in political experience and seemed hypnotized by the authority of the Moscow celebrities. The Moscow PF's Co-ordinating Committee continued through inertia to organize meetings without receiving any support or even gratitude from the 'Moscow group', which owed all its few successes to the masses' involvement.

The successes were, however, highly relative. A few eminent liberals who had been included on some commission or other removed from the decree on state crimes Article 11, which contained a blatantly absurd formulation forbidding the discrediting of social organizations. Thousands of people at meetings declared their readiness to support the bloc of progressive deputies by any means, but the deputies themselves clearly did not know what to do and confined themselves to general arguments to the effect that the next Congress would be better.

Disillusionment in the Congress was growing. On 11 June, the TV programme, *Vremya*, reported that in sociological surveys a majority (about 42–43 per cent of respondents) had a negative assessment of the Congress. The following day, the weekly *Argumenty i Fakty* solemnly announced that a tendency to a more positive evaluation of the work of Congress had been discovered in Alma-Ata, Tbilisi and Tallin. 'At the same time there have been changes in the opposite direction in the assessments of Muscovites, Leningraders and Kievans.'[15] It was thus quite obvious that the Congress was being positively appraised only in those parts of the country where confidence in the official structures had been definitively undermined during the events of 1986–89 and where, to all appearances, even worse had been expected! On the other hand, in Russia and the Ukraine, where significant illusions in the Gorbachev reforms still persisted, the disillusionment was terrible. The developing mood was vividly expressed as ever by Mikhail Zhvanetsky:

Idiot. I hoped for little: laws, decisions . . .
What utter rubbish! We got more than that: a massive and beautiful picture of a working machine producing no results. The mountain gave birth to the abolition of Article 11, which had already been abolished a long

time ago. To our delight and applause, the mountain gave birth to nothing.[16]

After the Congress had ended the deputies of the liberal group began to give numerous interviews where, while repeating the ritual phrase about a 'certain move to the right', they argued that, in the final analysis, nothing catastrophic had happened. In reality, the outcome of the Congress was perhaps even more lamentable than many pessimists had assumed. It was not so much a matter of the composition of the Supreme Soviet or of specific decisions that had been taken on particular questions (including Gorbachev's election as President of the Supreme Soviet since he, as a deputy from the Plenum of the CPSU Central Committee could, in accordance with existing legislation, be recalled at any time). The Congress had simply been unable to become a real political power. The real centres of decision-making remained just the same as before. With the best will in the world, a second Congress would be incapable of correcting this failing of the first, since the general rules of the game had already been fixed and the level of popular support and popular expectations could no longer be the same as they were in May–June 1989. Disillusionment in the Congress meant a sharp decrease in the chances of a peaceful evolutionary change. A majority of the country's serious problems remained unresolved just when the masses' faith in the parliamentary road, and in the possibility of finding solutions in a wise centre, had fallen precipitously. The deteriorating economic situation, the growth in the number of labour conflicts, worker discontent at market reforms which only profited the leaders of co-operatives and a section of Soviet managers, the absence of progress in resolving national conflicts all promised us a far from peaceful development of events in the near future.

The first Congress of People's Deputies was a unique phenomenon in the history of our country. Never again will there be such a fantastic, universal interest in the deputies' discussions and in each word enunciated in the conference hall of the Palace of Congresses. Never again will there be such bright and naive hopes in wise legislators, who would settle our fate before our very eyes. Never again will the liberal elite enjoy such great influence and authority in our country as it gained either justifiably or unjustifiably during the Congress's first days. Never again will we have a popular leader like Yeltsin, capable of winning to his side almost all of the capital's inhabitants. Never again will liberal figures be able to rely on the loyal and unselfish assistance of the Left, which they enjoyed in the spring of 1989.

The Congress of People's Deputies turned out to be a congress of disappointed hopes and missed opportunities. Gorbachev reached the high point of his political career, becoming the country's 'constitutional' President and the liberal elite gained the most political influence it could have hoped to achieve. But this was the beginning of the end. Further on, the road leads inevitably downhill. Henceforth the masses will not listen with hope or trepidation to what is happening in the Congress; but the deputies will have to react to the stormy events occurring in the country and which are passing them by. Perestroika has come to its logical and natural end. Without waiting for renewal, society has lost faith in the goodwill of wise leaders. But, over the past months, people discovered a faith in themselves, and they had no intentions of giving up one iota of their rights. There could be only one result: an exacerbation of the crisis and a deepening of the struggle.

NOTES

1. Compare the polemic between *Pravda* and *Izvestiya* which arose after the meeting of 21 May. Baltic newspapers claimed there were significantly more than 100,000 people at Luzhniki (see *Tartuskii Kur'er*, 1989, no. 1) but Western journalists, on the other hand, tended as a rule to underestimate the numbers of those present, mentioning a figure of roughly 20,000.
2. *Tartuskii Kur'er*, no. 1, 1989.
3. *Nedelya*, no. 22, 1989.
4. See *Izvestiya*, 26 May 1989.
5. Ibid.
6. *Moskovskie Novosti*, 9 July 1989, p. 16.
7. *Izvestiya*, 29 May 1989.
8. *Literaturnaya Gazeta*, 21 June 1989, p. 11. The extent of the mutual hostility between the Muscovites and other deputies, especially those from Central Asia, is splendidly revealed by one of the Congress's most comical episodes. G. A. Amangel'dinova, a teacher from Kazakhstan, declared that 'I, as a woman, am even afraid to sit among the Moscow delegates' (*Izvestiya*, 30 May 1989).
9. *Molodezh' Estonii*, 30 June 1989.
10. *Izvestiya*, 11 June 1989.
11. *Nedelya*, no. 23, 1989, p. 3.
12. Ibid, p. 2.

13. *Knizhnoe Obozrenie*, 2 June 1989, p. 2.
14. *Izvestiya*, 4 June 1989.
15. *Argumenty i Fakty*, no. 23, 1989.
16. *Moskovskie Novosti*, 9 July 1989, p. 16.

=10=

Onward, Onward, Onward . . .

By failing to solve any problems, the Congress of People's Deputies reinforced the masses' politicization. In a sense, the history of the Nineteenth Party Conference was repeating itself. The general excitement
and hopes for a quick solution to painful problems, which were simply
left unsatisfied by the Congress, made for a highly explosive situation.

It would be incorrect to explain all of the troubles which befell the
government in terms of the masses' disillusionment in the Congress.
It was not just a question of confounded expectations but of the Congress's
inability to take a single decision to change the overall situation even
a little. And this meant an unavoidable and natural escalation of all the
conflicts which were unfolding in the country, and a deepening of the
crisis.

All processes continued to take their course irrespective of the pleas
for calm and self-control which could be heard from time to time from
the Kremlin. On the one hand, national dissension continued to provoke
new and bloody clashes. Even while the Congress was in session, Uzbek
nationalists began reprisals against Meskhetian Turks in Fergana. Troops,
thrown into the disturbed region, clashed not only with an enraged crowd
but also with an armed nationalist militia capable of doing battle with
the regular army. In Kokanda 'extremist' detachments not only put up
resistance to the troops, but even attacked military units themselves. *Izvestiya* reported actual battles with the deployment of helicopters and the

landing of forces – just as in Afghanistan. Meskhetian refugee camps, guarded by government troops, came under siege.

The clashes in Fergana were stopped only after a week of bitter fighting and a large number of casualties, but the problem itself was not resolved. The Georgian leadership did not want the return of the Meskhetians deported by Stalin and, even worse, public opinion in the republic was on the whole extremely ill-disposed towards the Meskhetians. Neither did plans for resettling the Meskhetians in Russia meet with the rapturous delight of local inhabitants. The Meskhetians' position remained catastrophic but the authorities did not even want to begin a serious campaign of explanation in Russia or Georgia in order to create a more favourable psychological atmosphere for this people. Just as before, they tried to resolve all problems by purely administrative methods, but even these were applied indecisively and inconsistently.

Liberal circles in Moscow maintained a deathly silence on the question of the Meskhetians, deciding not to criticize either the Georgian leadership or the Georgian Popular Front. In turn, a peculiar united front was formed in the republic between ruling circles and the opposition in respect of the national minorities. The Georgian opposition, while striving for sovereignty and even autonomy for itself, and decisively and uncompromisingly in favour of democratic rights for its own people, could find nothing good to be said for the national minorities either living now or formerly in the republic and, on this question, had no desire to make the slightest concession. Attempts by representatives of the Moscow Popular Front to arbitrate did not, and could not, bear any fruit. The Georgian national intelligentsia felt it had the support of Russian public opinion on the major question of national sovereignty and did not want to make concessions on details.

The upshot of this policy was the formation of the Popular Front of Abkhazia, which was supported by part of the Abkhazian nomenklatura and emerged as a direct adversary of the Georgian Popular Front. The Meskhetians, Osetians and Abkhazians were forced to struggle against the flouting of their rights by the ruling Georgian nation just as the Georgians themselves were experiencing one of the most tragic moments in their history.

By June 1989, the Abkhazian struggle for their own national rights had in fact grown into an armed uprising. Thousands of holiday-makers, who were sent as usual at this time to the region of Sukhumi, discovered quite unusual holiday conditions. Here and there explosions, bursts of gunfire and single shots could be heard. Train-drivers refused to drive trains in the region affected by the fighting and many holiday-makers had to resort to sunbathing on the rails beside the stationary trains.

In the first clash between Georgians and Abkhazians, which took place on the evening of 15 July, 11 people were killed and 127 wounded. The occasion for this was the opening in Sukhumi of a branch of the Tbilisi State University. In the tense atmosphere of the summer of 1989, however, anything might have served as an excuse for carnage.

The number of weapons fired by both sides came as a very unpleasant surprise to the authorities. There was little to distinguish the battles between Georgian and Abkhazian militias from regular army engagements. 'I have not seen anything like it since I served in Afghanistan', claimed Major-General Yuri Shatalin, who was at the scene of the events.[1] The investigation conducted in July revealed that the police and 'executive workers', both from the Georgian and from the Abkhazian sides, had actively assisted in the formation of the militias' arsenals. Fifty-six automatic weapons, forty pistols and three rifles had been removed from police-stations for the purposes of arming the militias of both sides. Fighting detachments, numbering several hundred people, took part in the engagements. Troops sent to the scene uncovered stores of explosive, where dozens of kilograms of ammonite, Bickford safety fuses, detonators, and so on, were neatly packed. According to the most modest figures, the militias had in their possession thousands of firearms of all systems and calibres from hunting carbines to modern American automatics!

As in Fergana, the regular army was able to re-establish order after a few days. The presence of the troops did not, however, resolve the conflict and the fighting detachments were neither disbanded nor routed. If, in the 1960s, Latin American radicals threatened to create 'fifty Vietnams' for North American imperialism, then by the summer of 1989 Gorbachev had gained at least a half-dozen Ulsters without any interference from radical 'subversive' elements.

As with the British troops in Ulster, the Soviet Army was forced into policing operations in its own country, formally under the slogan of maintaining law and order and in the capacity of a neutral force between the conflicting parties. But as the military–police operations were not accompanied by any serious efforts at a political settlement, the army found itself drawn into an endless conflict and coming under more and more blows from all sides.

Straight after the clashes in Fergana and Abkhazia, skirmishes between Tadzhiks and Kirghiz flared up in the region of Isfara. The impetus for this was given by the unorganized reclamation of waste land, which had begun in Kirghizia (the Kirghiz feared that Moscow might use it to resettle refugees from other regions). Conflict arose after the Kirghiz began to a acquire barren plots on Tadzhik territory.

Although clashes over a whole series of disputed parcels of land and the distribution of water on the border between the two republics was nothing new, the equilibrium had been so clearly disrupted this time that, as the newspapers put it, 'reprisals from the Tadzhik side' rapidly followed.[2] The Matocha canal between the republics was destroyed and filled with stones, as a result of which serious damage was done to agriculture on the Kirghiz side of the border. After this, on 13 July, a bloody battle occurred between members of neighbouring communities on the border. Thousands of people took part in the engagement and both firearms and sidearms were employed. According to official figures, nineteen were wounded with one person subsequently dying. As usual, Moscow reacted to the conflict by imposing a curfew and dispatching troops to the affected region.

Events developed along similar lines in the Kazakh town of Novy Uzen' where clashes occurred between native inhabitants and temporary settlers from the Caucasus, who had come to take up jobs. This time, as before in Turkmenia, the wrath of the crowd fell upon members of co-operatives. The owners of co-operative stores, who were charging excessively high prices for their goods and prospering in the midst of a general crisis, became a kind of symbol to the masses of social injustice. Wherever shopkeepers and their customers were of different nationalities, the social contradictions threatened to turn into inter-ethnic discord.

Set against the confrontation between Georgians and Abkhazians and the carnage in Central Asia, the habitual conflict in Nagorny Karabakh already seemed comparatively under control. The regular strikes by the Armenian population of Stepanakert had caused rather more harm to the local inhabitants themselves and Moscow had resigned itself to them, not even undertaking any special measures to curtail them. The economy of the region was in ruins. Nevertheless, in July, this conflict entered a new phase. On the region's streets a 'war of stones' began. The link between Armenia and Karabakh was finally broken. Convoys of vehicles crossing the territory of Azerbaijan were subject to attack. 'It's just like Leningrad during Hitler's blockade', a representative of the Armenian national movement in Moscow told me in despair. Unfortunately, the situation of the Azerbaijani minority in Karabakh was no better. While the Azerbaijanis were blockading Stepanakert, the Armenians were attacking transport going to Shushu, the stronghold of the Azerbaijani community in Karabakh. The troops tried somehow to relieve the tension: additional military posts appeared everywhere; and in a number of cases military convoys delivered provisions and raw materials to local enterprises.

Izvestiya wrote that in Karabakh

> wooden doors have been replaced by steel ones better able to withstand the pressure of the crowd. However, you cannot sit out your life in a flat 'built like a safe'. Therefore, at night, the men don't sleep – they jump at the slightest noise so as to run out on to the street to meet the approaching danger with their neighbours. In many homes they have a knife, an axe or a club at hand, or even something a bit more serious. Checkpoints on the roads remove weapons and even homemade explosive devices from passing Azerbaijanis and Armenians. Night is the most anxious time and so citizens stand guard until morning and in the villages self-defensive sentry posts keep watch. The troops are troops but God helps those who help themselves'.[3]

The situation was tragic for mixed families; Armenians had virtually left Shushu altogether, and Azerbaijanis had left Stepanakert. Each day brought reports of new victims. The troops, while playing no role in the clashes, suffered losses. In Kel'badzhar, a military helicopter crashed onto a stadium, crushing eight children to death.

For more than a year, the ruling circles had been promising that all of the accumulated problems would be resolved at a special Plenum of the CPSU Central Committee on the national question. This Plenum was regularly postponed, primarily because neither Gorbachev nor his close advisers had any firm ideas with regard to the national question. The authorities could not bring themselves simply to wash their hands of it and thus travel further along the road of dismantling the empire – thereby at least removing from Moscow the responsibility for the endless political catastrophes in the borderlands – but nor could they propose their own initiatives without deciding to support one side against the other or at least take on the role of intermediary. No one proposed to the warring parties that they sit round a negotiating table, and Moscow avoided contact at any level with representatives of the mass national movements, who were quietly left to their own devices. Moscow's 'passive intervention' into the conflicts was the worst possible alternative. Instead of a more or less regulated dissolution of the empire or an active struggle to maintain it, the Gorbachev leadership was drawn into a senseless process of 'Lebanonization' of Soviet society. Every national community, every bureaucratic mafia realized that their interests could be preserved by enhancing their own powers. Just as in the Lebanon, small militias began to form which had every chance of growing into real private armies over time. Help was no longer expected from the central state and they were not afraid of it. The best the weaker side could hope for was that Russian soldiers would defend it from violence. No one was able, and no one tried, to prevent the national conflicts.

The latest postponement of the long-awaited Plenum on the national question followed in July against the background of catastrophe in virtually all republics. As before, Gorbachev and his entourage were patently unprepared for a serious dialogue with the national movements. However, whereas the Plenum's deferment had previously been accepted comparatively calmly because hopes were still retained in the Congress of People's Deputies, this time the authorities were so overtly acknowledging their own powerlessness that it only served to provoke new crises.

Nor was the state of affairs in Russia especially heartening for Gorbachev's group. The seat of the most profound political crisis was Leningrad, where ruling apparatchiks had suffered a disastrous defeat in the elections. At the end of June 1989, the founding congress took place of the Leningrad Popular Front (LPF), which was swiftly gaining strength after the elections.

Although the Leningraders were a month behind the Muscovites, their founding congress was rather more representative than ours. According to the figures of the organizing committee, about five thousand activists participated in electing the Congress's seven hundred delegates. Even if these figures were exaggerated (which some leading members of the Leningrad PF candidly admitted), it is still quite obvious that the numbers taking part in the movement there were roughly three times greater than in Moscow where the number of activists in the Moscow PF did not exceed 1,200. Unlike in Moscow, where the local media had boycotted the PF conference, the Leningrad press could not but take notice of the Popular Front. In fact it was the Leningraders' success which helped the Muscovites to break the information blockade – after the Leningrad congress, reports of the Moscow PF and its founding conference belatedly appeared in the pages of Moscow publications.

The ideological struggle within the Front in Leningrad was also rather less intense and outwardly the Leningrad PF seemed rather more homogeneous than the Moscow PF. As in Moscow, the documents presented to the congress reinforced the movement's socialist orientation but, unlike Moscow, they were not subjected to criticism either from the Left or from the Right. But, to make up for it, in Moscow, the programmatic documents were rather more carefully rewritten and the socialist orientation rather more emphasized. Workers' self-management was mentioned in the LPF documents, but it was clearly not the key link in the proposed strategy. In first place were general demands for civil liberties and declarations about the need for the foundation of a legal state. The foremost practical task was clearly the removal of the discredited city Party leadership and, above all, the *gorkom* First Secretary, V. Solov'ev.

On the whole, the Leningrad documents displayed the obvious influence of the ideas of social democracy, but even more so the influence of the programme and experience of the Estonian Popular Front. The social-democratic ideas were here presented in their 'Estonian' interpretation (combined with utopian projects for 'regional self-financing', about which none of its advocates could say anything more definite). At the same time, unlike in Moscow, no one directly demanded that the Front repudiate socialist ideology since, on the whole, ideology was here of little interest.

One could say that the already well-known difference between the ideologically motivated and radical Muscovites and the moderately pragmatic Leningraders was once again being displayed. Moderate pragmatism also distinguished the leaders of the Leningrad movement in their relations with the state. In their conflict with the local bosses, the LPF preferred not to provoke the central authorities and avoided radical demands of a general political character. Anti-Gorbachev feelings, typical of many activists in Moscow, were almost invisible here.

Forms of practical activity were also different. In Moscow, the meeting campaign and the struggle for power on the streets in May and June 1989 showed the Front's real strength, while the Leningraders preferred to put the emphasis on educational work and the meticulous organization of election campaigns. While being outwardly more homogeneous, the LPF was not devoid of internal contradictions. There was a total lack of long-term strategy and the leaders could only suggest in an embarrassed fashion that this would be drawn up at the next stage. As in Moscow, few workers had joined the movement and support groups in the enterprises were noticeably less developed than the territorial groups. Despite the predominance of intellectuals in the movement, a shortage of competent political cadres and lack of theory was also felt.

Paradoxically, irrespective of all the ideological and political differences between them, all the Popular Fronts were the same type of organization. While the national factor in the Baltic republics permitted such a movement, and not without the help of part of the local apparatus, to gather strength, their establishment in Russia progressed slowly. A crisis would frequently develop so rapidly that some forms of mass democratic movement would become obsolete before they were able to fulfil their potential. This is precisely how things went with the Popular Fronts.

Sensing a growing danger in Leningrad, both conservative and liberal circles in the apparatus began to take their own steps. The Lengingrad Workers' United Front (LOFT) was formed with amazing rapidity in parallel to the LPF. The Leningrad press impassively asserted that both Fronts 'proclaim generally identical programmes', but at the founding conference of LOFT 'Nina Andreeva's intervention was greeted with applause. Furthermore, Nina Andreeva was proposed for the Front's council, but she declined to accept.'[5] The foundation of LOFT seriously altered the situation. For the first time, an organized Stalinist opposition which endeavoured to base itself in the working class appeared alongside the liberal Fronde, with its base in the mass media, a dissident movement like the DU, nationalists grouped in various versions of *Pamyat'* and left-wingers, who gravitated towards the Popular Front.

LOFT's leaders declared it to be an organization representing, above all, workers and defending the traditional values of Soviet society. While sharply condemning the political struggle of the Popular Fronts, LOFT simultaneously called for unleashing a struggle for workers' economic rights. Agitation in favour of purely economic strikes to destabilize the economy fitted quite naturally into the Stalinists' political doctrine, but the appearance of LOFT signified a new headache for liberal apparatchiks in Moscow. For all the sympathy of many bureaucrats at the centre and in the localities for the new organization, it was patently not just a simple puppet of the conservative wing of the apparatus. Uniting, in the first instance, the ideological intelligentsia close to the apparatus – who for a long time had been nourished on the teaching of 'social sciences' according to Stalinist textbooks and were unsettled and craving revenge – this movement became a serious political problem primarily for the liberal section of the nomenklatura. Combatting this new organization meant, in a sense, firing at one's own troops, but to allow its free development was also risky – the outbursts of LOFT's 'lumpen-bureaucrats' had been overly threatening and irresponsible.

The Workers' United Front rapidly formed a branch in Moscow and also established links with the conservative Stalinist leadership of Intermovement in the Baltic republics. On this basis the All-Union Workers' United Front (VOFT) was founded in June.

Alas, this was all of little comfort to Solov'ev and his crew in Leningrad. Gorbachev and his entourage had drawn their own conclusions from the Leningrad crisis. After Gorbachev's sudden 'raid' on Leningrad, Solov'ev was removed from his post and replaced by Gidaspov. In his first interview, the new Party leader declared his intention to collaborate with the Popular Front, but was immediately corrected by Gorbachev sitting next to him: 'with both fronts'.

Although neither LOFT nor its Moscow branch were in a position to enlist the support of a significant number of workers, LOFT's agitation among the workers and its co-operation with Intermovement in the national republics clearly exposed the Popular Front's weakness. While it had no intention of creating a firm base in the enterprises and remained purely 'communalistic' and organized along territorial lines, the PF movement did not have sufficient opportunities to oppose LOFT effectively in the localities. Only the common sense displayed by the workers and the growing consciousness of their own genuine interests hindered the success of the Stalinist agitation. Meanwhile, it was becoming more and more obvious that it was precisely the workers' support which would determine the success or failure of the new democratic organizations.

The liberal deputies of the 'Moscow group', however, thought rather differently. Even after the strike movement had added to the unrest on national soil, liberal leaders continued to seek salvation in purely parliamentary combinations. All endeavours were directed primarily at replacing the compromised facade of the 'Moscow group' with something more effective. The 'Inter-Regional Group of Deputies' was formed, which united progressive deputies naturally on the basis of support for the Muscovites' platform. Here a small number of radicals, particularly from the provinces, found themselves, as at the Congress, playing the role of extras.

'If the Congress had proceeded along the path we proposed, there would have been neither strikes, nor excesses in Abkhazia', solemnly declared Gavriil Popov, who was presiding at a meeting of the group and thereby indirectly acknowledging the Congress's failure. The progressive minority did not, however, wish to take upon itself the responsibility for that failure. Nor did it throw down an overt challenge to the ruling circles. Having created a parliamentary minority fraction, the liberals continued to repeat like an incantation: 'We are not the opposition!'[6] And this did indeed correspond to reality. A rebellion on one's knees cannot turn into a real political struggle.

The elections for the group's president proved another unpleasant surprise for its organizers. The provincials who had joined the group voted overwhelmingly for Yeltsin. For purposes of balance it was decided to have some joint-presidents, which allowed Popov and Afanasyev to have their share of power.

Yeltsin's unity with the liberals in one fraction proved an unsatisfatory solution for both parties. On the one hand, Yeltsin would now in reality have to take responsibility for the economic projects of the Moscow liberals, which clearly had nothing in common with the notions of social justice popular among his supporters. On the other hand, the liberals themselves, having let Yeltsin be elected president of the group, were once again permitting the disgraced Party leader to demonstrate that he was the dominant figure in the opposition and the only conceivable alternative to Gorbachev in the present situation. The only trouble was that Yeltsin's success as leader of the parliamentary opposition was achieved against a background of universal disenchantment in the peculiar bureaucratic parliamentarism which had emerged during the Congress of People's Deputies. The role of leader of a disjointed and ineffective opposition in an impotent and undemocratic parliament could scarcely be called especially advantageous.

The belated consolidation and political manoeuvrings of the 'Inter-Regional Group' did little to change the overall balance of political forces. Time had been lost. The actual founding of the group, which during the Congress or at least immediately after its close would have proved the most prominent political event, now failed to attract any special attention from the public. Even liberal newspapers did not risk publishing front-page reports of its founding meeting and only gave attention to it alongside other, clearly more important happenings: the murder of the journalist, Vladimir Glotov, who had come into conflict with the mafia; meetings, disturbances and demonstrations in various parts of the country. Henceforth, the growth of the workers' movement was becoming the key factor in the political process. The future course of events depended heavily on its development.

NOTES

1. *Izvestiya*, 22 July 1989.
2. *Pravda*, 15 July 1989.
3. *Izvestiya*, 17 July 1989.
4. See Boris Kagarlitsky: *Leningradskie zametki* in *Levyi Povorot*, nos 7–8, 1988.
5. *Smena*, 18 June 1989.
6. *Literaturnaya Gazeta*, 2 August 1989, p. 2.

11

Yet Another Hot Summer

The summer of 1989 proved, to all appearances, to be a turning-point in the process of social struggle gripping our country. On the one hand, national conflicts reached an unprecedented acuteness and led to armed clashes in the USSR's southern republics; and on the other, the country was shaken by workers' strikes, which were incomparably stronger and better organized than before. Large-scale strikes had taken place previously – one has only to recall the strike in Novocherkassk in 1962, which ended in mass disturbances and the massacre of strikers by troops. Numerous strikes also spontaneously occurred subsequently. This time, however, it was not a question of isolated enterprises but of whole regions.

It would have been easy to predict the inevitable growth of a strike movement in a worsening economic crisis, but what did take many by surprise was the speed and scale on which it took place. The hopes of those who believed that the Congress of People's Deputies would lead to a swift change in the situation were patently unfounded. The pseudo-parliamentary struggle was a brilliant show for millions of TV viewers, and no less exciting for its participants, but the battles conducted in the Kremlin in no way affected the masses' real situation and gave no hope for a rapid and genuine improvement. It became evident to the masses that neither the Moscow liberals nor the highest echelons in Moscow could or, indeed, did wish to help them. All that remained was to rely on oneself and to act independently.

The strike wave was initiated by the actions of the Mezhdurechensk miners, who demanded an improvement in living conditions, a change in the wage system, and the granting of economic autonomy to the mines and other enterprises owned both by the state and by collective farms. The miners allied with workers in other enterprises in the town to demand from the authorities the immediate promulgation of a law on strikes and 'to publish in all the central newspapers' an appeal to the Supreme Soviet, adopted at a strikers' meeting on 13 July.[1] The workers formed their own strike committee, later renaming it a 'workers' committee'.

The crisis in Mezhdurechensk was brought under control comparatively quickly and the official organs promised to 'investigate' and examine the miners' demands 'according to established legal procedure'. The most straightforward economic demands were satisfied at once. By midday on 13 July the strike committee had already called on the miners to resume working and a large number of strikers began to return to the coalface. Nevertheless, in a situation of growing social tension, the Mezhdurechensk strike acted as a spark in a powder-magazine. One after another, strikes began in the mines of the Kuznetsk coalfield (Kuzbass). Strike committees formed in Kiselevsk, Prokop'evsk, Novokuznetsk, Kemerovo, Leninske-Kuznetsk, Anzhero-Sudzhensk, and other places. Each instance brought forth its own particular demands but, on the whole, the majority of collectives strove for one and the same thing. In Prokop'evsk, a regional strike committee was formed. The authorities naturally did everything in their power to bring the conflict under control as swiftly as possible but, by the time the strike had come to an end in Siberia, miners in Donetsk and Karaganda, and then the Western Ukraine and Vorkuta, were on strike. This chain reaction was caused by the fact that, initially, the authorities published no information about the content of the signed agreements. After work came to a halt in the Donbass, the official press claimed that the strike was 'snowballing'.[2] Worst of all for the authorities was the influence the miners were having on workers in other industries. Many workers declared that, in the present economic climate, it was better to strike than to work since chaos would still increase anyway. Appeals for strike action began to be heard on the railways and airlines. In the latter case, the newspaper *Vozdushnyi Transport* (Air Transport) had to acknowledge that 'strikes are, in no sense, evidence of the collectives' extremism, but are first and foremost the result of the impotence of the economic planners, Party and social organizations'.[3] The uncertainty of the situation heightened tension. No one was able to clarify whether the agreements reached in one region would be extended to others.

The strikes progressed in an unexpectedly organized fashion. Efim Ostrovsky, an activist in the Moscow Popular Front, who happened to be in Prokop′evsk in the very first days of the strike, declared that he had the feeling of being in a scene from Andrzej Wajda's film *Man of Iron*. As during the Polish strikes of 1980, the sale of alcoholic drinks was stopped by order of the strike committee and the workers themselves maintained order on the streets. A massive placard on the railway line into town announced: 'Prokop′evsk is on strike'. People gathered in Lenin Square, where in effect an uninterrupted meeting was going on. Many remained there for days on end. The strike committee also met there. Events in Mezhdurechensk had earlier taken a similar path. In Anzhero-Sudzhensk, however, it was decided to assemble people in the enterprises as, in the strike committee's opinion, this permitted 'better control of the situation'.

As local newspapers acknowledged, the strike committees had become 'the actual centre of popular power'. 'Life in town under strike conditions demanded great organizational efforts', reported the newspaper, *Kuzbass*, on 20 July,

> and the solution of hundreds of problems, large and small: supplying the town; unloading food that had been delivered; helping the villages; maintaining the mines in a state of operational readiness. Members of the committee undertook this all themselves and coped with it not at all badly.[4]

By decision of the strike committee, some enterprises did not stop work since their normal functioning was essential to ensure the population's normal daily routine. Transport continued to operate and the pharmaceuticals factory did not cease activity although its collective had declared its support for the strike.

The strike committees even undertook the function of struggling with corruption! In Anzhero-Sudzhensk large stores of goods in short supply, hidden away by speculators, were unearthed. The central press reported with alarm that, in Prokop'evsk, workers had independently conducted an inspection of the flats of a number of 'leading workers'. *Trud*, the organ of the official unions, citing these facts, stated that 'events are assuming a dramatic character'.[5]

From the very beginning, the attitude of the local authorities to events was ambivalent. A significant section of the apparatus of economic management openly supported the miners when it was a question of a struggle against the 'departmental colonial policy'.[6] The First Secretary of the Kiselevsk *gorkom* of the CPSU, Yuri Torubarov, while declaring that he considered strikes to be an 'unacceptable' form of struggle, at the same time conceded that 'Many of the demands advanced by Mezhdurechensk, and which judging by preliminary discussions are also supported by our miners, are justified.'[7]

In a majority of cases, the Party organs not only avoided, as far as possible, direct conflicts with the strikers but also strove to use the strike to achieve the fulfilment of their own particular demands from Moscow in the form of additional funds, resources and supplies. The director of one enterprise even joined the strike committee with the right to a consultative vote and he endeavoured to have included in the list of demands a production inventory, which had to be supplied to the mines and which he had, for a long time, been unable to obtain by 'normal' bureaucratic means. While collaborating with the strike committees, 'executives' were simultaneously concerned that the strikers did not display any 'extremism', did not advance any 'unacceptable' political demands and did not come into contact with 'trouble-makers' from unofficial organizations and movements.

At the same time, some steps were taken to frustrate the strike. Goods in short supply unexpectedly appeared in shops. The inhabitants of the mining settlements considered such a miracle to be nothing other than an attempt to draw people away from the meetings. In an interview with the local paper, *Shakhterskaya Pravda*, the president of the union committee at the Dzerzhinsky and Prokop'evsk mines reported that 'my wife was able to buy mayonnaise freely in a dairy shop'.[8] But there were also more serious matters. The prosecutor of Seleznev *oblast* turned to the strikers and declared that 'strikers are committing unlawful acts, in particular the picketing of places of work'.[9] Typically, the decision, which in fact banned the picketing of state enterprises and institutions, had been taken earlier in order to restrict the activity of informal political groupings, and especially the ecological movement, which had frequently adopted such methods. It now became clear that this same law could also be turned against workers if so desired.

Despite the fact that, on the whole, the Party apparatus successfully prevented the promotion of political demands, conflict between workers and apparatchiks periodically came into the open. Time and again, the workers would begin to demand the dismissal of one functionary or another and some 'leading cadres' would begin to justify themselves. The above-mentioned Torubarov appealed to a miners' meeting with the words: 'My dear fellows! Am I really to blame for the fact that our town is considered the most difficult in the Russian Federation?!' 'We're tired of being patient!' roared the crowd in reply. 'Talks between the First Secretary and the assembled miners did not, unfortunately, take place', the local paper stated phlegmatically, 'The other leaders decided not to continue the dialogue'.[10]

The official unions found themselves in the most difficult position. The strike began against their will and members of union committees not only did not join strike committees but were often the last to find out what was happening. The president of the local territorial committee of the mineworkers' union, M. Grinenko, explained in the pages of *Shakhterskaya Pravda* that he had simply not been in Prokop'evsk during the main events, but he was found guilty by journalism: 'I saw you in a shop, you bought some sour cream (*smetana*)' (for some reason the subject of purchases in dairy shops cropped up repeatedly in conversations between journalists and trade union officials). While not denying that he had bought the *smetana*, Comrade Grinenko insisted that at that moment he knew nothing about the strike. 'Then I found about the strike, but I didn't go there immediately. I just didn't know what to do.'[11]

The trade union apparatus, nevertheless, managed to overcome its initial confusion and 'jumped on the bandwagon'. While not adopting a clear position *vis-à-vis* the strikes or taking part in their organization, the official unions did not come out against the workers. They organized the supply of hot meals at meetings, paid for out of union funds, and, meanwhile, launched an initiative at a higher level. The central committee of the mineworkers' union proposed its own five demands to the Ministry of the Mining Industry, which generalized the miners' basic demands: the pit collectives themselves to be allowed to determine the regime of work and rest; the introduction of a common day off on Sundays; the payment of evening and night shifts at the higher rate established in 1987; the introduction of payment for time lost by miners travelling from the pit-shaft to their workplace and back; and the assignment of priority investment to the social sphere.[12]

These demands reflected the workers' real interests but were advanced too late, at a time when the miners were already able to manage quite well without the mediation of their union. Neither in Moscow, nor in the localities, did official union organs play any serious role in the negotiations, which were conducted directly between representatives of the authorities and the strike committees, which in reality looked after the workers' economic interests.

The reaction of the official press to the strikes was contradictory. It was a fact that July 1989 was not the first time the miners had been on strike. Over the preceding months, dozens of local miners' strikes had taken place and some, for example in Norilsk, had been very tense affairs. The official press had kept silent about all this. But this time keeping quiet was inconceivable. The papers not only reported on the strikes but wrote sympathetic articles, emphasizing the restraint and discipline of the workers. The journalists were particularly pleased that, in a majority of cases, the strike committees did not advance political demands. At the same time, the papers did not let slip the opportunity to mention the economic harm being inflicted by the strike. *Pravda* reminded its readers that 'this is already threatening to lead, in the next few days, to serious disruption of the work of ferrous metallurgy and thermal electric power stations, which utilize Kuznetsk coal'.[13] Immediately following this, letters from workers condemning the strike began to appear in the pages of *Pravda*. Similar items appeared in the local press. At the same time all the strikers' demands to be given the opportunity to express themselves directly in the pages of the central or republican press were ignored.

It was not surprising, therefore, that, despite the comparatively objective account of the course of the strike in the official press, the miners' dissatisfaction with newspaper articles intensified. This was felt especially acutely outside the Kuzbass, where the newspapers in the mining communities at any rate published all the documents of the strike committees. In Kazakhstan the position of the republican and central press was one of the causes of the strike. Even official organs were forced to recognize this:

> Representatives of labour collectives, which have halted the extraction of coal, justified this decision on the grounds that not all the points of the Kuzbass miners' demands had been published in the mass media. Discontent has also been provoked by the absence of guarantees in the declarations made at a session of the USSR Supreme Soviet that the satisfaction of the demands of workers in the Kuzbass coal enterprises would be extended in full measure to miners in the Karaganda coalfield'.[14]

In a majority of cases, despite the readiness of part of the local bureaucracy to support the miners, conflicts arose with one organ or another of local power or with specific bosses. The official press asserted that

> Things today are rather more serious than they might seem ... Today, there are few explanations to the effect that the strikers' conception of how to get out of the economic and social collapse in which the people of Novokuznetsk have found themselves reflects that of the town authorities ... There are also few declarations to the effect that Party and economic leaders in the town are at one with the strikers.[15]

These declarations were often uncorroborated. In Karaganda, a functionary of the CPSU *gorkom* admitted to me in a private conversation that the Party apparatus had given instructions to 'its people' to join in the strike, help maintain order and, at the same time, avoid the promotion of extremist demands. However, judging by the reaction of rank-and-file miners to the speeches of Party apparatchiks, such a position was no guarantee that the authority of official Party organs would be strengthened among the masses. Meanwhile, the administrative apparatus in the localities was often even less capable of political flexibility and frequently only increased the number of conflicts. For example, the director of the Karaganda mine and a majority of the managerial and engineering workers who supported him refused to collaborate with the strike committee in the maintenance of order at the pit, after which the strike committee actually dismissed the administration. Its president, Marash Nurtazin, then assumed the powers of director, declaring that he had no intention of giving in to them after the strike had ended: the workers themselves could cope perfectly well with all the tasks of management.

Demands were spontaneously advanced for the management to be elected and for self-management; much was said about the right to strike, about independent trade unions, and also about guarantees that participants in and organizers of the strikes would not be victimized. Workers insisted on the removal of some of the most unpopular economic – and sometimes even Party – leaders. On the whole, however, the miners did not go beyond economic questions, insisting primarily on an increase in wages, the granting of autonomy to the mines, an improvement in food supplies to the mining villages and towns, the introduction of additional measures for the protection of labour, pensions and social security, and so on. Demands relevant to the Soviet Union as a whole were often advanced. Thus, alongside its demands affecting the coal industry, the Karaganda strike committee insisted that all women 'should be paid an allowance for child-care over three years at a minimum wage rate no lower than the price index established for each region'.[16]

Despite the fact that the strikers had made a declaration about miners' solidarity, direct links were not established between the various regions' strike committees. Participants in the movement knew little about what was happening in other places. When Efim Ostrovsky and I brought a bundle of newspapers into Karaganda with information from the Kuzbass, this was seized by members of the local strike committee with great enthusiasm, but the strike committee itself still did nothing to establish links with other centres of the strike. Moreover, on the few occasions when the collectives of industrial enterprises intended to join the miners, the strike committees met them with a rebuff. This happened in Kemerovo and a few other places.

Many of the demands advanced were naturally repeated by different strike committees in different parts of the country, but each time the overall list was altered. In some cases, the demands were not well-formulated and were open to various interpretations. For example, in Karaganda, the 'regulation of prices' was demanded simultaneously with the demand that prices should be set according to the minimum wage (when it is precisely the minimum wage that depends on the level of prices and not vice-versa). Addressing the miners, deputy T. G. Avaliani declared that 'the strikers' demands have not been thought through to the end and they are not clearly formulated. It will take a minimum of 24 hours to finish them off'.[17]

In the end, the strike committees gained a degree of freedom by selecting from among the demands and slogans voiced during meetings or proposed by pits those that seemed the most important or the most acceptable to the authorities. The Kuzbass regional strike committee, headed by Avaliani, found itself in a paradoxical situation: on the one hand, its leaders to a significant extent determined independently the basic tasks of the strike and took decisions which frequently did not enjoy the support of a large section of the miners. On the other hand, replacing the strike committee, even in those instances when the masses were displeased, did not occur to anyone. No mechanism had been worked out for the masses' control over their representatives. The strike committees were indeed elected democratically, but events developed so quickly that the strike committees began to lag behind them. Lack of political experience and expertise and skill in handling negotiations had an effect and was felt especially keenly by the end of the strike.

Official propaganda continually frightened the workers with visions of extremists and 'informals', travelling the country and inciting the people to revolt. Particular reference was made to the activities of the Democratic Union. In Kemerovo, there were actually a few members of the DU, but they played no special role during the course of the strike. We were unable to discover any followers of the DU either in Prokop'evsk or Karaganda where members of the Moscow Popular Front and Committee of New Socialists were present.

The strikers were extremely wary of the 'newcomers'. Strike leaders were afraid of the strike's politicization. Joint work with representatives of the government had given them hope of a quick settlement of all demands and any political activity, in their opinion, could ruin the achievement of an agreement. In Karaganda, the initial appearance of members of the Moscow PF provoked enthusiasm in the strike committee and one of its members even copied out credentials for the newcomers, declaring that the strikers needed consultants. A while later, however, the strike committee president, Petr Shlegel', insisted that we leave the committee meeting. The local newspaper rushed to report this, quoting

Shlegel' as saying: 'We don't need any help from the Moscow Popular Front, we can deal with our own problems ourselves.'[18]

The mood of rank-and-file miners was rather more radical. At a meeting in Karaganda, the audience actively supported Ostrovsky, who spoke about the impossiblity of demands being limited to the purely economic, and they would not listen to a speaker who then tried to argue with him. Many wanted to find out more about the Popular Front and the emergent Socialist Party. References to Gorbachev, as a rule, only provoked annoyance.

A three-day meeting in Karaganda, at which I managed to speak myself, reminded me of films of the 1917 Revolution. Some miners remained in the Square for all three days so as not to miss anything. They were tired and hungry but didn't want to leave, as if a few people departing might change something. In Prokop'evsk, the official unions at the last moment had the sense to begin providing hot drinks. But nothing like that happened in Karaganda, though the miners lived for three days in the central square.

The most important thing was that people felt they were free. The people I spoke with in Karaganda repeated unanimously that if, even the day before, they had been told they would be on strike, they would not have believed it. I was told this not only by rank-and-file miners but also by members of the strike committees, even the most radical ones. In Karaganda, I was impressed by the miners' internationalism: Russians, Kazakhs, Germans, Crimean Tatars, Caucasians were all united. Against the background of the numerous national conflicts which were gripping the country, the miners' movement demonstrated traditional proletarian values.

On the whole, the movement was becoming politicized. Miners from Vorkuta and the Western Ukraine, although the last to join the strike, already spoke openly about free trade unions. The authorities, in their turn, insisted that political demands would not even be considered. Paradoxically, the government had driven itself into a corner: if political demands were 'impermissible', then the economic ones would remain, to a large extent, unrealizable. The country did not have the means to satisfy completely the multifarious demands of workers in the coal industry. But, in the meantime, the threat of a rail strike compelled the start of negotiations on raising wages in that sector as well. It was not only the danger of inflation that limited the authorities' potential to make concessions. People were demanding real goods: food and soap. But no goods were available – they could only be transferred from one region to another, which only destabilized further regions of the country!

At first, the government entered into separate negotiations with each regional strike in isolation. This gave the government commissions greater room for manoeuvre and reduced to a minimum the risk of the appearance of a single, leading centre or the advancement of common political demands. Second, the government commissions promised to satisfy almost all the workers' demands even when they realized that, most probably, they would not be completely fulfilled. It was assumed that the miners would be satisfied with the first package of immediate measures agreed at the negotiations with the strike committees, and that the more complex questions would be postponed. The most important thing in this situation was to bring an end to the strike at any price.

On the whole, this tactic worked quite well. Both strike committees and workers suspected, however, that the questions postponed till later would, most likely, not be resolved at all. The strike committees demanded the right to supervise the implementation of the agreements and declared that they reserved the right to resume the strike. The authorities were even prepared to go that far while simultaneously taking measures to 'tame' the workers' leaders. The miners, in turn, felt increasingly mistrustful of the strike committees.

The sharpest conflict broke out in Prokop'evsk. We will let *Shakhterskaya Pravda*, which published an hour-by-hour chronicle of events, have its say:

The loudspeaker voice continuously reports that an agreement, meeting 70 per cent of the workers' demands, has been signed between the Kuzbass strike committees, the CPSU Central Committee Commission, USSR Council of Ministers and the All-Union Central Trade Union Council. But the loudspeaker voice is not being heard. No one is listening to it. They are talking among themselves.

But now it has all calmed down. Over the radio can be heard the town strike committee's appeal to the workers: the strike is temporarily halted from 8 a.m. on 19 July 1989.

A murmur rolls across the Square: 'This is disinformation! Our strike committee hasn't signed any agreement! It can't do that without consulting with people.

'Any proposal to end the strike must be put to a general vote. But if the committee really have signed an agreement behind the backs of the people, then it means they've deceived us.'

VOICE FROM THE LOUDSPEAKER: 'Comrades! We ask you all to vacate the Square and turn up for work!'

'It's a provocation!'

WHISTLES. SHOUTS.

The square is getting agitated. 'Volodya, tell us: is this what happened? Have you signed an agreement?'

The microphone is silent. Strike committee members spread their hands helplessly. They say neither 'yes' nor 'no'. They are not yet ready for a frank discussion with the people.'[19]

It was only at the expense of considerable efforts that the strike committee managed to force the Prokop'evsk miners to return to the coalface. Similar conflicts arose in one form or another at all centres of the strike. In the Donbass, it took the strike committees several days to persuade the miners to resume working. In Karaganda, the Kostenko pit, which was one of the last to join the strike, refused to go back to work along with the rest.

Nevertheless, once the agreements had been signed the miners had little option but to return to work. Only a unified national miners' organization could have prolonged the struggle and such an organization had not been created during the strike. As a result, each pit and each region finally found itself in a one-to-one situation with the authorities and everyone realized that there was no point in continuing the strike in isolation.

The outcome of the strike once again showed the necessity for the formation of a unified political organization capable of undertaking co-ordinating functions. The new workers' movement had neither national leaders nor experienced activists able to defend workers' interests *politically* and at a national level. There were not only no free trade unions but also no unified organizational centre which could further the creation of such unions. True, in the spring of 1989 in Moscow, the Association of Socialist Trade Unions of the USSR (Sotsprof) was founded, whose activity was closely linked to the efforts to create the Socialist Party. Such organizations were, however, as yet unable to gather strength, develop their own political profile or declare themselves a national force.

The liberal Moscow public did not conceal its hostility to the strikers. Well-known economists argued in the pages of *Izvestiya* that the mass movement 'is no better than administrative diktat'. P. Bunich, one of the experts in the Moscow deputies' group, called on the workers 'to refrain from such extreme forms of protest. Strikes do not bring us any nearer to a normal life, but take us further away from it'.[20] In Bunich's opinion, all the workers' hopes should be placed on various parliamentary commissions which would, in the near future, prepare salutary new legislation capable of bringing the economic crisis to an end.

Appeals for moderation patently missed their mark. If Bunich had been in the mining communities, if he had listened to miners speaking at meetings, if he had thought even a little about the real problems of their lives, he would probably have been ashamed to come out with such arguments. The needs and troubles of 'ordinary' people are, however, of little interest to the rising stars of the new Soviet parliamentarism.

Unfortunately, the mass radical movements like the Popular Fronts were also divorced from the workers' movement. In Estonia, where the majority of workers were Russian, the Popular Front came into conflict with the strike committees, which were acting chiefly in defence of the national rights of the Russian minority. On 24–25 July, strikes began in Tallin in protest at the new Estonian electoral law which, on the basis of a residency qualification (five years in one place or fifteen years within the republic) deprived about 100,000 of the republic's Russian inhabitants of the right to vote. The leadership of the strikes remained, in turn, in the hands of management or the Stalinist-minded leaders of Intermovement, who as a rule gave very little thought to the workers' class interests.

The Popular Fronts in Russia also played no major role in these events. Workers who had joined the Popular Fronts were generally in a minority with very little influence over the Fronts' activity. Workers had shown positive support during the meetings and electoral campaigns organized by the PF in various parts of the country, but the PF's activity remained very distant from the day-to-day problems of people in production. The powerful electoral movement which the Popular Front had gradually become was incapable of resolving the tasks of free trade unions or of substituting for a Socialist Party. Precisely because the formation of such a party had already commenced within the ranks of the Moscow Popular Front – the Moscow Committee of New Socialists – we were more or less ready for a dialogue with the workers.

The fact that the growth of the strike movement opened up new prospects for left-wing socialist forces did not escape Gorbachev's attention. Speaking at a session of the CPSU Central Committee at the very height of the strikes, he acknowledged that 'left-radical moods' had begun to grow in the country. The leader of perestroika quite correctly saw in this a threat to his economic course and rushed to accuse the Left of profiting irresponsibly 'from demands for social justice in the spirit of universal egalitarianism'.[21] In reality, it was precisely the policy of social irresponsibility, the implementation of reforms in the interests of the ruling apparatus, privileged strata of the capital's intelligentsia and the 'new rich' at the expense of the masses, which had provoked the workers' increasing discontent. For Gorbachev, the danger of the left-wing alternative consisted in the fact that the Left posed the question of changing the goal of reform and its reorientation from the interests of privileged layers to the interests of the masses. Such a reorientation was, however, unacceptable to Gorbachev's circle, who saw the spectre of 'wage-levelling' in any attempt to defend the lower orders' material interests.

All things considered, the leader of perestroika was deeply worried. On television he seemed dismayed; he started grumbling in his speeches. Gorbachev complained about the press for undermining the Party's authority, appealed to everyone for consolidation, but proposed nothing specific. It was evident that he had finally lost control of the situation.

Meanwhile, the Supreme Soviet, to which not one of the leaders of the Moscow group had been elected, underwent an unexpected radicalization. Apparently, the absence of eminent Moscow orators had in no way prevented a sharp discussion. The stormy arguments in the Supreme Soviet with regard to the miners' strike led to calls for the foundation of genuine organs of self-management for independent workers' organizations and free trade unions – which the government had striven with all its might to avoid in Prokop'evsk, Karaganda and the Kuzbass – being heard on television across the entire country during broadcasts of Supreme

Soviet sessions. At the same time a sharp fall in interest in 'parliamentary' discussion was revealed. Although sessions of the Supreme Soviet had rather more substance than sessions of the Congress of People's Deputies and decided concrete questions, universal attention was no longer paid to them. This time it was not the country which followed the deputies' debates, but the deputies who endeavoured in their parliamentary interventions to keep up somehow with the country. The country's fate was clearly being decided neither by the deputies nor by the pseudo-parliamentary bodies established by Gorbachev.

The position of the General Secretary himself did not, however, become any easier because of this. In striving to keep up with events, the deputies demanded fresh concessions from him. The radicals Uoka and Boiko secured the recognition, if only in principle, of the workers' right to independent organization. Other deputies demanded the holding of local elections as early as possible and more democratic electoral laws.

Although the Party leadership had declared, immediately after the Congress of People's Deputies, that elections to city and local soviets would take place no earlier than the spring of 1990, Gorbachev was this time constrained to make concessions and to promise that elections could be held earlier. For the local Party and state apparatus, who had almost no chance of being elected, this signified the approach of a catastrophe. Meanwhile there was the threat of a resumption of the strike movement at any time. Both authorities and miners, not to mention workers in other branches, saw only a temporary compromise in the agreements that had been achieved, after which a fresh struggle would follow.

The strikes had definitively shown the groundlessness of hopes in a peaceful parliamentary and evolutionary path of moderate reform of which both progressive Party functionaries and Moscow liberals had dreamed. Events were gathering pace. The unstable compromise, which had enabled the strike to be ended, could not be maintained for long. Numerous new conflicts began to arise between the workers' committees and the authorities, after which followed fresh strikes or threats of strikes. As circumstances turned out, the miners simply had no other means of fighting for their rights. In Vorkuta and in Rostov province, strikers persisted in advancing political demands and set about the creation of new trade unions by establishing contact with Sotsprof.

The sympathetic attitude of many local officials to the strike could not prevent a number of contradictions. In fact, in the strike regions a situation of dual power came into being. 'Although the committees reject power', wrote *Literaturnaya Gazeta*, 'they have in fact had to assume some of the functions of soviets. Complaints from citizens, which previously would have been sent to Party organizations and Soviets, now come to the Kemerovo town strike committee'.[22] The co-existence of two centres of power in one territory could not continue without problems. The natural logic of events pushed both sides towards a resumption of the confrontation. What was happening was much closer to a revolutionary crisis than to 'restructuring' or the repeatedly promised but not yet delivered 'revolution from above'.

It was henceforth impossible to determine the course of events without the masses' participation. The time of the liberal project was at an end. But a new radical project was still only on the drawing-board. Society found itself in a very dangerous situation. The liberal circles, having monopolized the public consciousness and blocked as far as possible the normal development of left-radical tendencies, were unable to avert the failure of their own policies, but they hampered to the utmost the search for an alternative.

NOTES

1. *Znamya Shakhtera* (Mezhdurechensk), 15 July 1989.
2. *Sotsialisticheskaya Industriya*, 21 July 1989.
3. *Vozdushnyi Transport*, 18 July 1989.
4. *Kuzbass*, 20 July 1989.
5. *Trud*, 15 July 1989. The Kemerovo regional strike committee subsequently denied that it had supposedly organized an 'inspection of refrigerators' (see *Literaturnaya Gazeta*, 2 August 1989). More likely such actions were carried out without the authority of the regional strike committee.
6. *Kuzbass*, 20 July 1989.
7. *V boi za ugol'* (Kiselevsk), 15 July 1989.
8. *Shakhterskaya Pravda* (Prokop'evsk), 19 July 1989.
9. *V boi za ugol'*, 18 July 1989.
10. Ibid.
11. *Shakhterskaya Pravda*, 19 July 1989.
12. See *Trud*, 11 July 1989.
13. *Pravda*, 16 July 1989.
14. *Kazakhstanskaya Pravda*, 21 July 1989.
15. *Kuznetskii Rabochii*, 20 July 1989.

16. *Industrial'naya Karaganda*, 22 July 1989. Curiously, Gorbachev had spoken of this before, but later forgot his promises.
17. *V boi za ugol'*, 18 July 1989.
18. *Industrial'naya Karaganda*, 22 July 1989.
19. *Shakhterskaya Pravda*, 20 July 1989. Lack of confidence in the strike committee began to be displayed even before the agreement with the authorities was signed. Avaliani declared in this regard that 'work is being conducted in a very nervous situation' (*V boi za ugol'*, 20 July 1989).
20. *Izvestiya*, 22 July 1989.
21. *Izvestiya*, 19 July 1989.
22. *Literaturnaya Gazeta*, 2 August 1989, p. 2.

=12=

Farewell, Perestroika?

All observers are agreed that 1989 was one of the most dramatic years in the history of Russia and Eastern Europe. Europe has not known a year so packed with events at least since the end of the Second World War, and the last three months proved to be even more stormy than the whole of the preceding year.

Beginning in early spring, the severe and all-embracing crisis of the Soviet political system produced one shockwave after another, giving sustenance to the international press and completely muddling the maps of politicians accustomed to the traditional notions of a stable balance of forces in the USSR and Europe which had been maintained for decades.

First of all, there were the elections to the Congress of People's Deputies, the thousands of authorized and unauthorized meetings, the rise of the Popular Front movements in the Baltic republics and the calls for independence, no longer emanating from 'extremists' condemned by official organs, but in fact from the national Party-state apparatus itself. There was the Tbilisi tragedy – the massacre of unarmed demonstrators by special army units – and the Fergana tragedy – where troops were unable to get to the scene in time to prevent the pogroms. Abkhazians battled with Georgians, Tadzhiks with Kirghiz, Azeris with Armenians. The conflict between Russian settlers and the indigenous population of Estonia led to a general strike of the Russian-speaking working class, and in Lithuania, the traditional antagonisms between Vilnius and

Moscow were supplemented by the Polish–Lithuanian conflict which, it seemed, had receded into the past forty years ago. In this year, probably more blood has been spilt in the country than in any other year since the death of Stalin. The price of reforms? Or the price people are paying for their failure?

Then the first Congress of People's Deputies began – a brilliant television spectacle lasting for days which is preserved in history and in people's memories precisely as a media event, and which fired our imaginations but changed nothing in our lives. Dramatic debates between deputies began to be commonplace. The formation of the Inter-Regional Group of Deputies (IRG) – the first officially recognized political opposition grouping – could only be good news in that we now have an officially recognized opposition. That's all. However, the days of the Congress remain in our memories also thanks to the hundred-thousand-strong meetings at Luzhniki organized by the Moscow Popular Front – which demonstrated graphically to their participants that their opinions, their demands and their hopes were not reaching the ears of the people meeting in the Kremlin, whether supporters of 'The Government' or of 'His Majesty's Opposition'.

The result of the disillusionment in the 'constitutional creativity' of the élite and the 'constructive criticism' of the speakers of the 'parliamentary' opposition was the rise of the mass workers' movement in the summer. The miners' strike, unquestionably the biggest spontaneous strike in post-war European history, ended in a compromise agreement which both sides knew from the outset could not be implemented.

After the first Congress of People's Deputies and the wave of miners' strikes there was a brief lull in the political life of most of the country. Meetings at Luzhniki ceased; posters were torn down or removed from walls, but new ones no longer appeared in their place. Reports of mass actions came only from the Baltic republics where the anniversary of the signing of the Molotov–Ribbentrop Pact served as grounds for massive demonstrations by supporters of independence. Nevertheless, there was no drop in the political tension.

After everything that had happened in the summer, no one expected that autumn in our country would be peaceful, but the subsequent exacerbation of the political crisis proved even more serious than could have been predicted. By signing the summer agreement with the miners, the authorities had placed a time-bomb under themselves. By insisting that the workers confine themselves to economic demands and not advance political ones, the government was committed to implementing numerous measures to raise miners' living standards, although it was evident that there was neither the money nor the resources to carry them out. When it was discovered in October that the agreements were not being implemented, the government came under fire – and as a consequence was faced with both economic and political demands. Everything they had tried to avoid in July happened in November, only in circumstances even more difficult for the government. On 7 November, instead of the usual triumphal reports, the press was forced to give coverage of unofficial demonstrations, the sacking of the Ministry of Internal Affairs (MVD) building in Moldavia and the strike in Vorkuta. In Tbilisi and Yerevan, demonstrators burnt Soviet flags and, in Riga, activists of the Latvian national movement attempted to wreck the parades of the 'occupying forces'. Reports came in of strikes at several pits in the Donetsk coalfield where, instead of the customary holiday festivities, clashes occurred between workers and the forces of order. The major event was the strike at Vorkuta. This time, the miners were demanding the removal of Article 6 of the USSR Constitution on the leading role of the CPSU and the separation of Party bodies and state power. Concretely, this meant Gorbachev's resignation either from the post of President, or from the post of General Secretary of the CPSU Central Committee, and direct and equal elections to the Supreme Soviet.

Gorbachev was no longer making patronizing speeches about the miners. The Supreme Soviet passed an anti-strike law on labour conflicts, which was immediately employed against the Vorkuta miners. The strike was deemed to be unlawful and its participants were subjected to fines, and deprived of bonuses, privileges and the right to obtain accommodation within the time promised by the government.

The press was no longer talking about the prowess and virtues of the Soviet worker – the reports from Vorkuta were saturated with hatred for the strikers, who were depicted as being solely responsible for all of the country's ills. The time when the regime safeguarded glasnost had clearly receded into the past. The authorities strove to remove Vladislav Starkov – editor-in-chief of *Argumenty i Fakty*, one of the most radical and indisputably the most serious newspaper in the country – from his post. The attacks on Starkov were not the 'machinations of conservatives' and 'enemies of perestroika' – mythical figures, whom free-thinking journalists had been unsuccessfully seeking for some years (evidently through the lack of the KGB's competent assistance) – nor was there any reason to blame the 'arch-villain' Yegor Ligachev. This time, the person trying publicly to obtain the dismissal was the 'architect of perestroika' himself, 'the outstanding leader of the Soviet people', the initiator of new thinking, the father of glasnost and democracy, and the star of Western television – Mikhail Gorbachev. The authorities were patently striving to take the press into their hands and force it to serve the new tasks, to make it an instrument of normalization and to cut short any criticism of the reforms.

The strike at Vorkuta suffered defeat. This served as a signal for a spontaneous counter-attack by the bureaucratic apparatus on the workers' committees founded by the miners during the summer strikes. The formal task of these committees, which remained the sole officially recognized form of workers' self-organization, was supervision of the implementation of the summer agreement between the miners and the government. But immediately after the end of the Vorkuta strike, the creation of state social committees was announced to which the functions of supervision would be transferred. This meant that the workers' committees were automaticaly deprived of their legal status. In the Kuzbass, the authorities did not feel strong enough to disperse them directly, and proposed to the committees that they be absorbed into the structure of the official unions. In Karaganda, 'Order No. 325' was promulgated in which the administration simply annulled its former position on the workers' committee.

In the committees themselves a split was taking shape between moderates inclined (on certain conditions) to submit to the new situation and radicals intent on resistance and the preparation of new strikes. Meanwhile, the weaknesses of the committees were revealed to the utmost extent. During the strike, the movement's leaders could rely on the masses in their thousands. But when people returned to the coalface, it became clear that the committees had no apparatus, no links with the pits and were unrepresentative of people's moods. The lack of competent cadres, the poor supply of information and the undeveloped communications between committees at different levels began to tell. An attempt to solve this problem was the declaration of a Kuzbass Workers' Union, a new organization summoned to replace the crisis-ridden workers' committees. Moreover, the Workers' Union had to help overcome the gulf between the miners and workers in other sectors. It was not just the case that workers in many enterprises believed the propaganda against the miners, but that effective workers' solidarity would only become possible through the joint elaboration of demands, constant co-operation and exchange of information.

The apparatus's counter-offensive coincided with the more profound crisis of the liberal opposition. Sensing a loss of popularity, the leaders of the Inter-Regional Group, Gavriil Popov and Yuri Afanasyev, attempted to draw attention to themselves by making radical speeches and they even called for a two-hour 'warning strike' on 11 December in support of the Group's demands. Although several of these demands enjoyed the support of the workers – miners' leaders had called decisively for the repeal of Article 6 – the strike call revealed the complete impotence of the 'official opposition'. The strike simply did not take place. Even in work collectives where supporters of the IRG were in a strong position, people limited themselves to sending telegrams to the opening of the Second Congress of People's Deputies. Worker-activists referred to the appeal by IRG leaders as an attempt to 'manipulate the workers' movement'. 'If they had really wanted to march side by side with us', remarked a member of the Prokop'evsk workers' committee, 'they would have been here in the summer.'

The death of Andrei Sakharov on 15 December was yet another great blow to the liberal group. Of all the figures in the IRG only Sakharov enjoyed the indisputable authority of a moral leader, standing above personal ambition and factional squabbles. It was precisely his participation in the group that turned it from a coalition of discontented pretenders to power into a real political movement.

The second Congress of People's Deputies did not provoke either mass enthusiasm or even interest. The Moscow and Leningrad intelligentsia continued to follow the debates in the Kremlin, but in the mining centres broadcasts from the Congress were watched primarily by women and children. The preparations for the elections to the local republican soviets were also progressing limply, and many observers feared the disruption of the elections through voters failing to turn out. People no longer had any faith in the reforms.

The organization of local meetings to nominate independent candidates for the 1990 elections proved rather more difficult than during the previous year, although the unofficial organizations themselves had become stronger, had recruited new members and gained experience. A large number of independent candidates were still nominated and registered in many parts of the country, but this had little in common with the situation in spring 1989. Activists of the various political groups were increasingly enthusiastic about the new elections at which their organizations were granted a first opportunity to gain a number of seats – but, alas, the electorate did not display a similar level of enthusiasm.

Conflicts within and between unofficial organizations were exacerbated. The Moscow PF Co-ordinating Council in practice ceased to meet and the basic core of activists who had founded the organization a year before were either busy in the support groups for democratic candidates in their districts or placed their hopes in the project to create a Socialist Party. The exhaustion of the old forms of organization and struggle, typical of the 'epoch of perestroika', was evident to the overwhelming majority of the Left.

Good news was coming in from the 'fraternal countries' of Eastern Europe. One bureaucratic regime after another was collapsing like a set of dominoes. In Poland, the elections conducted on the basis of a compromise between the regime and the opposition – a compromise reached to ensure the maintenance of 'the leading and directing role of the sole and ruling party' – led to the formation of a Sejm which happily removed that party from power. Then the 'leading and directing' party in Hungary fell to pieces in an attempt to reform itself and become more social-democratic. Then came the hot autumn. Hundreds of thousands of people thronged the centres of the main cities demanding an end to party dictatorship and the reign of the political police. The model police regime in East Germany tumbled like a house of cards. Not even a month had passed when the same fate struck the Czechoslovak government, which had prided itself on being able to feed the country without any reforms or restructuring whatsoever. In Bulgaria it was just the same and, by Christmas, Romania had risen up.

The Baltic republics suffered a certain shock. The leaders of these countries and the leaders of their democratic movements felt that the events in Eastern Europe were rapidly passing them by: striving to catch up with and overtake their neighbours turned into the driving force of political action. The Lithuanian Communist Party, which was increasingly losing its influence over the masses in the run-up to the elections to the republican Supreme Soviet, declared that it was leaving the CPSU – a move that meant, in conditions where the structure of power and the structure of the party still coincided completely, that it was in fact leaving the administrative structure of the Soviet Union. However, this was no longer sufficient. The Party split and, in Lithuania, political pluralism emerged in the shape of two communist parties. A formal declaration of independence was next. Neither Gorbachev's trip to Lithuania nor the arguments of Western politicians who attempted to show, in the pages of the Soviet press, that the Lithuanians' separatism would undermine perestroika, could halt the spontaneous process any longer. Without the use of force, Moscow could no longer have any influence on the course of events and there was neither the political will nor a favourable situation for decisive military action. However, the more the empire slid into chaos, the more dangerous the situation became and the greater became the inclination of those involved in confrontations to resort to force.

In the autumn of 1989, Georgia had became the first republic to declare its intention to form its own army. Azeri youths were not turning up at Soviet Army call-up points, and began to form Azerbaijani armed forces in preparation for a campaign against Armenia. In its turn, the Armenian Supreme Soviet announced the inclusion of Nagorny Karabakh within the republic and Armenians on the border began to take up arms on a wide scale. In January 1990, in Karabakh itself, the crackle of gunfire and the rumble of explosions could already be heard. Soviet Army patrols tried unsuccessfully to remove the weaponry, which included ground-to-ground missiles brought into Karabakh from Armenia. On 14 January, anti-aircraft guns were employed for the first time by the Azerbaijani side. An army helicopter was damaged and put out of action. Army units, transferred to the scene of events, could not break out beyond the airport at Kirovobad. The names of soldiers and officers who had been killed began to be seen in the pages of newspapers. No one knew the number of Armenian and Azeri casualties – most probably no one had counted them.

Events were acquiring a truly global scale. The success of revolutions in some countries provided the impetus for uprisings in others. Demonstrations even began in Mongolia, and in January 1990, the Albanian regime, in its turn, promised reforms after reports of protest demonstrations. It was no longer easy to tell to what extent the force of example, or to what extent 'internal factors', were in operation. The mass movement on the Soviet–Iranian frontier, where peasants tore down border fences and cut the barbed wire, might appear a distant echo of the destruction of the Berlin Wall, although in reality other considerations were also at work – the Azeri peasants, apart from anything else, were endeavouring to take possession of waste lands which had been withdrawn from circulation because of the existing procedures for guarding the frontier. Now it seemed anything was possible. The system of fear had collapsed, and along with it any notions of the limitations of the real world. When Iranian border guards began to open fire to halt the crowds crossing the Soviet frontier, the insurgents expressed their surprise – they had not given a thought to the fact that in other countries there are also border guards and a system for protecting the frontier.

The belief that the impossible no longer exists is one of the most dangerous illusions generated by the events of 1989, and the course of events quickly demonstrated this. The bloody battles on the streets of the Romanian capital were, of course, an exception but they must force us to stop and think about the real essence of the processes occurring in 'our camp'. The overthrow of the dictatorship did not signify the end of the political crisis. Already in January, new incensed crowds were appearing on the streets of Bucharest, and this time they were protesting against the policies of the new regime, demanding reprisals against supporters of Ceausescu, and calling for the banning of the Communist Party. The demand for the prohibition of the Party was conceded, but this did not solve a single one of the country's problems. The crisis continued to deepen. Vaclav Havel, just elected President of Czechoslovakia and himself a former dissident, also came in for criticism. The government formed in Poland by leading figures of Solidarity adopted, at the recommendation of the International Monetary Fund, one unpopular crisis measure after another, as a result of which popular living conditions detiorated still further. The old nomenklatura proved better prepared than the others for the new situation – the selling of shares in state enterprises and the abolition of state control over economic activity untied the hands first and foremost of the corrupt 'bureaucratic bourgeoisie'.

Generally, what we are witnessing in practice in all of these countries is not the transfer of power from one political force to another, not the victory of the 'opposition' over the 'government', but a power vacuum and looming economic disorder – the collapse of the old power structures without their replacement by new ones. It is reminiscent of Russia in February 1917. But the real, not the mythical, February was in no sense the triumph of democracy but simply chaos which had arisen as a consequence of the downfall of the 'old regime'.

The power vacuum is only one side of the coin. No less important is the economic collapse, whose chief factor is the paralysis of the system of managing the national economy. 'It is impossible to reform chaos', remarked one of the new leaders of Romania – and especially with the currently fashionable market methods. In conditions where the economy is lying in ruins even capitalist governments have inevitably been obliged to resort to the 'administrative methods' so condemned today.

Naive hopes to the effect that, through the 'liberation of market forces', the means for overcoming any difficulties will be successfully uncovered are contradicted by the reality of the worsening crisis. Attempts at 'simple market solutions' lead only to rising inflation and unemployment, foreign debt and dependence on the West, and the transition of the East European countries to the status of Third World states. As the experience of Poland, and in part Hungary, shows, increasing chaos actually hinders the formation of any sort of normal market relations.

If 'spontaneous market forces' cannot in themselves assist in overcoming the crisis, the question of power advances to the forefront – what political and social forces will be able to lead the process of transformation and begin consistently and consciously the work of overcoming the chaos.

The mafia and the old bureaucracy are the only genuine sources for the formation of a 'new bourgeoisie'. Only they have the means to buy shares in the enterprises being sold off and to acquire securities. They head the numerous mixed enterprises, which as a rule produce nothing and only ensure a steady income to their participants from all possible means of legal speculation. The power vacuum is being filled not by new forces but by social groups and clans which took shape within the old oligarchy.

The guardians of old ideas can talk about the restoration of capitalism, but the fact is that this social milieu is incapable either of creating from within itself a modern Western-style bourgeoisie or of 'building' developed capitalism. The most of which it is capable is forming a dependent, poorly developed society with a parasitic ruling class combining all the negative features of both the 'Eastern' and 'Western' models.

To one degree or another, these tendencies have been observed in a majority of the countries of the Eastern bloc. But if, in 1989, Eastern Europe discovered the joy of victory over dictatorships, then Soviet society had to share with neighbouring countries their problems and ills but not their triumphs.

The natural reaction is bitterness; disillusionment; protest. However, there are different forms of protest. The Workers' United Front which arose in summer 1989 is the logical result of mass dissatisfaction at the outcome of the liberal changes: if the changes have not improved the lives of ordinary people, would it not be better to return to the past? In the final analysis, there was no Sumgait pogrom under Brezhnev; no such severe situation in the economy; no strikes. The trouble is that today's catastrophe is the unavoidable consequence of the development of the very system to which the defenders of the good old days are summoning us to return. It is the catastrophe of a system which proved unable to construct the promised socialism but which is, in any case, no longer even capable of a transition to 'civilized' capitalism.

Appeals to 'follow the West's example' in the end leave us with the realization that we are strikingly unlike the Western world, and cannot become a part of Europe without a radical resolution of our own problems for which Western 'medicine' is inappropriate in principle. We have yet to realize fully that we are needed by the centres of contemporary advanced capitalism only as a supplier of cheap resources and as a massive (one sixth of the world!) rubbish heap for filthy technologies; and that, having lost our former strength as a superpower, we have in fact become part of the oppressed and backward majority of humanity, the Third World, with whom which we must seek our own way out of slavery and poverty.

The failure of perestroika from above has been distinctly demonstrated by the results of 1989, which patently did not coincide with the plans and calculations of its architects. Today it is already difficult to find people who are not conscious of this to one degree or another. But the coming year forces us to acknowledge another aspect of the problem: the vacuum of an alternative.

Who can fill this vacuum? The Workers' United Front with their orthodox slogans? The liberals, who have clearly exhausted their potential both ideologically and politically – in the past year they have called for progress along the same road as we are already travelling only 'more swiftly and more decisively'? The economy is on the edge of a precipice, we must take a bold step forwards!

An alternative must be created. An alternative is being born in the workers' movement, which in 1989 showed its combativity and independence. But this objectively existing social alternative must be organized and shaped *politically*. The first steps are being taken in this direction. On the one hand, an alternative trade union movement is arising independent of the state – the Association of Socialist Trade Unions (Sotsprof). On the other hand, a Socialist Party has begun to be formed – at the very end of the year, on 23–24 December, an All-Russian Committee for a Socialist Party (ACSP) was established in Moscow, at which members of the miners' strike committees were present. In the face of the masses' growing disillusionment in liberalism, increasing discontent at social injustice, and protest against the humiliating state of helplessness, backwardness and dependence in which our country (only yesterday proud of its role as a superpower) still finds itself, socialists are the sole democratic force capable of strengthening their position. If they are not successful, the vacuum will be filled by the Stalinist demagogues of the Workers' United Front and the nationalist instigators of pogroms of any nationality.

The organizational and political formation of all basic tendencies – from today's liberal opposition to extreme right-wing nationalists – is inevitable. Also inevitable is political differentiation between them. One more illusion that has died in the past year is the illusion of the 'United Front'. Now all political forces are obliged to define themselves. Confusion is at an end – as are political games, and dilletantist electoral campaigns under the slogan of 'elect good people for deputy!'. A genuine political struggle is beginning that is bitter and hard. And conclusions have to be drawn from the overall political choice made by each political organization: where do we go along with others and where do we differ in principle from our recent colleagues in the 'movement in support of perestroika'?

It is reasonable to ask: where is the 'leading and directing' party on this spectrum, what is its role in events? Alas, the CPSU has no special role in the new conditions: having become part of the state machine, it has long since ceased to be a party. Today we are witnessing not the crisis but the disintegration of the CPSU. In the ranks of the former 'single party' can be found representatives of all conceivable currents from liberals to fascists. The question of 'the Party's role in perestroika' can no longer be posed: there is no role because there is no Party.

Some will be drawn (are already being drawn) to the socialists; others will stand beneath nationalist banners. At the end of January, representatives of the various opposition groups active within the official party gathered in Moscow and announced the formation of the 'Democratic Platform of the CPSU'. The demands of this new opposition were little different from the slogans of other democratic groups which have spoken about free elections and pluralism of parties. By the very fact of its appearance, 'Democratic Platform' has once again confirmed the existence of a split within the ranks of the Party, but has proved at the same time extremely heterogeneous itself. All of the contradictions in evidence within the 'big' CPSU have been reproduced in essence within Democratic Platform: here were liberal Westernizers, social democrats, advocates of the rebirth of Leninist Bolshevism, and socialists. In this situation the radical representatives of Democratic Platform declared that the CPSU is irreformable in principle and that they supported the Committee for a Socialist Party. From amongst the founders of Democratic Platform, Mikhail Maliutin and Igor Yakovenko joined the ACSP.

In February, the disintegration of the Komsomol began in practice. A section of those who were discontented declared, in place of the collapsing official youth union, the formation of the Federation of Socialist Youth. The centre was the Komsomol committee of Moscow State University. One of its leaders is Efim Ostrovsky, who has only just recently been depicted by *Pravda* as a firebrand attempting to force the Prokop'evsk miners to act against their own communist party.

On 4 February, a demonstration of 300,000 through the streets of Moscow demanded the repeal of Article 6. The following day, the CPSU

Central Committee Plenum promised the population a multi-party system and the repeal of the notorious Article 6 – and Yegor Ligachev, who had always symbolized conservative and orthodox tendencies, suddenly declared his sympathy for social-democracy. The opportunity to form hundreds of new parties did not, however, generate much enthusiasm among a population weary of standing in queues. For a majority of people, democratic rights remained abstract and useless if they did not allow them to defend their immediate interests. On 9 February, when delegates to the Plenum were speaking on the TV programme *Vzglyad* ('Glance') about the 'democratic revolution', a multi-party system, and so on, the interventions by representatives of the socialists and the Kuzbass strike committee were censored on transmission of the programme for being too dangerous and going beyond the bounds of an abstract ideological game. But if democratization is still a game for professional politicians and intellectuals, then nothing good can be expected from the changes. For the time being the workers' movement remains behind the establishment, but the first rolls of thunder can already be heard.

The Republican and municipal elections are conducted in a strange atmosphere. It has been decided that I should stand as a candidate for the leftwing community group 'The City for its Citizens'. My strongest opponent is not the official candidate, who will certainly be defeated, but a nationalist who helps to edit a journal for the Orthodox Church. The unreal aspect of the campaign is that it is conducted against a background of menacing events and circumstances which could so easily rob the results of any significance. The representations of the national movements in the Caucasus and the Baltic are met with crude bullying and threats. In their own way these movements can also be intolerant but they enjoy real popular support. We hear that in Baku the attacks on the Armenians were the responsibility of Azeri refugees who had themselves been ejected from Armenia. Apparently the Azeri Popular Front had already succeeded in restoring order before the troops were sent in. Gorbachev tries to deal in a more moderate way with Lithuania because he knows that they count for more with the West than the Azeris. A cumbersome proposal has been rushed through the Supreme Soviet admitting the possibility of secession – but it seems that the process will take at least five years, and require the consent of a majority in other republics.

Another constitutional change being rushed through is the creation of a Presidential Council which would confer large powers on Gorbachev. Some of his advisers want him to use his new position to impose 'Polish' shock therapy. The effect of ending all subsidies from one day to the next could only be to triple prices and throw millions out of work. Other advisers warn of the social resistance this would provoke. Against a background of wild rumour and continuing everyday problems of every sort, the electors doubt the significance of voting. While some people still come to meetings there is much suspicion and apathy. We also learn that both the central government and the old municipal authorities are taking out insurance against defeat by reducing the powers of the municipality and transferring its funds to other bodies.

When the results come in we are surprised that the turn-out remains quite high. In Moscow, Leningrad and many other places the democratic opposition groupings are well-placed to win while the Russian nationalists do not score as much as many had predicted. Together with other members of 'The City for its Citzens', I go through to the second round and, eventually, am elected. But the largest group of democratic deputies intends to ask the free-market economist Popov to form an administration. The plans they discuss are really no different to those being canvassed by the presidentialist camarilla around Gorbachev. In private they will readily confess that perestroika has failed and that something new must be tried. The more honest of them no longer speak of socialism. But even these often seem to have lost touch with the reality of our country, and have fallen in love with an imaginary model of capitalism that corresponds neither to our possibilities nor to the aspirations of ordinary people. Today the liberals have much shallower support than a year ago. The death of Sakharov is a big blow to them; Yeltsin simply cannot replace him.

And so, the year has come to an end, the decade has come to an end, and perestroika has come to an end – or, more precisely, is in its death agony. One can truly say it's not a pity. The 'epoch of perestroika' has been a time of woolly political slogans, of contradictory and impotent reforms 'from above' inducing euphoria among intellectuals, and rapture among the Western press; of the rise of corruption under the cover of a struggle for 'purification'; of unrestrained demagoguery; and of amorphous mass movements possessing no clear structure, nor a worked-out programme or a firm ideology. It has been a period of breakdown passed off as reforms, and of reforms which have led only to breakdown. There will be few who will feel sorrow at the passing of this time.

Perestroika has ended by turning into bloody chaos. But the real fight is only just beginning. The illusions of the 1980s are no longer operative in 1990; the masses are beginning to grasp much better who are their enemies and who are on their side. An alternative has yet to be created. Before us are hard times. But before us is the future. We live, we act and that means we have hope.

Index